Method and Perspective in
ANTHROPOLOGY

WILSON D. WALLIS

METHOD AND PERSPECTIVE IN ANTHROPOLOGY

Papers in honor of
WILSON D. WALLIS

edited by Robert F. Spencer

THE UNIVERSITY OF MINNESOTA
PRESS, Minneapolis

PRINTED AT THE NORTH CENTRAL PUBLISHING COMPANY, ST. PAUL

Library of Congress Catalog Card Number: 54-8210

PUBLISHED IN GREAT BRITAIN, INDIA, AND PAKISTAN BY
GEOFFREY CUMBERLEGE: OXFORD UNIVERSITY PRESS, LONDON, BOMBAY, AND KARACHI

THIS VOLUME IS DEDICATED TO

WILSON DALLAM WALLIS

AS A TRIBUTE BY THE UNIVERSITY OF MINNESOTA

TO ONE OF ITS DISTINGUISHED PROFESSORS AT

THE TIME OF HIS RETIREMENT

WILSON D. WALLIS *joined the faculty of the University of Minnesota in 1923; he has been chairman of its Department of Anthropology since 1939.*

During his years of University service, Professor Wallis has pursued with unremitting devotion and diligence his studies in anthropology, as reflected in the extensive bibliography of his scientific and scholarly writing. During these years he has likewise been the respected teacher of hundreds of students, many of whom were stimulated by him to prepare for careers in anthropology.

Professor Wallis, it would be agreed by all who know him, is characterized by an inquiring, active mind that always is seeking new facets of problems for study. This volume draws together materials relating to one of the most significant of these problems — method in anthropology. Those responsible for its preparation are hopeful that the contents will worthily symbolize the critical attitudes that Professor Wallis, through his own work, has done so much to evoke and perpetuate.

PREFACE

THIS volume honors Wilson D. Wallis on the occasion of his retirement from active service as professor and chairman of the Department of Anthropology at the University of Minnesota. Although Professor Wallis leaves the teaching position he has held for
thirty years, his professional career in anthropology — as outstanding scholar, theorist, and indefatigable field worker — is by no
means at an end. He is at present engaged in preparing for publication the data collected on recent trips to the Canadian Dakota and
Micmac tribes. At the same time, a wider public than that of
anthropology awaits the results of his labor of recent years — an
attempt to determine the place of science in primitive cultures.
While the University of Minnesota has never boasted a large department of anthropology, the many professional anthropologists
whose interest in the field was first sparked by Professor Wallis
attest to his success as a teacher. His Minnesota colleagues will
miss his calm presence, his democratic leadership in departmental
affairs, and his remarkable depth of scholarly knowledge.

While, as an ethnologist, Mr. Wallis has devoted his primary
attention to the life of primitive peoples, he has also made significant contributions to social and cultural theory, not to mention physical anthropology. Grounded originally in philosophy,
Mr. Wallis found his career as an anthropologist when, as a
Rhodes scholar at Oxford, he came to study under the late
R. R. Marett. Ethnographic field research among Canadian Indians culminated in his doctorate at the University of Pennsylvania. Since that time he has published widely on an amazing
variety of subjects. The careful ethnographer, endowed with a
high degree of insight, is reflected in his monographs, while in

his many books — *Culture and Progress* (1930), *Religion in Primitive Society* (1939), *Messiahs — Their Role in Civilization* (1943), not to mention the numerous textbooks in both anthropology and sociology — the finished scholar appears. Mr. Wallis's papers in learned journals, too many to be listed here, are significant not only as contributions to social science and anthropology in general but very frequently as level-headed warnings to the too audacious theorist. How, then, to honor a man whose range of interest has extended from sneezing customs to kingship among primitive peoples, and from anatomical measurement to sociological analysis?

It was with the thought in mind of somehow bringing together a series of papers in anthropology reflecting Mr. Wallis's wide range of endeavor that the present volume, *Method and Perspective in Anthropology*, was conceived. In all his work Mr. Wallis has concerned himself with the "hows" of knowing, with the selection and rejection of evidence. Of anthropologists in the United States it has been not incorrectly said that a major preoccupation has been with "fact-gathering" in the field, an interest which has worked to the detriment of theory.* It is now clear, however, that the anthropologist in America is beginning seriously to attempt a reappraisal of his field and to designate with somewhat greater exactness his areas of interest. Through the years, anthropology in America has been characterized by the appearance of sudden, often short-lived preoccupations. Although, since some of the earliest writing of Boas and Kroeber, an attempt at refinement and application of the concept of culture has been primary, historical ethnology has given way to functionalist studies, to research in acculturation, personality approaches, and normative appraisals. Anthropology, it is true, has been obliged to suit its methods to its many and varied problems. It can be argued that, as the study of man, the areas of concern to anthropology are boundless. But in another way, despite this inherent eclecticism, the core of the discipline and a more precise definition of its preoccupations have begun to emerge.

* David Bidney, *Theoretical Anthropology* (New York: Columbia University Press, 1953), pp. vii–viii.

PREFACE

Only recently has the field of anthropology begun to subject itself to inventory and to raise, with somewhat greater detachment than had hitherto been possible, questions as to its theoretical premises and its methodology. There is the example of the recently published and encyclopedic *Anthropology Today* (Kroeber *et al.*, 1953), which chooses as its major themes the problems associated with historical approaches, with process, and with application, and stresses method, theory, and result in its treatment of aspects in each category. It is clear that there is no longer a question as to what anthropology is or as to its place in the realm of human knowledge. The present symposium, while admittedly not encyclopedic in scope, does seek to come to grips with some of the precisely defined areas of interest to contemporary anthropology and its related fields, and it does try to sharpen further some of the tools used by the science. Despite the recognition accorded anthropology and its established share in the social and physical sciences and in the humanities, much remains to be said concerning the ways in which anthropologists work, how they define their problems, and how they establish acceptable frames of reference in which to solve them. Mr. Wallis's consistent concern with just these points, his long-time interest in problems of method, justify a tribute to him in the form of papers treating these general themes.

The contributors to this volume are those who, over the years, have had personal contact with Mr. Wallis, as students, colleagues, and friends. The subjects with which they have chosen to concern themselves reflect a wide range of interests. In anthropology the analysis of human achievement everywhere in the world — in short, ethnology itself — remains basic. Hence these essays begin on the level of the anthropological interest in primitive man and so spread broadly into the areas of differing treatments of the concepts of culture and society. Through these papers, however varied their subject matter, runs the common thread of concern with method. But lest the community of purpose be lost, the editor has sought to restore focus by requesting Professor A. L. Kroeber to discuss each presentation. The result has been to lend additional perspective to the methods of modern anthropology.

METHOD AND PERSPECTIVE IN ANTHROPOLOGY

The editor wishes to express his appreciation to Dr. Elizabeth Colson for her assistance in preparing the manuscripts for the press, to Miss Sachiko Kaneko for her technical help, and especially to Mrs. Doris Franklin, of the University of Minnesota Press, for her cheerful and immeasurable aid in seeing this book through publication.

R. F. S.

March 1, 1954

TABLE OF CONTENTS

Ethnography

Cultural Anthropology

xi

TABLE OF CONTENTS

Prehistory, Linguistics, Ethnogeography

A Related Behavioral Field, Sociology

Conclusion

ETHNOGRAPHY

by MELVILLE J. HERSKOVITS

Some Problems of Method in Ethnography

Tʜᴇ relation between research design and theoretical terms of reference in shaping ethnographic studies has many facets. Outstanding is the fact that the conceptual scheme of the student deeply influences not only the execution of a given field problem but also the way in which it is formulated and planned. This has not had full recognition, though it is some time since we have heard charges that earlier examples of systematic field work consisted of no more than random "fact-gathering" — research guided by no principle other than to describe a given way of life. For while a work that is solely one of description may, from the point of view of the theoretical structure of a discipline, lodge on a relatively low level of scientific analysis, yet no one would today fail to perceive that the data are ordered in accordance with a definite schema, however implicit this may be, and thereby represent the results of systematic research.

Some examples of the relation between theory and method may be indicated to make our initial point. Thus, the approach of a student who holds that culture is to be broken down into traits must, of necessity, be quite different from that of the investigator who conceives of a way of life as an integrated whole, no part of which is to be understood except in its relation to the totality of which it is a part. This is patent if, for instance, the procedures employed in the studies whose aim was to collect trait lists, initiated

3

and carried out by students at the University of California, are contrasted with the field techniques of those who termed themselves functionalists and who conducted their investigations at about the same period. The significant factor in making the collection of trait lists was the hypothesis that culture is an historical phenomenon which can be understood if the contacts of peoples, as reflected in similarities and divergences in the component elements of their respective ways of life, are reconstructed, and that these ways of life consist of items sufficiently discrete to be set down separately and manipulated in mathematical terms. On the other hand, the theoretical position of the functionalists, which maintains that the fabric of a culture is so tightly woven that to separate a single strand from it is to do violence to the whole, meant that the very concept of the trait was inadmissible, since the aim was to gather materials which revealed the totality of the existing patterns of behavior. Here, therefore, the aspect becomes the unit of study.

It should be made clear that the point at issue has nothing to do with the validity of either of these positions; in fact, time has brought us to the realization that each contains elements of value for the description and understanding of the phenomenon of culture, which both study. What is significant is that the actual modes of field research differed in the two cases, and that this difference was directly traceable to the underlying assumptions as to the nature and significance of culture held by those concerned with planning and executing the research.

Another instance is at hand if we consider studies made by anthropologists who take as their organizing concept the term "society," as against those whose investigations are focused on the concept "culture." The former characteristically tend to delimit the area of research to those institutions which shape the contacts between members of a given society, describing and analyzing their functions as media through which the relations between those who make up a given aggregate are ordered, and are commonly lodged on a single time plane. The student who conceives of his research as a study of the culture of a people, in contrast, tends to be more holistic in his approach, taking any type of socially sanctioned behavior as lying within the scope of his analysis. In these terms, he often moves even further, to record behavior that goes beyond the limits of customary sanction, as a means toward understanding the dynamics of the situation with which he is concerned, and adding the dimension of time depth.

Here again, the methodological divergences that are apparent arise from different theoretical approaches. The student who is concerned with structure will pay more attention to data obtained is response to the "What?" questions than the one who centers his attention on dynamics and seeks answers to questions which lie in the "Why?" category. This does not mean that, as far as scientifically acceptable field procedures are concerned, students who take either position will not obtain data of validity and ethnographic accuracy; or, indeed, that their actual procedures in the field will differ to any great extent — certainly not as much as those of the trait analyst differed from those of the functionalist. Yet those elements in the life of a given people which will attract major interest, where emphases will be laid in formulating the kind of questions asked of informants and the type of activity each elects to observe, must differ quite appreciably.

In short, we must accept the postulate that the term *method* implies more than the actual procedures employed in prosecuting a given research project. This is why the present discussion, which will in the main be concerned with these procedures, begins with the reminder that techniques are essentially no more than ways of implementing the testing of hypotheses, and that there is no hypothesis which does not arise from a body of theory and concept. Even research reports which merely present the data gathered and are thus purely descriptive are framed in terms of concepts of what comprises the way of life of a people, how it is to be divided for purposes of presentation, what are the critical items that are to be given priority, and what relationships are to be noted. It is therefore no anomaly that developments in procedure have closely followed the development of theory. The early evolutionists had little need of field research at all, because their method was dominated by the comparative principle and the doctrine of survivals. The emphasis of the diffusionists on the need to differentiate the cultures they studied into traits rather than to integrate their observations in terms of aspects arose from their conception of culture, phrased in terms of the ability of independent cultural items to travel on their own, so to speak, and thus reveal the historic past of nonhistoric peoples. The stress later laid on the importance of the total situation and the use of documentary materials was contingent on the development of a theory which held that cultural behavior, to be understood, must take into full account the psychological component involved, and that the dynamics of change, no less than the statics of institutionalized procedures, must be grasped if the nature of culture and the human relationships that exist under it are to be revealed.

Once the relation between theory and method is clear, it becomes possible to approach more realistically the problems of field techniques, and the question of the means by which field data are best to be deployed in presenting these materials. This holds especially when we consider the differing objectives of students whose research derives from varying assumptions about the nature and functioning of human society and human culture. It then becomes patent that the methods to be used, insofar as they reflect differing conceptual schemes, will differ in their point and stress. And it follows that, if scientific objectivity, to the degree this can be obtained in the study of men by men be the end of our investigations, there is no single method any more than there is a single problem. The present discussion, therefore, will be oriented about and informed by this fundamental methodological fact.

2

The problems centering on field research that have been most discussed are those of duration, of communication, of rapport, of comparison, and of historic depth. Of these, the first three must be taken into account in the execution of any project; whether the final two enter is dependent largely on the approach of the student. We may consider each in turn.

The length of time to be spent on a field project has perhaps been the subject of more controversy than any single phase of field method. Here considerations of a practical character enter significantly — distance from the field, financing, possibility of release from conflicting calls on time, and the like. Ideally, there can be little doubt that a longer period is better than a shorter one, though even here it is necessary to qualify and add "other things being equal." We may, however, raise with cogency the question of how long work can be carried on among a people before a kind of secondary ethnocentrism sets in, so that the student takes the culture he has studied as a point of departure for his later generalizations about culture as a whole and thus forfeits the basic advantage of perspective that is an important end of cross-cultural research. Other questions may also be raised. Is a continuous period of residence among a people to be preferred to shorter periods spread over a number of years? Is it better to budget one's time to a single community than to range more widely among different villages of a given society?

Continuous residence, over a year or more, permits the observation of the annual round as manifested in economic pursuits and ritual sequences, to name only the two most obvious items of this kind. A classic example of the handicap an inability to do this imposes is to be had in the fact that it was years before students of the Navaho observed and recorded the winter ceremonies, because all field work, dictated by the exigencies of the academic calendar, had to be carried on during the summer. Yet, though this is an extreme case, the fact remains that in many societies there are certain rites that are performed only once every several years, and that even in a period which permits the observation of the ordinary annual round, especially in a small commmunity, there may be no marriage or no death.

There is a consensus on this matter of time that can be distilled from the numerous expressions on the point that have been registered, a consensus that reflects, more perhaps than anthropologists are aware, the fact that far greater support for field research has become available than in earlier years, when studies had to be made during vacations or near at home. That the period of research should be long enough to permit the observation of the normal course of the annual cycle of life is regarded as desirable by all; that it should not be so long or so continuous as to blunt the psychological distance with which the student approaches the phenomena of his concern is also agreed on. For the rest, individual differences in perceptiveness, in flexibility, and in insight enter to a decisive degree. Alertness to cues to behavior will in the case of one student permit work to be done in a shorter period than that of another who responds more slowly, but for whom a longer period of residence will permit the achievement of results of comparable worth. For one person residence in a single village might result in tensions that would materially affect the nature and quality of the data; yet this might be an optimum procedure for another student having different personality characteristics or working among a group that accepted the outsider more readily.

Our implicit assumption thus far has been that the field project envisages work among peoples whose cultures either are not known or have not been previously subject to scientific study. Yet there is the whole range of problems that involve the investigation of particular segments of a culture, to be studied in societies previously described. These may have to do with any aspect of life — the music of a people, or their political structure, or their material culture, or their literary products. There is not much question that, though the time required for adequate study varies greatly, much more can be accomplished in less time in researches of this sort than where the understanding of an entire way of life must be achieved. This does not overlook the fact that no body of custom, in all its variation, has ever been completely probed. The dynamic character of culture, the fact that one member of a society never reacts precisely as does the next, the presence of local variants, are only a few of the obstacles to achieving completeness. Yet with the basic patterns in hand, the specialist in one phase of culture can go into the field equipped to analyze the manifestations of his particular specialty in a given society much more quickly than where a knowledge of these patterns is lacking.

Indeed, where these are not available, the student interested in one phase of the life of a people often finds himself, of necessity, spending his available time doing general ethnography.

Whatever the time given to carrying out a particular field project, the factor of communication must enter. The problem here turns on the degree to which control of the language spoken by a people is essential for an understanding of their culture. Again, ideally, there can be no question that command of a language facilitates cultural comprehension; this is so elementary as scarcely to need stating. Yet the matter is not so simple, and the proposition, so appealing on the face of it, that one must be conversant with the speech of a people if he is to master their modes of thought raises many questions when subjected to critical analysis. For to learn the turn of phrase, the idiomatic use of a word, the figures of speech that are as essential a part of linguistic expression as are a common vocabulary and the accepted rules of grammar is difficult, indeed. The use of slang terms or of local or occupational or class dialects further complicates the picture. The question can be fairly raised whether or not the law of limiting returns does not set in after a time; whether, in terms of the scientific problems of cultural and social significance to be studied, it does not take too much time to attain this theoretically complete knowledge of the language to justify the additional results it yields.

The importance of understanding the language of a group as an aid to adequate ethnographic research has long been recognized, and early students in the United States, at least, attempted to meet the problem by recording textual materials. There were disadvantages to the process, however; it was difficult to take dictation at the customary rate of conversation, so that the presentation became truncated, and the flow of expression stilted. Nonetheless, the texts that have been gathered from peoples all over the world are valuable documentation and stand as raw data that permit checking as to meaning and relevance in a way that few other materials in the ethnographic repertory allow.

Certain minimum requirements can be stated. It is unthinkable that any competent ethnographer should go into the field without

9

equipment in linguistics which will enable him to hear and set down in proper phonemic terms the critical words, the textual materials, requisite for the study of his problem. Because of the confusion of terminology and the need for clarification of designations when applied in particular cases — words such as *family* or *fetish* — it is essential that native terms be precisely recorded and their meanings analyzed as comprehensively as possible. Place and personal names, names of deities, spells and formulas, designations of kinship, and a host of other types of documentation must be taken down to prevent ambiguity and to permit further discussion in terms meaningful to the member of the society with whom they are to be discussed.

This brings us to the moot point concerning the use of interpreters. There are few ethnographers who, in actuality, do not use them. The question is really the extent to which they should be employed and the best techniques for utilizing them. It is agreed that reliance on a single interpreter is dangerous. Yet a principal interpreter may be so infected with enthusiasm for discovering the unsuspected implications of his own culture that he becomes a most valuable aide in ways that far transcend his original function. The employment of pidgin dialects or of a *lingua franca* is analogous; where better understanding through their use can be established, they are well worth employing.

Thus, here again, no single formula can be offered. Some students are more gifted at learning languages than others; some have more time to spend on the task of acquiring a language; in some instances, especially among peoples living in remote areas, the question may become academic because no interpreter can be found. The test of a given field procedure, whether linguistic or other, lies in the validity of the results. Good field work has been done by students whose knowledge of the language of the people being studied has been slight, as is the case in many researches into American Indian cultures. Granting that critical words must be recorded, that as much comprehension of current speech as is necessary to control what is being discussed by interpreter and informant or to grasp the main outlines of a situation being observed is essential, then the minimal requirements are met. Beyond this, the more the knowledge of the language, the better — if, however, the very important inner controls by the student over his own competence are exerted so that he does not assume a greater understanding of a language than he actually has or does not believe that he can express himself more effectively than he actually can.

3

The question of rapport, in essence, goes beyond training and enters into the difficult and subtle field of the individual sensitivity of the research worker. It involves the ability to adjust to new situations and to personalities that express themselves in ways that are strange; to grasp cues to behavior and attitudes that are being newly encountered. This does not presuppose any element of mysticism, for to be effective, rapport must be controlled; and much of anthropological training is designed to inculcate the cross-cultural point of view that is essential for scientific ethnography and that on the ideological level most markedly differentiates the ethnographer from other observers. Given this point of view and the intensive training in field procedures that the field worker has had, then its implementation must be developed in the experience of the student himself.

Thus, from this point of view, it is taken for granted that the people who are being studied are fully adult and that their ways have a rationale that gives them meaning and stability, in addition to such obvious matters as the need to respect beliefs and follow established rules of etiquette and comportment. But there is more than this. To make oneself a member of a community where one is a stranger and perhaps a representative of a group whose common practice is to be circumspect and even politely hostile, to be able to empathize with the personal triumphs or difficulties of those with whom one lives as well as with the broader satisfactions or problems of the group as a whole, to be able to discern the individual differences and to stress similarities between one person and another — these are some of the things that are involved in the ability to achieve rapport. Without these, and more that might be named, the length of stay will be of little help, and even the student who is linguistically best equipped will meet with evasion and prevarication, if not with outright hostility.

The degree to which the student must have a knowledge of his own biases, of his own motivations and drives, before he can effectively carry on work in the field has been much debated; and there is little question that an ability to discount one's prejudices and understand characteristic reactions to situations and people is of help in the field. The problem is how to achieve this. It has been suggested, for example, that no field work should be attempted unless the student has been psychoanalyzed or has subjected himself to other psychiatric tests which determine the nature of his personality and the manner in which he might be expected to respond in his interpersonal relations with those he studies. It is pointed out, however, that the results obtained by students who have not been analyzed, on balance, suggest that there is little significant difference in the scientific value of their reports and those of students who have had such analysis. Certainly everything is to be said for any element in the training of the field worker that will make for a pre-established sensitivity to persons and situations and that will help him to obtain a psychological distance not only toward behavior outside the expected range of his own culture, but in the face of the irritations that inevitably arise in the course of field research. Perhaps here again one must be eclectic, recognizing that while in some cases it is desirable that the student know his unconscious responses to people and situations, in others this is not needed. Or it may be that while it is desirable for those whose research problem is essentially psychological to undergo analysis, in the case of those concerned with other questions this is not necessary. The problem posed is a real one; it would seem that no over-all solution can provide the answer to it.

The problem of rapport takes on added significance in view of certain new techniques of field research that are being urged on ethnologists as the study of large populations and the search for quantitative data involve radical departures from the customary techniques of ethnography, directed toward obtaining qualitative findings. One of the instruments most favored for this newer approach is the questionnaire or, if this is not feasible, the short interview. Both instruments, employed to obtain mass data, derive from the assumption that where questions are clearly and simply phrased, and of direct import, valid answers can readily be obtained. These data can then be manipulated statistically, and thereby yield results of greater reliability than can be had from the customary ethnographic technique of investigating cross-cultural phenomena through the intensive study of small social units. This approach is especially favored in research which is concerned with the sociological and economic aspects of the lives of peoples being investigated, such as studies of standards of living, or in demographic inquiries into family size, birth and death rates, and the like.

Yet in many societies — and many of those experienced in employing these methods would by no means except those of Europe and America — a direct question is an invitation to give a distorted answer. One may refer to census projects in various parts of Africa as a case in point; the difficulty in obtaining data that approximate reality has long been recognized as of the first order. The care with which the Nigerian census of 1952–1953 was organized is evidence of this. Thus, for example, officers charged with collecting the data conducted classes where the African enumerators were not only trained in the correct manner of setting down the answers given, but were taught the meaning of the questions themselves so that they could rephrase them if necessary. A campaign of publicity, which enlisted the aid of African public figures in whom the people had confidence and which broadcast their appeals for cooperation in printed form and through the radio, was initiated. It was explained at length that this census would form the basis, for two decades, for allocating public funds to each district for such desired ends as schools, roads, hospitals, and other public works. Intensive sampling was done to predict the validity of the final results. Nonetheless, a fear that the count might be the basis for levying taxes, so that to indicate the number of persons in a household might thus lay open its head to greater obligations than he had hitherto assumed, was only one of the reasons that caused those in charge of the work to be anything but certain that the count would have the accuracy it might have in countries where the tradition of census-taking was well established. And initial publication of certain of the results brought forth immediate charges of inaccuracies on the part of Africans, some of whom documented their charges with cases of evasions that, if general, might materially affect the validity of the final figures.

It is scarcely necessary to raise the question of the extent to which the ethnographer, who will hardly have the resources of publicity or the support of leaders among the people he is studying to aid his endeavor to employ questionnaires in obtaining mass data, can gather materials which will not be subject to a considerably greater degree of error. Yet there is no need to be negativistic concerning attempts to employ techniques of this sort. What would seem to be required is a series of test studies which might check this method against the results to be obtained from researches in depth into identical phenomena.

This brings us to the question of sampling, which has been increasingly posed to ethnographers by their fellows in the social sciences whose work does not involve a cross-cultural component. The turn which the questions tend to take on the level of method is logical enough, given the assumptions of those who ask them. Most often they raise the issue of the extent to which an anthropologist, working not only in small societies but in those which may comprehend thousands if not tens of thousands of members, can be sure that data gathered from a single village, or from a single quarter of a town, or from a single district of a widely spread, nomadic group, will be representative of the civilization of the people as a whole. It must be granted that anthropologists have well earned this skepticism, since there has been a tendency, which still persists in too many quarters, to speak of the customary modes of behavior and belief of a local unit in terms of the traditions of the entire people of which they form only a small part; often, indeed, without any attempt even to indicate whether or not local or class variations exist. Yet this failure to make clear the limits of a given study only increases the obligation to clarify the methodological assumptions of the ethnologist which, in his own thinking, justify him in representing the culture of a people to be what he has found in a segment of it.

The matter turns largely on the nature of ethnographic truth. It is not likely that any student of culture would maintain that the variations that are at the base of the question here being discussed do not exist. Yet, it should be made plain that the issue of the comparative importance of small variations is crucial. From a cross-cultural point of view, it has been made amply clear that local differences within a culture are in no wise of the same magnitude, nor are they significant for the same problems, as are the differences between the modes of life of peoples having different cultures, when considered as wholes. Certainly it is important, especially when questions of cultural dynamics and cultural variation are under study, to obtain a sense not only of local and class differences, but of the range of individual, even of idiosyncratic behavior. This, which might be termed the micro-ethnographic approach, is, however, quite another matter from the approach to be made toward those macro-ethnographic questions that deal with the total range of variation in human behavior, and which have proved to be essential in the study of such problems as the nature of cultural learning, of cultural patterning, or of the relationship between individual behavior and the pre-existing conventions of the society into which a person is born.

Increasingly, the question of sampling is being resolved by the work of ethnographers who supplement the intensive study of a single group in the total society with which they are concerned with shorter, "spot" studies whose aim is to reveal differences that arise out of the class structure of a society, or its local specializations, and the like. It is well to take cognizance of the fact, however, that the assumption which led ethnologists to accept the analysis of a restricted group as representative of an entire people remains valid within limits. This validity may even be extended to data furnished by a single informant, as where one member of a faraway society, hitherto unstudied, becomes available to a university department, and some member of its staff, or one of its advanced students, employs this individual as an informant. Granting the defects of this procedure, which is to be followed only where more adequately controlled data are not to be had, its utility in the hands of a trained investigator has been demonstrated. It is scarcely necessary to draw attention to that specialized aspect of culture, language, to make the point. Many grammars of unwritten languages have been written on the basis of work carried on with a single speaker, far from his home. And just as it has been established that no human being can make up a language, so it can be asserted that no individual can make up a culture, though he may distort detail.

The psychology of cultural learning is too well known to permit us to conclude otherwise, and in the same way the ecology of culture is too well understood to accord validity to arguments which overemphasize local differences and fail to recognize similarities. It would be unrealistic to disregard either of these factors, just as it would be equally unrealistic to insist that every local group be studied before valid — or valuable — conclusions can be drawn regarding the worth of the intensive study of an individual community. In effect, the proposition is not the qualitative approach as against the quantitative study of mass data; the ideal situation is where both can be applied. In the final analysis the problem to be attacked must govern the methodological tools to be employed. Where, as in most studies of culture, ideal situations do not exist, experience has proved that intensive analysis yields insights that extensive research can never give. And in the light of this experience, it would seem that intensive analysis, in depth, must continue to be given the priority in the anthropological repertoire that long use has taught us to accord it. The answer to the question regarding the validity of ethnographic studies, that is, lies in the nature and functioning of culture itself, and can only be understood if those who raise the issue are willing to learn the methodological no less than the conceptual implications of the term.

The degree to which team research can achieve ends that are

beyond the competence of the individual ethnographer raises analogous points. A considerable number of researches, carried out by specialists in various disciplines and pointed toward a more complete understanding of a single culture or of the way of life of a single community than can be attained by a student working alone, have been carried out in the Americas, in the Caribbean, in Africa, and the South Seas. These team researches are not numerous enough, however, to enable any definitive judgment to be drawn concerning the value of the results obtained when compared to those gathered by individual research workers. The degree to which participants who are not ethnologists are trained in the basic principles of ethnographic method and the cross-cultural approach is of great significance. Given this, and the willingness to recognize that generalizations drawn out of the study of Euroamerican culture are to be regarded as hypotheses for cross-cultural testing rather than as principles whose validity must be documented, there can be little question that this multiple approach must yield significant results.

One practical question of field procedure where team research is envisaged, must be raised. In any society the student is an outsider, usually a stranger. The resistances which the ethnographer must overcome to have himself and his study accepted are many times compounded when a group project is undertaken. There is evidence, indeed, that this holds for other than cross-cultural field situations and is true of communities in America and Europe where group research is prosecuted. The questions raised in the minds of the people being studied concerning the presence of a single ethnographer — which, incidentally, few who have studied non-European societies have failed to encounter — become the more pressing when a group of students appears on the scene. Concomitantly, the time-honored formula of interest in ways other than one's own as a means of inculcating a broader knowledge of man comes to hold less conviction as the number of researchers increases. Moreover, with more members of the team, the problems of interpersonal relations between them and the community become more complex, while the question of the influence which the injection of a considerable number of students into a homogeneous community may have on its life is not one that can be disregarded.

Here these points can only be raised; we are not in a position as yet to answer them. Much depends on the selection of personnel and on their training. Alternate procedures may meet these problems, as where the members of a research team may be distributed among different communities of the same society, once the relative unity of the underlying patterns of belief and behavior for the group as a whole has been established. Basically the methodological question reduces itself to the same issue which questions as to the use of mass data and of adequate sampling raise — that of intensive as against extensive approaches. Since the specialist sees problems and commands special techniques which the student of whole cultures does not have, it follows that the application of the concepts and methods of other disciplines to the broadest range of cultures is desirable. Whether this can be achieved through team research, in which an anthropologist and a number of specialists work together, or whether the specialist can best work alone after being trained in the cross-cultural approach and its methodology, again depends on the total framework within which the research is to be carried out. Here again, no single answer can be given; it is enough that we comprehend both the advantages and the difficulties involved in team research.

4

We may now turn briefly to the methodological problems presented by the factors of comparison and of historical depth. In earlier research these were integral elements in accepted procedure. The comparative method constituted a clearly defined attack on the question of how institutions develop, through the use of excerpts from any reports available regarding the ways of life of peoples all over the world; its eventual rejection, indeed, resulted from a realization of the heterogeneous nature of the data employed and the disregard for cultural context that characterized their use. The historical approach, insofar as it implied the world-wide reconstruction of history, in most cases involved a similar methodological attack, with no more satisfactory results.

With the development of acculturation studies, however, a new tool came to hand. The essence of acculturation studies is their concern with dynamics; this is implicit in the very concept of cultural contact as a moving force in cultural change. Their appeal for anthropologists lies in the fact that scientific controls are far more readily achieved in such researches than in those where the study of process is approached through assumed historic contacts between peoples, assumptions that were always subject to debate because documentation was lacking. In the study of acculturation, that is, the historical foundation is assured; for all studies of this kind take as their point of departure established historical contacts, the results of which are analyzed in terms of the cultural reorientations that are to be observed.

Comparison here takes on a character that differentiates it from earlier uses of the "comparative method." This difference, in part, is expressed in the concept of the "base-line" from which documented change has occurred; in part through the study, either in the field or by use of the documents, of the nature of the cultures that were in contact and thereby took over elements from one another. The methodological principle involved here seems simple when it has been stated, but it took years of research to force a realization of its importance. How many studies of Indian cultures in Latin America recognized as having been influenced by contact with the Spanish, have been made without supporting information to be derived from field research in Spain? How frequently, in earlier years, was the character of New World Negro culture assessed without knowledge of the African elements that entered into the final picture? How many instances can be cited of studies of contemporary North American Indian cultures which have been made with little or no reference to the situation in which changes that diverge from aboriginal custom were brought about?

One of the contributions of acculturation research to the methods of anthropology, indeed, has been to put the historical component in anthropological science on a sure footing. Out of this development came the contemporary technique of ethno-history — that welding of the ethnographic data from the peoples concerned with a given contact situation, to the information from the historical documentation, that explains the nature and intensity of the resulting changes.

It is, of course, no more difficult to carry on ethnographic research in a society where the culture is of obvious multiple derivation than it is to study a people in an "undisturbed" state, whose culture, indeed, must similarly be assumed to have been more remotely influenced by its contacts. The real methodological distinction arises out of the complexities that enter when the resulting amalgam has not developed into a smoothly functioning series of institutions, each with its sanctions capable of explicit statement. Where the culture is in a state of flux, moreover, the number of variables to be taken into account increases. Differences in attitude and behavior between generations, for example, have far greater significance than in a society whose culture is stable, while the existence of orientations focused on the same aspects of life that differ from one group to another, such as follow on a realignment of social and economic classes, materially alters the nature of the field situation with which the ethnographer must deal.

Most research into changing cultures has turned on the contact between native and Euroamerican custom, and this has had a result that in turn develops out of the fact that there are few students of culture who, for historic reasons, do not derive from the Euroamerican stream. Thus emphasis has come to be laid on change, while the other side of the acculturative picture, equally important from a methodological and theoretical point of view, the element of cultural tenacity, has tended to be relegated to a minor position. From a scientific no less than from a practical point of view, this is unfortunate. It needs but a moment's reflection to see that both of these must be taken into full account if scientifically valid findings are to issue. One result of this attitude, to which it is important to give explicit expression, is the tendency to take Euroamerican procedures that have been adopted by non-Euro-americans. It has often become apparent, on analysis, that these presumably Euroamerican elements in a changing culture represent inner realignments whose significance, when probed, affords rich insights into the processes of cultural change.

It is out of the study of situations of this kind, for example, that generalizations regarding the relation between cultural form and meaning have been derived, in terms of the concept of reinterpretation. Originally held applicable to the analysis of change under acculturation, it has become apparent that it applies with equal force to the inner dynamics of culture as well. The basic methodological principle involved is a simple one whose very simplicity, perhaps, caused it to be overlooked. One tends to take more elements in a situation under study for granted than is ordinarily realized; and it is reasonable to hold that the more commonplace the phenomenon, either to the student or to the people being studied, the greater will be the chance for this mechanism to come into operation. It is apparent that the application of the principle of taking all cultural elements into account in any research operation will further enrich our methodological resources as concerns the data in hand and will make for greater perceptiveness in their interpretation.

5

Fundamental to scientific procedure is the principle that data must be presented in such a manner that they can be checked by independent observers; that, in addition, these checks should come into play before the validity of the results of research is to be accepted. The principle, which has come out of the laboratory sciences, presents a real challenge in the study of man, and it is pertinent to inquire, in concluding our discussion of method, what steps have been and can be taken to implement this requirement.

We recognize, with all candor, that the principle of checking data has not been applied to the degree that is scientifically desirable in any of the sciences that deal with human social life. In all likelihood the ideal is not attainable, in view of the impossibility of maintaining the degree of control over the human being that can be exercised over nonhuman forms of animal life or over inert matter. This holds not alone for the study of culture. All disciplines that have attempted to by-pass psycho-cultural dynamics have merely given an apparent scientific stamp to a particular type of controlled unreality. For if the need to conduct research so as to enable it to be repeated is accepted as a basic tenet of science, it is just as basic to recognize and admit the limitations of a technique which yields results that, despite their appearance of regularity and accuracy, are, at base, spurious. This does not mean, however, that an awareness of difficulties is inimical to a search for solutions to them, and it is in these terms that this problem is approached.

It is not so long ago that to initiate work among a people already studied was regarded as in the nature of a vote of no confidence. This, in all probability, resulted from the fact that there were many societies where no work had been done and that not enough trained personnel capable of studying them was available in the first instance. With the increase in the number of anthropologists, however, this is changing. The number of researches that are being carried out among peoples previously reported on, or in the same region where earlier investigations were made, is an encouraging sign that this tradition of what might be termed the possessive "my-people" concept is losing force among scientific students of culture. This new tradition will undoubtedly be extended as more anthropologists become available and as prior research is subjected to scrutiny by literate members of the nonliterate societies on whose cultures published reports are at hand. There can be no doubt that such checking is needed; it is not necessary to document this need by citing instances in which presumed discoveries of mechanisms and processes in some "primitive" society have gone beyond the bounds of anthropological discussion and, for the public at large, have become guiding principles, without ever having been checked as to their validity. On the other hand, the larger number of cases in which, either through the mechanism of the repeated study or of research among a related group, the accuracy of ethnographic presentations has been established have confirmed the validity of the approach and methods of scientific ethnography.

Granting the need to control the reliability of studies of culture by means of repeated analyses of the same phenomena, what are some of the difficulties that must be taken into account in attaining this end? Here the dynamic factor in culture, which arises out of the fact that it is learned and therefore does not have the order of stability of inborn traits, enters as a critical point. Let us assume that one student repeats the study of a society investigated two or three decades earlier by another. Even where the society has been relatively undisturbed, the propensity of its members to develop new ideas and new techniques and the contacts they have had with neighboring folk in the meantime will to some degree change the picture. Morover, the very fact that a student has lived among the people he studies sets up a kind of feed-back reaction that may well influence the course of cultural change. On the other hand, the stability of culture in terms of its over-all patterning has been fully established, and this means that, in large measure, the broad outlines of the culture as described by the first student should be found by the second. If fundamental differences are found by the second, various hypotheses may be advanced in explanation. Some far-reaching historic occurrence may have taken place; this, however, over a period such as we are considering, should readily become known and be taken into account in evaluating the differences found between the culture in its earlier and later manifestations. Where this has not occurred, the matter then becomes a question of the accuracy of observation of the two students and can only be resolved by further independent checking.

There is another way in which results can be checked, though this does not have the validity of restudy of a given people. This has to do with the comparison of the findings of independent observers among neighboring groups. The fact of cultural diffusion is fundamental in ethnological theory, and from this it follows that societies that are near one another will share many cultural elements. It is on this basis that the theory of the culture area is founded; it is this theory that makes the student who expects to go to a people hitherto unstudied read the literature on other societies inhabiting the same general region. Hence, where two cultures not too far removed from one another are studied with results that differ more than theory would justify, the presumption must follow that these divergences are to be accounted for through rechecks on the data of either or both investigators.

Without explicit expression, this has been perhaps the method of control most widely employed in ethnography, and needs only to be extended and regularized to bring it to its full effectiveness. It is for this reason that it is important, in the presentation of field data, that the regional cultural matrix in which they lodge be given adequate expression. Despite a tendency to reject all kinds of comparative analysis and to present in great detail the data from a single society without reference to historic background or relation to other peoples in the same area, it is to be anticipated that the utility of this well-grounded tradition of anthropology will cause it to prevail. With the development of the type of study that provides an independent check on earlier data, methodological devices will then be in hand that should advance the study of man a further step toward the attainment of that objectivity which is the aim of its scientific methodology.

NOTE. Since this paper was written in the field, the citations to the literature that would ordinarily have been given are regrettably, but necessarily lacking.

by SISTER M. INEZ HILGER

An Ethnographic Field Method

A FIELD assistant and I set out to record the ethnography of primitive Indian child life as reflected in the milieu of the tribal culture. Our method was that of personal observations and personal interviews with Indian informants in their native habitat. The method, which is described in the following pages, grew out of what we set out to do. To a large extent it developed out of our field experience.

Our studies covered mostly past ethnography — that is, such customs, beliefs, and traditions as were remembered by informants, especially by old men and old women. The psychoanalytical approach was not used. Since, in instances, we recorded present-day ethnology, it might possibly have been used. However, I felt insecure in its techniques. I also feared to be unjust in the inferences or conclusions that I might draw from its findings. Since culture and psychology are interdependent, an interested psychologist, I believe, will be able to deduce certain psychological information from our studies, especially from the verbatim quotations of informants.

NOTE. The work spoken of in this paper was made possible by the following grants: the field work among the Chippewa in 1939 and that among the Arapaho in 1940 and 1942 was subsidized by the Social Science Research Council; that among the Arapaho in 1941 and research in libraries and museums in 1942, by the American Council of Learned Societies; that among the Araucanian of Chile in 1946–1947 and among the Araucanian of Argentina and Chile in 1951–1952, by the American Philosophical Society (Grants No. 805 and 1341, Penrose Fund); the work in 1951–1952 was also supported by the Wenner-Gren Foundation for Anthropological Research.

ETHNOGRAPHY

By an ethnographic method, then, we studied the Chippewa of Minnesota, Wisconsin, and Michigan; the Arapaho of Wyoming and Oklahoma; and the Araucanian of Chile and Argentina.

PREPARATION FOR THE FIELD

My field assistant and I set out for field work with stiff-covered notebooks, a steel measuring tape, my Field Guide, several hundred pieces of paper 4 by 6 inches, a camera and photographic attachment, films, a published work on the tribe we were to study, colored prints and photographs of Indians, gifts, and money in cash.

We chose stiff-covered notebooks because we knew that notes would have to be written when the occasion arose. This might be while we squatted or stood, or rode in automobiles, boats, or ox carts. A flexible-rigid steel rule gave us measurements of cradleboards or looms, or anything we wanted to measure on the spot, in feet and inches; measurements by informants were usually handspreads or arm-lengths.

A Field Guide which I have compiled during my years of field experience (1932–1952) covers leads to the beliefs, customs, and traditions in the theory and procedure related to the development, rearing, and training of the child, and also the areas of the child's cultural background. Before leaving our residence for the day's field work, I usually typed short leads from the Guide on 4-by-6-inch pieces of paper so as to have them ready for the interview. Unfailingly I carried with me a copy of the Table of Contents of the Guide. If leads became exhausted or the arrival of transportation to another area was hours late, a glance at the Table of Contents gave me new leads. Then, too, small papers and the few sheets of paper (5 by 8 inches) of the Table of Contents were less formidable-looking than the two loose-leaf notebooks forming the Guide.

Photographs had to be taken when the occasion was present; hence, our camera was always in readiness. "I just finished setting up this loom in good sunlight so you could take a picture of it. I expected you to pass by this way today." Always several unused films were placed into our supply for the day's field work.

Seeing printed material about their own tribe roused immediate interest on the part of the informants; it also gave leads for conversation. "Right here [I pointed to the place, p. 723, in Cooper's *The Araucanians*, 1946] are names of kugas of the Araucanian. What is a kuga?" We took Densmore's *Chippewa Customs* to the Chippewa, Kroeber's *The Arapaho* to the Arapaho, and Cooper's *The Araucanians* to the Araucanian. Photographs that I myself had taken and colored prints such as the Great Northern Railroad publishes on the Blackfoot Indians of Montana stimulated interest and questions. "Look at the way those western Indians dress. That man has feathers on his head and back. They wore buffalo hides; we Chippewa wore deer hides. I never saw any beadwork like that. I make designs of flowers and fruit in beadwork."

Since giving or accepting anything generally indicates good will on both sides, we carried gifts with us. An unfailing one was tobacco, either smoking or chewing tobacco, or both. Local storekeepers told us which kind the Indians in the area favored. Always, too, we took hard mixed candies or all-day suckers. Other gifts we found to be acceptable were scarfs, beads, dime-store jewelry, neckties, handkerchiefs, and similar inexpensive items.

We needed ready money to pay both informants and interpreters. Small coins were handy in the event we wanted to pay children. We paid informants and interpreters at the end of each interview. Believing that there is a point of justice involved, for time and information given we paid in money by the hour or the day at the rate laborers in the area were being paid, unless non-Indian persons engaged in the service of the Indians advised against it — drinking to excess, it was known, sometimes followed payment in cash. In such cases we paid in food or clothing or some other material thing, maybe a work tool or kitchen wear. Commercial informants, such as offered services at stipulated prices, were strictly avoided.

COLLECTING INFORMATION BY INTERVIEWS AND OBSERVATIONS

I learned early in my field experience that accuracy and reliability in collecting information are of prime importance — decidedly less checking has to be done if they are provided for. Essentials I found to be: (1) honest, clear-minded, and willing informants; (2) keenly alert and honest Indian interpreters who speak the language of the people and speak fluently one of those I speak; (3) a competent field assistant; (4) contact-making that establishes rapport from the beginning; and (5) a system of interviewing and note-taking agreed upon by my field assistant and myself.

Selection of informants and interpreters. I selected both informants and interpreters carefully. I compiled three lists of informants and three of interpreters from names suggested by three separate groups, namely, the personnel of the offices of Indian affairs in the local government, the missionaries on the reservation, and intelligent Indian men and women. Always the lists contained a number of identical names. Quite obviously these were the persons to be contacted. Also, while in conference with each of the three groups, I inquired after the location of that section of the reservation in which the tribal religious ceremonial was still being observed. I had learned that in this particular area lived the group that clung most tenaciously to old customs and beliefs. Old men and old women from all areas had information that we wanted, but in this particular area there would be younger persons, even children, who could be helpful.

I found it advantageous to let the interpreter choose the informant for whom she wished to interpret. Thereby rapport existed between them from the beginning, and knowledge was seldom withheld; in fact, the informant usually had much to tell to the interpreter herself, because "that young generation knows so little about the old ways, that it is a pity!" Then, too, difficulties because of in-law taboos or feuds between families were not encountered.

The field assistant. In the selection of a field assistant I looked for a person who had an interest in people and who regarded Indians as persons endowed with the same mental abilities all other persons are endowed with; for one who realized that the culture of the Indians with whom we were about to work was as precious to them as ours is to us; for one who admired the intelligent manner in which these Indians had adjusted to their way of living. She had to be an intelligent observer, one who had stick-to-itiveness, one with a sense of humor, and good mental and physical health. She had to be willing to take notes under my direction while I interviewed the informant; in fact, to assist me in any way necessary.

Contact-making. The field assistant and I together worked out a system of contact-making. We found the following to be important: (1) We learned from the interpreters, before we set out for work, what the contact courtesies of the people themselves were; we intended to use them. What were the native words used in greeting? (Chippewa: *Bojou.* Araucanian: *Mari mari.*) Should we or should we not shake hands? (Chippewa: not important. Arapaho and Araucanian: a custom.) What was the time for gift-giving? (Chippewa and Arapaho: after first greetings. Araucanian: at some time during the interview.) Was stereotyped conversation to be carried out? (Chippewa and Arapaho: no. Araucanian: most emphatically at the beginning of a visit.) (2) When the greeting at first meeting had ended, we took notice of something of interest near at hand, and we talked about it. This might be a baby, a toddler, a sick person, weaving, basketry, fish just brought in by the father. (3) Following this, in order to get the informant to talk, we asked for an opinion on some current topic (general elections, in Argentina; a recent earthquake, in Chile; a visit from the Sioux, among the Chippewa; a recent death of a favorite Sister among the Arapaho).

Note-taking. The field assistant and I also worked out a system of note-taking and of joint observation. A cue to the assistant for close observation of a performance, for example, was a remark from me calling attention to the action: "Did you see how grandma made the knots in that fishing net?"

While I did the interviewing, the assistant took notes. But notes were never written until the consent of the informant was obtained. Usually there was no apprehension on the part of the informant about note-taking, since Sisters who had proved trustworthy and helpful in need had introduced us and had explained our purpose in having come. Informants had been told by the Sisters that the information we were taking would be an addition to what others had already found worthwhile to write about their tribe, provided that we found the information reliable and truthful. "Anyway, who would want to tell something about the tribe that was not true? Later people would not think much of a tribe that had to lie about itself." They were also told that names of informants would be printed in a list at the beginning of the study so that great-grandchildren would know that their great-grandparents had contributed to the study. The study was to be left as a legacy to future generations of the tribe. No name would be mentioned in the text itself, unless the informant was willing to have it printed there.

Among the Argentine Araucanians there are no Sisters. I introduced note-taking there, if the informant was a man, by asking for information related to stellar constellations. I would say, making a diagram of the Big Dipper by placing an X in the position of each star, "In North America we can see a group of stars like this. We call it the Big Dipper. I am wondering what group of stars one can see here in Argentina." By this time the informant had taken a look at my diagram. In answer he usually took the pencil and drew a diagram also. "Here is one. We call it *rapultrelke*; that means 'a stretched hide.' And here is another (he drew the X's). We call this one *namun choike*, 'foot of the ostrich'." I would then take the paper again and say, "Will you please tell me those Araucanian names once more? I want to write them down." We then talked about the meaning of thunder and lightning. I would tell of the Chippewa belief regarding the Thunderbird, and sketch the Arapaho design of the bird. When we were both interested, I would say, "Do you mind if Margaret (my field assistant) writes down those Araucanian words you just spoke, and also your way of thinking about lightning? I brought her with me to help me." There was no objection.

If the informant was a woman, I introduced note-taking by sketching some patterns found in Chilean Araucanian weaving. This done, I would ask the informant to draw some patterns used by Argentine Araucanian women. We then talked about the mean-

ing of the various designs in the patterns. I wrote down the Araucanian words and their meanings in Spanish. Soon I could say,
"Will it be satisfactory if Margaret writes down some of the Araucanian words, and also the things we are saying? I do not want to
forget them." There was no objection. In fact, "Señorita Margarita
would make a good Araucanian señorita. She pronounces those
Araucanian words much better than you do!"

Once the informant consented to note-taking, the cue to the
assistant to do so was a sentence from me containing the word
"writing": "Grandpa says that he has no objections to your writing
this down." The cue that the conversation should be taken down
verbatim (in shorthand, if the assistant knew how) was a statement
that contained the words "most, most interesting": "Your statement about the way in which names originated is most, most interesting." The remark from me, "That is remarkable," was the cue
that I was doubting the informant, and that the note should be
preceded by a question mark. At times courtesy required me to
listen when I knew the informant was not familiar with the item
under discussion, or was intoxicated, or, as happened in several
instances, was fabricating information. Such information was carefully checked and the mistake pointed out to the informant; an
informant needed to be told of an error on his part, in the event
he had attempted to give misinformation.

One of the duties of the field assistant at some time during the
first interview was to obtain the name of the informant, his age,
his tribe, and his place of habitat when a youth. On one occasion,
after an hour's interview, we found that the informant, a Chippewa, had been reared among the Sioux, and that all his information was Sioux and not Chippewa.

On our arrival home, after an interview, the assistant and I
together — and the interpreter, if she could arrange to be with
us — wrote the notes taken that day in the field on 4-by-6-inch
pieces of paper. Each paper was headed with the informant's
name, his age, tribe, early habitat, present habitat on the reservation, the date on which we obtained the information, and a title
which indicated the subject matter of the information. Below this

we wrote the information that we had collected. If a disagreement arose between the assistant, the interpreter, and myself regarding any note, we cleared it at the next interview with the informant. We took with us the 4-by-6-inch paper containing the contested note. Also by sorting and assembling the 4-by-6-inch papers we could see the pattern grow from interview to interview. This practice also facilitated the checking off of sections in the Field Guide on which we had sufficient notes.

Motivating the informant. Before many interviews with any informant, he would take the lead: "Why do you want to know these things?" Here was my opportunity to tell him honestly and frankly that we wished to record some of the old beliefs and customs regarding his people. We were asking him because we thought he, being one of the oldest members of his tribe, would remember former customs that most younger men had no knowledge of; that we were especially interested in learning the old ways with regard to children, since very little had been recorded about the way their children had been reared. I showed him the published work on his tribe that we had brought with us; especially the plates, if he did not read English. At this point I laid emphasis on truthfulness, accuracy, and reliability. From then on I spoke of our study to the informant as "the book we are writing" or as "our book."

Once we had a frank discussion about our objectives with the informant, he usually acted as though he shared some of the responsibilities. "I have waited all week for you to come back. Now since I got started thinking about our old ways, I recall much." "What will the title of our book be?" In Chile an informant objected to the word "primitive" being used in the title. "And let us not have an Araucanian woman on the cover, like they put on Félix José's *Lecturas araucanas.* That is not the place for a woman's picture!"

After several more interviews came the inevitable question, "Who will get the pay for this book we are writing?" The unfailing answer was, "No one. In fact it will cost a lot of money to get someone to print it." Then would follow conversation on the value of the study and on its serving as a legacy to generations of his descendants, especially his great-grandchildren. He understood; after he was paid for the day's work, rapport was usually established for the next interview.

ESTABLISHING THE VALIDITY OF MATERIAL COLLECTED

Checking by interviews with participants or other informants; items personally observed. We drove to Anadarko, Oklahoma, to interview an eighty-year-old man. When we arrived, his daughter-in-law was sitting on the back porch of his house reading the Sunday paper; he himself, nearly blind, was sitting on his bed in his room, the front room, smoking his pipe. The daughter-in-law's husband and her children had left home to see a baseball game. Both received us with courtesy, but separately. Each gave us ethnological information, but each stayed in the place where we had met. During our interview with the old man, the daughter-in-law prepared the evening meal. When it was ready, she told the man's daughter (the woman who had brought us to see the old man) to tell her father to come to the kitchen table where she had set his meal. The old man went. The daughter-in-law left the kitchen, walked around the outside of the house, and entered the front room by the front door. This was done to avoid meeting the old man. When we were seated for another interview with her, she remarked, "I shall never again let both children go away at the same time; the poor old man sat here by himself all afternoon. I was so glad when you came. Whenever I wish to say something to him or he to me, we send the children back and forth. For instance, I sent the children this noon to tell him that dinner was ready. They did so and led him to the table. He and my husband and the children ate; I sat on the front porch until the old man was finished. Then he left the table and I ate. If I would talk to him or go where he is, he would think that I had no respect for him. That is what all the old people say. I would not talk to him unless it were really necessary. For instance, if he took sick suddenly and there were no one else here, then I would have to talk to him. Having to sit alone like this and not being able to talk to my father-in-law is really hard. He is a good man and I have always admired him. He is lonely now, too. He grieves because he does not know where his son is, the one in the army."

Another daughter-in-law of the old man who had accompanied us from Anadarko did not greet the old man when we arrived at his home, nor did she bid him goodbye when he left. She did not appear in his presence at any time. On our way home, she solicitously inquired of the driver, the old man's daughter, whether her (the driver's) father had failed any since she had last visited him. The following day, the old man's daughter explained to us in detail the Arapaho father-in-law daughter-in-law and the mother-in-law son-in-law taboos.

Checking by participating in an activity, writing up the activity, and then checking the notes taken by being a nonparticipant observer. I played a game of marbles with Araucanian school boys in Alepue, Chile. As they taught me the game, I dictated each step to my assistant. In the evening we wrote up our notes. The following day we observed the same boys and also other boys, play the same game. We made several corrections in our notes, and, as the game proceeded, added several details that I had missed on the previous day.

While on the Lac Court Oreille Reservation in Wisconsin, a Chippewa herbalist took the field assistant and me into the woods and through the meadows to find trees and plants which she used for medicinal purposes. She had us make a collection of them. As we chipped bark off trees, dug up roots, and plucked leaves off plants, she gave us the Chippewa name for each tree and plant and also the English name, if she knew it. She told us the manner in which she used the plant or bark and for what sickness it was efficacious.

That evening we classified the plants botanically and pressed them. A few days later we showed the pressed plants and the bark to another herbalist. She, too, told us their Chippewa and English names, their medicinal values, and the manner of preparing them for use. We then compared the information obtained from the two herbalists. In instances where it did not seem clear or we disagreed, we sought corrections or additional information from a third informant.

Checking an item through personal interviews only. I knew that I should not have an opportunity to see the religious ceremonial of the Araucanian; the time for celebrating it fell outside the period of our stay in the areas. Details were what we particularly wanted. I conferred with an informant in Alepue with whom we had established good rapport. He immediately volunteered to give us the information himself.—"I know it as well as any one here."— He added that it would take a long time to describe the ceremonial, that he would organize his knowledge in an orderly way and write down details before he came to talk to us; that he needed an entire afternoon to relate it; when should he report? He came at the assigned time with notes and a diagram. The diagram showed the location of the objects, the persons, and the activities of the ceremonial. He referred to the diagram continually during his narrative, showing the movements of activities and of participating persons. We took down his account verbatim. He halted after each explanation to allow us time to write.

I asked another informant in another area, Panguipulle, to prepare an orderly account of the ceremonial also. He, too, brought a diagram and gave us time to take down his account verbatim. From the two accounts, then, I worked out the essentials of the ceremonial and noted down carefully what seemed to be variations or complete differences between them. In still another area, Conaripe, I went, one by one, through the items that I had noted down as essentials, with a man on whose land the ceremonial was annually held. He, too, drew a diagram and then took each item that I had noted, discussed it, and placed it on his diagram. Variations again showed up. We also took his account down verbatim. Taking these three independent accounts from three separated areas, I worked out what I inferred to be the essentials of the tribal religious ceremonial. Variations and similarities are found in the verbatim accounts.

Discovering whether or not a trait is native. I was curious to know whether a statement that I had heard at the 1951 meetings of the Central States Branch of the American Anthropological Association was true. It was said that even though a field worker did not intend to use the Rorschach tests for studies of personality, he could by means of them elicit the informant's major interests. With this in mind I showed an Argentine Araucanian woman from Pilpil the small reprints of the Rorschach cards found on the last page of the protocol score sheet. I had cut these reprints apart and had pasted them singly on sheets of paper.

The informant looked at reprint No. 1 with these comments: "Have you more of these? Who made these? Were they made here? I have seen some like these." She continued to examine the reprint. I asked, "Where did you see these?" No answer. She was treating me as I had treated her. I asked, "What does this picture make you think of?" No answer. After a little time, "Have you any more?" She looked at each one of the ten, one by one, without any comment, then put them in numerical order, and said, "Girls make these. A girl will mix the black from the bottom of the tea kettle with water, just a little water, or use ink, if there is any around. She will put some of the wet smudge on one half of a folded paper, near the crease, fold the other half over it, and lay the folded paper under the pillow on which she will sleep that night. In the morning she will look at it and know from the picture that it has made what kind of luck she will have when she marries. If it turns out to look like a puma or dog, she will have bad luck. If it looks like the head of an animal or like a horse, she will have good luck."

She continued, "But let me look at your pictures again." She looked thoughtfully at each one successively, and made the following remarks: (For No. 1) "Like the wings of a bird, probably the wings of an eagle. The center part is like a little lamb." (No. 2) "A little bird. No, no, two men with hats." (No. 3) "Persons just like we." (No. 4) "Could be a bear." (No. 5) "A butterfly. Yes, a butterfly. Things will not go very well with the girl that gets one like this." (No. 6) "The top part is the head of an animal." She turned the card to the side, and added, "The two things on the sides are dogs." (No. 7) "These are two children with a house." (No. 8) "The top is a house; the bottom are cats and a puma. The girl who gets this will have a man like a puma." (No. 9) "A young girl in a house. She will have great luck." (No. 10) "A little sheep and rats and more animals. It means good luck for the girl who gets this one." The informant could give no further information regarding the custom except that "this has been done around here for many years."

Several days later I showed the reprints to an Araucanian woman in another area, Trumpul, not too distant from Pilpil. She merely remarked, "If you want to know what these mean you will have to go to one of two men in San Martin. No, these men are not Araucanian. Girls go to them when they want to know what theirs mean." Our oldest informants were certain that no one in the old days made marital predictions in this manner. No informant in the Pilpil and Trumpul areas was able to give us an Araucanian word for the custom nor a Spanish one. We checked in the areas of Malleo and San Ignacio also. Here informants were certain that the custom was not an Araucanian one, nor did we obtain here an Araucanian word for the custom. I was certain, then, that the custom was not part of the pre-Spanish Araucanian culture.

While making inquiries about the marital prediction by ink-blots, an old Araucanian man, with emphasis and assurance, told of a performance test that, he said, predicted personality. In administering it parents oblige a boy — he may be only four years old — to drink chicha or, more recently, wine until he is completely intoxicated. If the boy, when intoxicated, "runs around and yells and wants to fight," he will grow up to be an angry man, he will be jealous and quarrelsome. His parents, observing him in this excited state, are frightened and worried at the thought of his future, "but they can do nothing about it." If the boy lies down and sleeps, it is a good sign. I wondered whether this was a true Araucanian custom. We had not heard of it among the Chilean Araucanian after five months' intensive study among them. On the other hand, it did not seem to be of Spanish origin, for neither Argentines nor recently arrived Spanish persons knew of such a custom. Maybe it was borrowed from the Tehuelche, a tribe to the south. Occasionally the Tehuelche were mentioned by the Araucanian. But knowing the Araucanian to be a proud people, I doubted that they would adopt so personal a custom as this. They had adopted environmental ones.

If it was a true Araucanian custom, I reasoned, it should be found among the Chilean Araucanians as well. We had learned among the Chilean Araucanians that the father insisted, at times, that his school-age son drink to intoxication, but we had not heard that a personality-prediction test was attached to it. On our way home from the Argentine Araucanians, we stopped among the Chilean Araucanians (Panquipulli) to check this custom, along with several others. Our best informant's reply was: "One of my relatives tested his sons that way when they were small, and the forecast of their characters came true. The boy must not know that he is being tested. On a day he is given the seeds of miyaiya (not identified) with toasted wheat or barley. I do not know whether or not the miyaiya is toasted, also, but he is given this as his meal. This makes him drunk. His parents observe him in this state to see what he will do. If he picks up things around the place, they know that he will turn out to be a thief. If he acts toward other children as though he were going to fight them, he will be a fighter. If he tries to get near girls, he will be a lover. If he wants to drink everything in the place, he will be a drunkard. If he pretends to be playing the guitar, he will be a musician. Formerly nearly all parents tried to discover the character of each son. It was not so with girls; but a girl could have been subjected to the test, too, in order to learn what her character would turn out to be." We were certain now that the test on the performance of which personality was predicted was Araucanian. It would be interesting now to know whether the Argentine Araucanian at any time used the seeds of the miyaiya in place of the present-day chicha and wine.

Clearing published information that seemed doubtful. Did sibs ever exist among the Araucanians? Were the kuga, cuga, cunga, elpa of Cooper's sources merely kinship groups, or were they sibs? Quoting Cooper: ". . . there is no tangible evidence in our sources that any but real kin were members of any given kuga, and consequently no evidence that the kuga constituted a true sib. Each kuga had its own name, such as sky, sun, pillan . . ., stone grove, likan, pebble, sea, or lake, gold, bird of prey, eagle, river, water . . ." From both the literature and field work I was thoroughly acquainted with the Chippewa exogamic gentes, known to them as the dô'dàm. I knew that the exogamy of the dô'dàm extended to all the members of a gens in any Chippewa tribe anywhere. I also knew from field work and from Kroeber's account that neither clans nor gentes existed among the Arapaho.

The kuga *might* be a sib, I thought. Certainly the names of the kuga reminded me of the Chippewa gentes. I set about to find some tangible evidence of the kuga as a sib. I explained the clan and the gens systems to Araucanian informants, both men and women, in three separated areas in Chile: Alepue, Conaripe, and Panguipulli. I also conferred with Father Sigifredo de Fraunhäusl who had spent more than fifty years among the Araucanian. He had not heard of the kuga or cuga or cunga or elpa. He called in Domingo Wenuñamco (today known as Domingo Huenun). Both Father Sigifredo and Huenun had assisted Father Félix José de Augusta in compiling the *Diccionario (araucano-español y español-araucano)*. Neither had ever heard the words; neither one believed that a sib system ever existed among the Araucanian. Huenun noted that if *kuga, cuga, cunga,* and *elpa* referred to a naming system, the word *kunpém* should be added to them; that *kunpém* definitely referred to the naming system and had no relation whatever to a clan or gens system. I also asked teachers to have school children write down the name of the kuga or elpa or kunpém to which each belonged. No child had ever heard that it belonged to one of them.

Upon the basis of what we had collected, I made the following statement regarding sibs for the Araucanian of Chile: "No informant had heard of a sib system. The oldest informants — one older than one hundred years — did not know the meaning of the words *kuga* or *elpa*, terms found in the literature which might lead one to suspect a sib system. Cooper's more recent sources, too, noted

39

that they found no recollection of a sib system among their Araucanian informants . . . If kuga denotes a kinship system rather
than a sib system, it may persist in related family groups of the
present day."

While among the Araucanian in Argentina, I made further inquiries. No informant, not even the oldest, had even a vague notion
of the meaning of *kuga* or *elpa*, or of a sib system. (I should note
that the Argentine Araucanian are decidedly more acculturated
than are the Chilean.) Neither did Bertha Koessler-Ilg know of a
sib system or the meaning of *kuga* and *elpa*. She is a recognized
Araucanian folklorist who has lived among the Argentine Araucanian for more than thirty years. Her interest became intense, and
she made every effort to find the meaning of the words. She contacted Horacio Molinari, Secretary of the Sociedad Argentina de
Americanistas, who was in the Araucanian country in the interest
of the Academia Argentina de Letras making a comparative study
of Araucanian dialects. Molinari found the following in the *Revista
Chilena de Historia y Geografía*: "aillo: familia, linaje, del vo-
cablo quichua *ayllu* que los indígenas chilenos del Norte tomaron
de sus conquistadores peruanos en lugar de cuya, elpa, y cheun,
con que en lengua araucana se indica la misma idea." Neither
Koessler nor Molinari nor I interpreted this as throwing any light
on the sib system. I now believed that I could find no tangible
evidence for a sib system.

*Clearing doubts raised by information found in museum collec-
tions.* After field work among the Arapaho in both Wyoming and
Oklahoma, I studied museum specimens of both areas in the Chicago Natural History Museum, the United States National Museum, the American Museum of Natural History, and the University
of Pennsylvania Museum. Among the cradles labeled as Arapaho
there are two kinds, one made of canvas with quill-work decora-
tions, and the other an all-beaded one. I had suspicions that the
all-beaded one was not of Arapaho make. From my field work I
knew that the Arapaho women made their cradles ceremonially.
An all-beaded one would have taken too long to make, if accompanied by a ceremony such as had been described to me by old

women. However, I had every reason to believe that the collectors of the all-beaded cradles (Alfred Kroeber, Emile Granier, and P. H. Ray) were careful and reliable collectors.

I discussed my doubt with the curator of the United States National Museum. He had specimens of both types of cradles photographed. In 1942, during my last field trip to the Wyoming Arapaho, I showed the photographs to two old women. The quill-worked canvas cradle brought exclamations of pleasure and was pointed out as being an Arapaho one. All parts were examined and counted and commented upon, and the cradle was finally declared to have been correctly and well made. The women were emphatic in declaring that the Arapaho had only the one type of cradle. The other cradle, the all-beaded one, was Sioux, both insisted. They admired the beaded design and wondered where I had got the photographs.

Since I could find no cradle of either type extant among the present-day Arapaho, I had no way of clearing my doubts by personal observations. All informants were agreed that the last cradles had been bought by a white man who "used to come around here to buy up all the old Indian 'stuff'." In the fall of 1943 I had an opportunity to show the photographs to several old Sioux men and women of the Standing Rock Reservation of the Dakotas. All were agreed that the all-beaded one was a Sioux cradle. Obviously, then, the all-beaded cradle was not an Arapaho one.

Checking by procuring the native word. Whenever we obtained a native word for an object, a custom, a belief, or an activity, we had some assurance that we were dealing with a native trait. If no native word was obtainable, the trait was most probably a bor-rowed one. Whenever we drove through the country once occupied by the Argentine Araucanian, the driver pointed out groves of wild apple trees and remarked: "Wherever you find these wild apple groves, you will find a spring also. Those are the places where once Araucanian lived." No Araucanian informant, however, knew an Araucanian word for apples. Always the Spanish word, *man-zano*, was given. No Araucanian informant would admit that apples had not always been known to them. In fact, informants insisted that their people have always been called Manzaneros (apple-eaters or apple-growers). Non-Araucanians, conversant with the historical background of the area, believe that the Jesuit Fathers who crossed the Andes from Chile introduced the horti-culture of apple trees to the Argentine Araucanian.

Among other foods for which the Araucanian language provides no word and which are designated by Spanish words are butter, milk, and cheese. Among foods for which there is an Araucanian name, but no Spanish one, are funa poñü (fermented potatoes), ñachi (highly seasoned coagulated blood of sheep or lamb), and loko (dish of shellfish).

THE OUTCOME OF OUR METHOD

In collecting ethnographic information, then, we found the following helpful: making adequate preparation for field work; a careful choice of field assistant, informants, and interpreters; using a planned system of contact-making and one of note-taking; motivating the informant; and establishing the validity of the information we gathered through observations and interviews. Our procedure, we believe, brought about stimulated, interested, and intelligent responses from informants and interpreters. The results of our method are to be found in our ethnographic studies entitled "Chippewa Child Life and Its Cultural Background" (Bulletin 146 of the Bureau of American Ethnology, Smithsonian Institu-tion); "Arapaho Child Life and Its Cultural Background" (Bulle-tin 148 of the Bureau of American Ethnology); and "Araucanian Child Life and Its Cultural Background" (a forthcoming publi-cation).

by ELIZABETH COLSON

The Intensive Study of Small
Sample Communities

THE last few years have seen a resurgence of interest in the comparative method among social anthropologists both in Europe and America. Perhaps the greatest recent contribution to comparative research has been that of Murdock (1949), who used information drawn from 250 societies to test the degree to which various social factors were correlated with kinship terminologies. The recent interest in the comparative method undoubtedly reflects the fact that anthropology has reached a new stage in its struggle to become a "science." With the use of the comparative method comes the application of statistical techniques, although much of the information which is available at the present time was not collected with this end in view.

The new techniques of analysis, as well as the new problems with which anthropologists are engaged, have already affected the field work which is being done. Field workers are producing more and more meticulous descriptions with a good deal of quantitative material to back up generalized statements, and at the same time they are narrowing their areas of investigation. This, I think, reflects a general and important trend in anthropology and in the social sciences in general.

It is toward a consideration of these new demands upon the field worker that this paper is directed. Kluckhohn (1939) some years ago pointed out: "If we are to deal with any problem (such as that of the acquisition of culture by individuals) in a way which is reducible to actual human behaviors, generalizations must be given a quantitative basis" (p. 6). More recently Driver (1953) pressed this point home when he wrote, "If we are going to use more mathematics, we must organize field work with that in mind. We must obtain more quantification of every kind wherever it is possible to do so. . . . If one of the goals of ethnology is to arrive at patterns, configurations, or structures of cultures, these must be determined inductively from adequate numbers of actual facts if they are to satisfy the standards of science" (p. 53).

The worker in the comparative field is hampered very badly because he does not have "adequate numbers of actual facts" upon which to base comparisons. Instead he must rely upon generalized statements about social institutions and compare these on an all-or-none basis, though the generalized descriptions may be incomparable in actual fact. Thus, in her article on the Arapesh which appears in *Cooperation and Competition among Primitive Peoples* (1937), Margaret Mead follows the description of the formal organization of Arapesh society with the comment that the actual functioning of the society is "of a very different order than that implied in their structural arrangements" (p. 27). She further says that the formal structure is not observed in practice, unlike "many primitive societies, notably Dobu" (p. 27). If we had the same type of material for most primitive societies that Mead has for the Arapesh, it might well turn out that the formal structural arrangement of the society offers only a very general guide to behavior which does not jibe with practice to any exact degree, and that those societies where formal structure and actual practice largely coincide are the exceptions. At present we simply do not know, and the type of comparative work which Murdock and others have attempted to do becomes questionable when viewed against this background. Murdock uses the Arapesh as one of his sample societies. Presumably he works with the formal structure of Arapesh society as he does with the formal structure of the other societies in his sample. As things stand, we do not know whether or not he is comparing comparable phenomena. It is certainly not suggested

44

here that Murdock is unaware of this problem, witness his discussion of the criteria to be used in classifying a given society as polygamous or monogamous (1949, pp. 24–28). But much of the information available to him is inadequate for the purpose to which it is put.

I suspect therefore that the comparative method will contribute little further to our understanding of social organization and the field of cultural phenomena in general until we shift from the all-or-none classifications so largely used at present to a method based on the comparison of rates constructed from quantitative information collected in a systematic fashion. For this we need new standards of field work. Counting noses is a tedious and uninspiring job, but perhaps the new depths of insight into human organization to which it should lead will at least partially compensate even the field worker for the loss of some of his old freedom.

We want, then, quantitative material to back up qualitative statements: an analysis of actual residence to accompany descriptive statements about whether residence is virilocal, uxorilocal, avunculocal, neolocal, or what have you; of actual inheritance and successions to back up stated rules of inheritance; of the number of cross-cousin marriages expressed as a proportion of total marriages; and so on through the whole gamut of social facts used to characterize a society and thus to contrast it with others.

This development should enable us to test a large number of hypotheses which have been put forward over the years about the nature of social interaction. Monica Wilson (1951) has some extremely suggestive things to say about the importance of residence patterns in determining the nature and direction of witchcraft accusations. To test her hypothesis, we need some cross-cultural information, showing the actual composition of residence units and the number, type, and direction of witchcraft accusations made by members of these units. Does cross-cousin marriage solve some of the stresses that occur in a matrilineal society, as suggested by Malinowski? Some quantitative data on divorce frequencies for cross-cousin marriages as against non-cross-cousin marriages, as well some better information on the incidence of

45

quarrels between those united by a cross-cousin marriage tie, might help us to check this hypothesis. Does the joking relationship serve as a safety valve for people who are in some way in an ambivalent position with respect to each other? Radcliffe-Brown has made this suggestion, but nobody to my knowledge has actually tested it in a systematic fashion.

Nadel (1947), on the basis of his work among the various Nuba groups of the Anglo-Egyptian Sudan, has suggested that an intrinsic and logical correlation exists between social rigidity or inclusiveness and the incidence of suicide (p. 480). In this, of course, he is following in the footsteps of Durkheim. He points out that his information on the incidence of suicide for the different Nuba groups is inadequate. He usually cites the number of cases which his informants listed for him, or remarks that it was unknown or denied by informants of some particular group. This is enough, perhaps, to point the problem. But since he does not give the size of the population or the time period to which the information applies, it is impossible to construct a suicide rate for comparisons with other societies. I suspect on the basis of my own field work among the Plateau Tonga of Northern Rhodesia that their suicide rate is high, and I think that the frequency may be related to the diffuse nature of the social network in which the Tonga finds himself, where he lacks the security that a more rigid formulation of rights and obligations might provide. On the basis of my material, I may be able to work out a very crude rate, with number of suicides, size of population, and period of time taken into account. But until other anthropologists produce the same sort of material for the peoples with whom they are working, I am in no position to be sure whether the Tonga take their lives with any greater or less frequency than the majority of other preliterate peoples. The Nuba material as it stands is suggestive, but useless for comparative purposes. What is needed is material of a type which allows of a direct comparison of rates. This, of course, will give the information for only one of the factors involved in Nadel's hypothesis. To test the hypothesis itself, we shall also need some means of stating objectively the degree of diffuseness or rigidity of social relationships, and to state this in such a way that it will be possible again to collect the information which will allow of the construction of rates for cross-cultural comparisons.

Gluckman (1950) has suggested that frequency of divorce is correlated with social structures of a particular type, but with the crude information at his disposal he is able to do little more than state the problem. To test his hypothesis we need divorce rates, worked out in a comparable fashion, for a series of societies with different forms of social structure. Barnes has attempted to develop a method of computing a divorce rate for nonliterate societies where no records are kept of either marriages or divorces, and he has combed the literature for quantitative information on divorce.[1] Other anthropologists working with various societies in Central Africa, under the auspices of the Rhodes-Livingstone Institute, are collecting quantitative information on divorce in a standard fashion and will use the method worked out by Barnes for presenting their results. We shall soon then be in a better position to test Gluckman's hypothesis, and to refine upon it.

I have suggested (1951) that population movements may be related to strains within the social structure, and have characterized the Plateau Tonga as highly mobile, i.e., as making frequent changes of residence from one village to another. Although in the paper in which I put this forward, I gave a certain amount of information on the number of moves made by the people found in certain villages, the quantitative material is not expressed in a fashion which makes a direct comparison with other societies possible. For this it will be necessary to work out some method of computing a mobility rate. In any event, as matters stand, my assumption that the Tonga are highly mobile is only an assumption. When we have an adequate series of mobility rates for other societies, the Tonga may turn out to be unusually stable.

So far I have been speaking only of the utility of rates, and quantitative data in general, for cross-cultural comparisons. But they are equally useful to those who are concerned with a single society over a period of time. Even where a single anthropologist

[1] Barnes, 1951; Barnes, 1952; Mitchell and Barnes, 1950.

makes a return visit to a society which he studied ten to twenty years ago, he cannot be certain that the implicit standards against which his qualitative description was made have remained the same. The anthropologist who follows another into the same field has even more of a problem, unless his predecessor has made his yardstick explicit. Since anthropologists are today highly concerned with problems of culture change, some method of measuring trends must be developed, and I suspect that for this, quantitative information is again necessary. I have argued (1951) that as land shortage develops, the geographical mobility of the Tonga population will decline. I ought therefore to provide some measure of both land shortage and the rate of population mobility for the period when I worked with the Tonga so that anyone who works among the Tonga in the future will have a standard against which he can compare his own results.

Both the comparative method and the interest in problems of cultural or social change are therefore creating a new demand that the field worker collect information on critical factors in such a way that direct comparisons may be possible.

How the information is to be collected remains the problem, which is more or less pressing according to the size of the unit with which the field worker is concerned and the time that he has at his disposal. Some collection of quantitative data has long been part of the standard schedule of field work, and various suggestions for appropriate techniques have been made. Audrey Richards (1935) in the middle thirties recommended the adoption of the village census as a means of having some check upon the field worker's impressions. The census as a tool is admittedly most useful to the anthropologist working in an extant society, but Gifford (1926) has shown its possibilities even in situations where one is attempting to reconstruct a society with the aid of informants. Other survey techniques have also been used, and Streib (1952) has recently argued for their utility in studies of semiliterate societies, instancing his own work among the Navaho. Some form of census work is probably by now a standard technique among field workers, at least among those who are dealing with extant societies.

The real argument lies not with regard to the use of the census, but how it shall be used, to what units it shall be applied, and how it can be combined with other field techniques to produce the most adequate description of the society which is to be studied. The anthropologist who works within a restricted geographical area and with a population numbering only some hundreds, or at the most several thousand, can afford to ignore sampling problems. Since he can collect his information for every man, woman, and child in the universe with which he deals, the question of the representativeness of his material does not arise. Moreover, he can combine his census work with a close observation of the members of the society which he is studying, and this gives him a valuable cross-check upon the accuracy of the information supplied to the census questionnaire. The material derived from the census, from any other survey technique employed, and from detailed observations, combine into a unified picture of a single entity at the end of his study.

Most anthropologists today find themselves in a very different situation, even when they are still working with what may be termed preliterate societies. Those of us who have worked in Africa are usually faced with the problem of studying a tribe whose population may be less than a hundred thousand, but is very frequently on the scale of several millions. This population may be a highly differentiated one, showing both social stratification and geographical or local variations. Frequently no very obvious boundary distinguishes it from its neighbors. Instead there may be gradual changes in language and customs across an area of several hundred miles. At either extreme, the people may be very different, but at no one point would it be possible to say that one was now dealing with a different population, or a different society, or a different culture. Sheer size of population, sheer extent of geographical space, sheer degree of cultural differentiation, combine to make it impossible for the anthropologist to study and describe such a society in the same way that he does the small-scale societies with which most early field-workers were concerned.

In these circumstances it has frequently been argued that the census has little utility, since it is impossible to obtain a representative sample for the entire community which is to be studied, and that one must therefore confine oneself to qualitative descriptions of the way in which the society functions or of the different aspects of its culture. Attempts have been made to meet the objections on the score of representativeness, either through the use of a random sample or through some form of stratified sample. Neither one is particularly satisfactory.

Usually we have insufficient information about the universe from which the sample is to be drawn to allow us to apply sample techniques which would meet the standards set up for statistical analysis. In Central Africa, for instance, we usually lack even that vital necessity an accurate estimate of the total size of the population with which we are to work. In 1946, when I began work with the Plateau Tonga, official estimates of their population varied between 80,000 and 120,000. Information on the distribution of the population was no better. In 1946 I could find no maps which would give me the location of villages. Maps were available giving some rough indication of the roads, but I was told that I could not expect to find a road where one was indicated and that I might well find roads where none were shown upon the map. The official estimates of the population of the various chieftaincies into which Tonga country is divided for administrative convenience were no better than the estimates for the total population. Official records showed the theoretical size of each village, but these were admittedly very far from showing the true state of affairs. The records also listed by name all adult male taxpayers residing in each village, but a man listed officially under a village might be living anywhere else within Tonga country, or he might have gone away to work in the industrial areas, or he might be dead. Information on differences in custom, on the degree of missionary and other European influence, or on any other significant variables upon which a stratified sample might have been constructed was lacking, except for figures giving the amount of maize sold by each producer during the previous year. After several years in Tonga country, spent in touring from one area to another, collecting survey material, I might have been in a position to consider the possibility of obtaining a not too unrepresentative sample for census purposes, but this was only after I had completed most of my field work. My colleagues of the Rhodes-Livingstone Institute who went to other tribes in Northern Rhodesia, Southern Rhodesia, and Nyasaland found themselves in much the same situation.

We also had to face another problem in deciding upon the utility of a census technique, and that was whether or not we should be able to collect a sufficient number of cases in the time at our disposal to make the technique worth using. If we had to spend a good proportion of our time moving from place to place and in discovering appropriate people to question, it was obvious that at the end we should probably have little to show for our efforts. While we could count on two tours, of approximately twelve months each, time was still limited. Furthermore, each of us had only the assistance of a clerk-interpreter in making the study. These men were of varying abilities, but none was trained as a research assistant. As time went on and the anthropologist became fluent in the language of the area while the assistant came to know his job, it became possible to divide the work somewhat, and thus to increase the amount of information which could be collected. My own assistant became invaluable, and in the end was doing a good deal of census work independently, with an occasional check by myself so that I could be certain of his accuracy in recording.[2]

All these considerations forced us to consider carefully just what we were doing, and the units to which our final studies were to apply. We agreed that we ought to be able to compare our results, and this meant that we were to collect information on the same problems, and to present this information in as standard a fashion as possible. But we also felt that we had to relate our material to a given body of people. In a sense the result was that we tended to re-create the situation of the anthropologist who works within

[2] Eventually funds were obtained to employ and train a team of African assistants, to be attached to the various anthropologists working in the field and to collect quantitative information of various types under his guidance. But this occurred only after my own field work was completed and I had left Central Africa.

a small-scale society. We artificially delimited a unit for study, roughly a small geographical area containing a number of villages. Here we made the majority of our observations, and here we collected our quantitative material on a systematic basis. Or rather, we selected two or three such units, and cross-checked the information for each one against the other. Each unit was treated as a universe, within which we made no attempt to sample. Instead we collected information for the census for each individual in the area, returning again and again until each person had been interviewed. This took a good deal of time, and, indeed, it sometimes took more time to track down the one or two persons missing during the main census period than it did to do a census of all the rest of a village. It was not, however, time completely wasted, for every visit to a village could be used to build up a picture of the general background of those living within it and to add to information on points not directly involved in the census.

Since we were taking our quantitative material from the people within a small geographical area, the census could be easily incorporated with a set of other field techniques — observation, collection of genealogies, discussions with informants about matters of custom or the ordinary flow of daily events, attendance at rituals, etc. The problems of rapport were less because we were working with people whom we knew and who knew us. Moreover, since all were being subjected to the same barrage of questions, they minded it less than if one or two from a village had been chosen at random and they had had to wonder why fate had brought this infliction upon them and not upon their neighbors. Information obtained in the general give-and-take of daily life or during sessions when other matters were to the fore frequently gave a good check upon the accuracy of the answers obtained to census questions. Census information from several individuals also gave us some cross-check, as when a woman was asked for information on her children and it corroborated information that one of her sons had given regarding his parents and siblings. After the information was collected, we were able to get the maximum use from it because it applied always to people whom we knew and who were in the same social group as others about whom we had similar information.

After our first six months of field work, we arrived at a standard census form which could be used in all the areas we were working in and which contained questions directed at getting information that we all agreed was essential. At the same time there was sufficient space on the form so that the individual field worker could add additional questions as he decided that particular matters relevant to his field of inquiry needed systematic checking. Thus the final census form which each field worker used was adjusted to the particular problems of the area in which he worked, but at the same time certain relevant information was being collected in each area, and the information was being collected in a similar fashion so that comparable rates could be obtained.

The final census form that I used among the Tonga covered the following information:

Information on Kinsmen

Parents: names, clan and tribal affiliation, birthplace, present residence if still alive, cross reference to their census cards if they were in the census area.

Siblings: names, sex, residence if alive, final residence if dead, cross reference to their cards if they lived within the census area, names and sex and residence of their children if not in the census.

Spouse: names, clan affiliation, previous kinship term used, approximate date of marriage; if terminated, manner and approximate date of termination; number of plural marriages; whether or not marriage represented inheritance of widow.

Children: names and sex of children by each spouse or by lover or mistress, approximate birth dates, residence if alive, approximate date of death if dead and place of final residence, cross reference to their census cards if they were within the census area.

Personal Information

Name, alternative names, sex, place of birth, approximate date of birth, clan and tribal affiliation, where and by whom reared.

Place of residence: village, chieftaincy, number of hut against chart of village, kinship relation to the head of the household.

Physical defects.

Religious affiliation, amount of schooling, occupation or craft specialization, official status, any indications of economic status.

Previous places of residence, and their sequence; reason for present residence.

Marriage payment, amount and from whom assistance received; payments of damages for elopement or for the impregnation of an unmarried girl, whereabouts of child.

Details of puberty ceremony (from women only): length of seclusion, by whom secluded, number of animals killed at final ceremony and by whom provided, length of time elapsing between final ceremony and marriage.

Labor history (for men): place of work, type of work, manner of reaching work and how this was financed, wage earned, amount brought back to village and for what this was used, sequence of trips to work, reason for going (this last a fairly useless question).

Fields: number, how obtained, and from whom.

Crop sales: sales from the previous harvest of maize, beans, peanuts, and other saleable crops — amount sold and money received.

Succession: whether or not informant had ever succeeded to a position or inherited the name of a dead person, and if so, the kinship relation of the two.

House dedication: kinship category of the ancestor to whom the household was dedicated.

Household: number of people living in the household, and their relationship to each other.

In addition, if the informant had a sibling, child, parent, or spouse who was away at work, I tried to obtain details of the absent worker's labor history, including the length of time he had been gone, his present place of work, and whether or not he was in touch with his relatives and either visited them or sent them gifts of goods or money from time to time.

This may seem a long list of questions to batter informants with, but at the end my chief regrets were that I had not included more questions in the systematic check, that I included some of the questions too late to have a complete coverage for all the people in the census, and that occasionally I had grown slipshod and omitted a question or two during an interview. Some of the questions have little significance in themselves, but in combination with others on the schedule they may be used to throw light on a variety of problems.

In addition to the information about the individuals in the census area, further information about each village was included in the file containing the cards for each village. The headman and other adults in the village were interviewed to obtain the history of the village: the approximate date of its founding if this had occurred within living memory, its previous locations, the succession to the headmanship, and the relationship of the successor to his predecessor. By the use of genealogies I attempted to discover how each person in the village was related to all others resident there. A numbered hut chart was drawn showing the physical layout of the village at the time of the census.

Other information collected about the inhabitants of the villages was on a cumulative basis. Villages in the two areas chosen for intensive study were watched over a four-year period, and I recorded birth, puberty ceremonies, marriages, divorces, deaths, trips away to work, return of labor migrants, changes in hut sites, and changes in residence, throughout the four years. After the harvest and the sale of crops had been completed, we collected information each year on the amount that had been sold by each household. This material was either recorded on the census card or a cross reference was made to the place where it could be found in the file of other field notes.

During my first field tour I worked in four different areas, and planned to make these my unit of observation. In three I took censuses during that first year. Later it became necessary to reduce the number of areas to only two, and I chose one which was close to the belt of European farms and the railway line and one which was back in the reserve on the edge of the hills of the escarpment country. The two were contrasts in various ways: One was under Roman Catholic influence, the other under Seventh Day Adventist. One had only a small cash income from the sale of crops, the other had a much higher average income from crop sales and included a number of relatively wealthy progressive farmers. One was dominated by a government-appointed chief who lived in one of the

55

villages, the other had no chief resident within it. One owed allegiance to a rain shrine or set of shrines, and there was community-
wide participation in the rain and harvest rites, while in the other
few concerned themselves with the local rain shrine or with the
rites connected with it. One was considered by the Tonga to be
a conservative area where old customs were still followed, the other
was considered to be a progressive area where the people were
trying to be like Europeans. The two areas lay about thirteen
miles apart, and many of the people in the progressive area had
originally come from the conservative one.

I redid the census for these two areas in 1948, during my second
tour, and thereafter kept it up to date by constant visits. In addition to the information that I had for these two areas, I also had
incomplete census data from a third area studied in 1947, and
I supplemented this with further material drawn from a census,
carried out by my clerk in 1949–1950, of villages which lay in an
intermediate zone between the progressive and conservative areas.
In analyzing the data, I have first compiled the material by area,
compared the figures for the four, and if no significant differences
appear, then I have treated the material as a single body of data
and indicate that it relates to all four different Tonga areas to
which the census was applied. If significant differences appear,
then the material for each area is handled separately, and I am
concerned to find why the differences should appear and what
factors are involved.

My knowledge of the area visited only in 1947, and of the intermediate area added in 1949–1950, is much less than it is for the
two areas of intensive work, though even here the census material
pertains to known groups, of a known size, and to all the people
within the given areas. But I have made my formulation of problems and my analysis on the basis of my work in the two intensive
areas and have used the material drawn from the other two only
to test the wider applicability of the analysis.

The following discussion will show some of the uses to which the
census information can be put. I would suggest that cross-cousin
marriages are of most importance among the Tonga where people

are most dependent upon mutual assistance, and where they are least affected by the market economy and the possibility of developing ties with the strangers who work along the railway line. When I analyzed the crop sales for the three areas, I find that Area I (the progressive area) has the largest average income from this source; Area II (the intermediate area) has a significantly lower income; Area III (the conservative area) has the lowest income. The three areas are in the same order with respect to proximity to the railway line, Area II being only slightly further removed from the railway than Area I. From all the marriages of informants in each area, I extract the number of cross-cousin marriages and show it as a percentage of the total number of marriages. The results are given below:

	Area I	Area II	Area III	Total
Cross-cousin marriages shown as a percentage of all extant marriages....	18.56	17.69	33.63	23.43

There is a real difference between Area I and Area III in line with my original argument, but Area II seems contradictory, at least if crop sales are any indication of the influence of impersonal market relationships upon a people.

Material derived from the census is also useful for checking general impressions, and frequently a check of the data indicates a trend very different from that which has been assumed. I originally assumed that the period of seclusion for girls at puberty had been progressively diminished by mission and school influence. When I compiled material on the length of seclusion, classifying the material according to the decade in which the woman had been born, I found that there had actually been a progessive increase in the length of time of seclusion in all areas, but that this trend had been reversed for the last group of women to reach puberty. I now suspect that the increased prosperity of the Tonga due to the development of a market for their crops and the introduction of tools allowing a larger area to be cultivated enabled more families to indulge in the status-producing practice of lengthy seclusion, which indicated that the family had sufficient food and to spare. In early years, when the Tonga seem to have faced a hunger period as an annual event, since they did not produce enough grain to last from one harvest to the next, few families could reach the ideal length of seclusion.

Again, from the statements of informants, I believed that formerly Tonga women married much earlier than they do today and that girls were frequently married immediately after their puberty ceremony. Again, when the material on the length of time between the puberty seclusion and the marriage was analyzed according to the decade in which the woman was born, the facts were directly contrary to popular belief and my understanding of the situation. Today I find that when I make a statement about the Tonga, I am inclined first to check it against the material drawn from the census to see whether or not I am coming anywhere near the facts of the case. Impressions can be thoroughly wrong; so can the statements of informants. Getting out the material to check one's statements from the census forms may consume a good deal of time, but it also gives one some assurance that the statement is reasonably accurate, at least for the particular small group with which one has been dealing.

Whether or not my material for the areas studied is in any way representative of the Tonga people as a whole, I do not know. This is a problem which may be of some concern to the administration and to the technical assistants who are trying to deal with the Tonga as though they were a single unit. I do not think that it is a problem which needs to concern the anthropologist who is trying to make a study of the interrelation of social factors in a single social system. After all, each area studied does represent a unit in which the people are in close social relations with each other. The factors which exist within that set of relations can be dealt with as though one were dealing with an isolated society. The anthropologist certainly has a duty to outline his method and the area to which his information applies, and furthermore he ought to be able to give some indication of variations over the general area which might affect his analysis and make it inapplicable or applicable elsewhere. This seems to be about the limit to which he can go, with the time, the assistance, and the resources at his disposal. I see no reason why information collected on particular small units within a larger area which bears the same tribal name should not be used for comparison with information drawn from similar small units within other large areas which bear different tribal names. The result of the intensive study of small units may not make for the best description in the style of a standard ethnography, but it is most likely to provide us with the type of information we need for testing hypotheses and for formulating new research into the relation between various social factors.

by DAVID G. MANDELBAUM

Form, Variation, and Meaning
of a Ceremony

A FUNERAL is perhaps a melancholy subject, but it is a religious ceremony that lends itself well to general analysis. The ceremony that is the subject of this paper is one performed by the Kota of the Nilgiri Hills of South India. The following discussion is part of a larger design intended to describe Kota life and to develop some theoretical concepts in the light of the description.

The Kota live in seven small villages, each of which is located among villages of the Badaga, the agricultural people long resident in the area, whose population of some 50,000 is far greater than the Kota total of some 1,200. Even fewer are the numbers of the pastoral Toda, the third indigenous group of the Nilgiri plateau, who now number little more than 500. The fourth aboriginal people, the Kurumbas, are still jungle dwellers, too shy and too dispersed to be counted accurately.

These four aboriginal peoples lived in a caste-like interdependence atop the hills and in relative isolation until the British built roads and then a railroad up to the cool plateau. Then came many peoples from the plains; towns and markets developed. For about a century there was relatively little change in Kota ways. In the last few decades however, they, like many other aboriginal folk in India, have taken on a good many traits from the Hindu peoples with whom they are now in contact, mainly from Tamil-speaking areas. Some of these changes will be examined in this discussion of the Kota Dry Funeral, but it must be noted that much of this rite has remained unaltered within living Kota memory.

The account which follows begins with some general comments on funeral ceremonies and on the two kinds of Kota funerals. It next lists the roles involved in the ceremony. Then follows a brief synopsis of the action, the detailed description being omitted here. In considering the kinds of culture patterns involved in these roles and acts, we come to discuss form and then variations. The meanings entailed in performing the ceremony are examined, and finally the methodological relevance of these concepts.

1

All peoples have some formula for dealing with the death of their fellows. Those individuals who are bereaved, whose way of living has been drastically affected by the death, must be helped to fit into a new mode of life. The group as a whole must have a known way of compensating for the loss of one of its members, and so of re-establishing itself as a going concern.

For no matter how unprepared a person may be for the fact of a particular death, the group must be prepared always for the fact of death and have a set of culture patterns — a plan — for dealing with it in regular and satisfactory fashion. It is proper to say that every society "must" be so prepared simply because all societies have such plans or rapidly develop them when, for one reason or another, they may be lacking, as in a newly coalesced group or when former patterns for the occasion become unfeasible.

A society's plan for action on the occasion of a death may incorporate much more than such common elements as the consolement of the bereaved, the closing of the social gap, and the disposal of the corpse. Indeed, at the Dry Funeral among the Kota, there is no corpse, only a bit of skull bone, salvaged from the cremation at the first funeral, which symbolizes the bodily remains of the deceased. The first funeral is called *Pasdau*, "Green Funeral," and it is then, shortly after the actual death, that the body is cremated. The second funeral, *Varldau*, "Dry Funeral," is held for all the deaths that have occurred since the last Dry Funeral held the year, sometimes two years, before. The terms used for the first and second funerals refer to the analogy of a cut plant. The death is green and fresh in mind for the first funeral; it is dried out, sere, at the second. But the second funeral is as much a part of the Kota plan for dealing with death as is the first.

What then is this second funeral for? How does the second stage of the funeral plan incorporate special Kota phrasings of the usual functions of such plans, and what special Kota needs does this particular plan satisfy?

The manifest purpose of the Dry Funeral is readily perceived. Some of the prayers during the ceremony ask the gods to take the deceased on to *Amo·nad*, "Motherland." The animals sacrificed and the goods burned with the pyre are mentioned in the prayers as being provided to accompany the deceased to the afterworld. One man put it well when he explained that until the bone is brought across the brook which marks the bound of the cremation place used in the second funeral, "it is as though the Green Funeral were still continuing. The bone which equals the body is still with us. And on this side of the brook it is still not pure. As soon as we cross the brook, it is pure there and then only does the dead man reach God."

Until the second funeral the dead man still has certain attributes of social personality. It is as though in the performance of the Dry Funeral, society rather than nature made the final cleavage between life and death, a cleavage which was only begun by the physical demise. Thus a widow is still her late husband's wife until the second funeral is performed after his death. And if she becomes pregnant before that Dry Funeral, the child is his, one of his family, and shares in his property. In fact, the dead man's right to the children his widow bears ceases only when the widow has a menstrual period after the Dry Funeral. Should she become pregnant during the ceremony itself — and some widows, of sonless men, try to become pregnant then if not before — the child is still to the name of the dead husband.

Even a brief comment on the Kota way of dealing with death introduces certain of their dominant concepts, such as the great desire for children, which overrides considerations of biological fatherhood, and the emphasis on the individual's social personality, which continues beyond physical death until the Dry Funeral. But these are not reasons for staging the Dry Funeral.

The reason, as the Kota know it, is to speed the departed to the other world. The emphasis is much more on the process of release and take-off for the dead than on the "Motherland" beyond. There is little interest in the other world and only hazy ideas about its nature. But there are the clearest ideas about the necessary conditions of purity which must prevail in the group and be provided for the departed so that they may really depart this earth and life for good.

A proper departure is imperative because lingering spirits may be perilous for men. They must be sent off with decisive and effective action. That the immanence of the dead person, from the halting of his breath until the final rite of the Dry Funeral, is dangerous to the living, is indicated by the many elaborate ritual acts designed to make both survivors and deceased pure, i.e., safe, so that the former may continue their normal round of life and the latter may duly be dispatched to the bourne of the hereafter.

That the departure involves some abrupt snapping of bonds is symbolized at the climax of the ceremony, when at the signal of a smashed pot all — elders and youngsters, priests and villagers, mourners and visitors — run pell-mell back to the village without looking behind them.

That this severance is always successful is indicated by the fact that the spirits of the dead do not come back to plague the living. They may communicate to their descendants through a woman medium, but they cause them no harm as they do in many societies.

2

How, then, is this return for the quick and release for the dead accomplished? There is the ceremony — that is to say, a series of activities — which these people habitually perform for the purpose. The ceremonial performance, like a dramatic performance, has a known form and order which is enacted. As in a play there are various roles, each of which contributes to the ceremony and does something for the actor. Two sets of roles may be distinguished in the second funeral, those of the kinsmen of the dead person and those of his fellows in the community. The former are the bereaved who are being brought back to normal social life; the latter are those who help bring them back and ensure that the departed really departs.

The bereaved are mainly those of the deceased's household, spouse, siblings, children, grandchildren, and others in the joint family. The women among them begin to wail with the very first notes of the lament played on the opening day of the ceremony. They recall with an onrush of unsilenceable sorrow the enormity of their loss; they come out to sit on the verandah of their houses, closely draped in their outer cloths, and wail in a piercing keen through much of that day and the next. The men of the mourning household have much to do in the ceremony, arranging the necessary details and provisions, and they are not as free to sit and mourn aloud as are the women. But even they may stop to weep from time to time during the proceedings, especially when some sad tune or some trifle reminds them poignantly of their grief. Most grief-stricken of all the bereaved, at least in the formal context of the ceremony, are the

WIDOWS AND WIDOWERS. Much of the action revolves around them. Mourning taboos are girt most tightly about them as though their relation to the deceased were of a closer order and their loss of a higher degree than any one else's. Like the other villagers, those in the role of widow and widower do not eat after sunset during the days of the ceremony. Like other bereaved kinsmen, they do not bathe during that period; they wear old and dirty clothes as a symbol of grief, and those only the cloak and waistcloth of the traditional costume. But alone among the bereaved the widow must be carried by her brothers in the funeral procession, as though she were too distraught to walk, and a widower must be supported by his brother as he goes along in that procession. The earrings, bangles, and other jewelry worn by each are formally stripped in the course of the ritual and formally restored at its end, a rite not performed for any other of the bereaved.

Throughout most of the ceremony these mourners stay apart from other people. They come to see the dancing and singing, but do not participate until a final stage of the ceremony, when they are formally and completely restored to normal social life. And during the climactic night and day of rites at the cremation place they must remain secluded with only the Funeral Boys, whose role we shall soon describe, to keep them company. Their first meal after the night at the cremation ground must be symbolically prepared for them and for the Boys by the priest. And when all race back to the village, after the rites at the cremation ground have been completed, the widows and widowers must take a separate path from the rest of the people, for their jewelry has not yet been restored to them, and until that time they are not as yet one with other folk.

Widows undergo the same rites as do widowers. Thus neither they nor any others in the mourning household put up their hair in the usual style; the widow does not use the leaf bundle around which women normally roll their hair in back, the widower does not use the ball and string with which men usually fasten their chignon. Hairdress is a most significant symbol both of sex affiliation and of normal, as contrasted with ceremonially unusual and hence dangerous, states. Both widows and widowers are alike in ceremonial treatment here as in practically all phases of the ceremony. But in the next degree of kinship — next in importance of ceremonial role — a distinction of sex is made. The siblings of the deceased, his or her

BROTHERS AND SISTERS, take different ceremonial roles. The sister is part of the mourning household and, if she has married out of the village, returns for the Dry Funeral. But she has no specific ceremonial duties. A brother does have such duties, the difference being that in all ritual, active parts are taken by men, and only in a few instances does a woman initiate or carry through a ritual act. Thus a brother of the widower formally takes off his ornaments and, at the proper time, formally puts them on again. These rites are performed for a widow mainly by her deceased husband's brother, although her own brother may take some part in this and she is carried in the procession by her own brothers. The affines of the deceased man or woman, relatives through marriage, take only this minor part in the funeral ceremony.

If an unmarried boy or girl is being mourned, a brother takes the bath on the night before the first day of the ceremony, as do widows and widowers, rather than on the morning of the first day, as do other participants in the ceremony. This brother does not bathe again until the widows and widowers do. For a deceased who had outlived her husband or his wife, the eldest of their

SONS AND DAUGHTERS take the bath on the night before the first day and bathe in cold water when the widows and widowers do in the final phase of the ceremony. The son of the senior deceased male formally asks the elders for permission to hold the ceremony, but apart from these small bits, the descending generations of the dead person, his sons and daughters, their mates and their children, have no greater formal function than to abstain from bathing, from eating after sunset, and from putting up their hair during the mourning period.

The role of son mourning a father is of less importance than that of widower mourning his wife, as is shown in those cases when a man may be mourning both in the same ceremony. When it comes time for such a man to bow his head to the relics of the deceased — one of the most important stages of the ceremony — he bows first to his wife's bier, then to that of the senior male deceased of all those being mourned, and only then to the relic of his father.

Slight as is the formal role of the bereaved children, it comes to more than that of the dead person's

PARENTS. The father and mother of the deceased, and all his relatives of the ascending generations, do not observe the mourning taboos, nor do they have any special part to perform in all the long ritual. Among the Kota, as among other people, a mother and father who have lost a child may be as grievously rent as any person can be by such a loss. Yet there is no particular provision in the funeral plan for them, and they do not even act out the formal gestures of mourning.

Prominent are certain roles whose actors are not close kinsmen of the mourned. A leading role, in a literal sense of leading the funeral procession and initiating certain crucial acts in the ritual, is that of the

BOY WITH THE BELL. The term for this office, *melpačmog*, seems to mean "the boy who holds the bell," and one of his tasks is to keep tolling a bell through most of the funeral day and night without let or surcease. If the lad tires, some man may ring it for him, but he does most of the ringing, and the jangle he raises leaves an auditory image of the whole ritual which does not quickly fade from memory.

There are usually two such Boys, one who is from and officiates for the two larger clans in the village, and the other for the dead of the middle clan. That clan is supposed to have been of alien origin in the misty past and so must have a separate Funeral Boy and a separate pyre for its deceased. The Boy of the middle clan follows the other and performs exactly the same rites for his dead clansmen as the first Boy does for his.

The rites performed by the Boy are among the most important of the ceremony. He leads the procession when the relic is carried from the place of the first cremation to the place of the second cremation. He holds a chopping blade which he touches symbolically when the cows are sacrificed in the cremation ground, as though he, rather than the one who wields the slaughtering axe, were the real sacrificer. Moreover it is he who lights the funeral pyre, a task which he must do by thrusting the torch behind him, as though he should not look at the deed he does. These are acts which expose the doer to danger, and it may be presumed that the Boy is chosen to do these acts because, being a child, he is less vulnerable to supernatural reprisal than an adult, whose life has not been without transgression. Hence the boy chosen for this part must be, as one man put it, "a little boy, one who is innocent and doesn't know bad works."

Less vulnerable though he may be, he is nonetheless in an exposed position during the ceremony and so he stays secluded with the widows and widowers and with them eats of the special meal prepared by the priest. Later he breaks the pot which starts the flight from the cremation ground to the village; back in the village he has yet another rite to perform — the symbolic cooking of millet and throwing it away. Only after he sleeps that night in the house of the senior male deceased, is bathed and fed there the next morning, does he become just another child again.

There is yet another important role, whose incumbent does not become an ordinary person after the Dry Funeral is over, one whose place in the ceremony is part of the role he must play throughout his own life and in all seasons of the year. It is the PRIEST. As the Boy is leader in certain of the important steps of the ceremony, so the priest is leader in all the other major ritual acts. There are two priests for the triad of traditional Kota deities: the senior priest serves the elder male god and the goddess, the junior priest serves the junior male god. It is the senior priest who leads at every stage, the junior follows next, only repeating the senior's actions. All that is here noted about the priest applies to both senior and junior priests.

Thus it is the priest who, having seen the appearance of the proper new moon, gives word that preparation for the Dry Funeral may begin. During these preparations he leads a procession of men to clear the path to the cremation ground and the growth therein. He is the first to touch the memorial millet, the principal act of the first day. He leads the funeral procession when it leaves the village. He kindles the fire with which the funeral pyre is lit — or at least touches the fire-stick, which is then twirled by some other man more adept at the task. The touch symbolizes the priest's performance of the act.

The priest, again symbolically, prepares and partakes of the first meal eaten by the widows, widowers, and Funeral Boys after the pyre has been burned. They spend the night at the cremation ground; not so the priests. For the priest should not stay the night there nor indeed anywhere but his own home. His own house is sacrosanct and during the funeral period is not considered to be contaminated by the presence of death as are the other houses in the village. Thus when each of the other houses is touched with a purificatory pole in the final stages of the Dry Funeral, his is omitted, for it has no need of being so purified.

The priest must be segregate from the other villagers, must keep himself specially guarded against ritually defiling influences, not only for the ceremonial period but through all his life. Even if his brother should die, he does not loosen his hair and undergo the mourning taboos as do other bereaved siblings. However great his personal sorrow may be, his special relations to the supernatural demand that he not share in such mundane practices.

His role as priest overrides any role of bereaved, except when his wife dies. Then he takes the role of widower at the funeral and fulfills all its requirements, but at that time he is no longer priest. In the case of a priest whose wife has died, his official role is overridden and canceled. From the moment she dies he is no longer priest but only a widower, and a new priest must be ordained in his stead.

But so long as he is priest, he is guarded against contaminating influences. Thus only once does he touch his forehead to the relics, being first to do so after they are taken out. But he does not do so again later in the ceremony as other men may. After the other participants have bowed to the relics, these mementoes no longer are pure enough for the touch of the priest. That the priest bows to the relic of the deceased at all may be evidence of the great importance attached to this gesture symbolizing social affinity.

In very many other ways, the priest is guarded from influences and contacts repellent to supernatural forces. And it would seem that just because he thus is less vulnerable to injury from the supernatural and has superior sacred resources in his person, he is fit to be the ceremonial leader, to stand and act first among his fellows in all their relations with the supernatural. Almost all, that is. For in the Dry Funeral there are certain ritual acts apparently so fraught with peril — the lighting of pyre, for example — that not even a priest may do it. Only the specially chosen Boy, who has not yet had opportunity to be defiled and displeasing to the supernatural powers, may perform them.

There are three other officials, one for each of the traditional gods, who are also guarded against contaminating influences. Each is a

DIVINER. Through each, in appropriate times and circumstances, the voice of a particular deity speaks and makes known its will to the people. In a good many ceremonial situations, the diviner has the center of the ritual stage and his role is crucial. But, interestingly enough, he plays no part in the Dry Funeral. It is as if this ceremony required no assurance or guidance from the supernatural for its purpose to be accomplished. The diviners attend the ceremony and follow the priests in order of precedence. But only in the village of Kurgoj, whose rites differ in certain details from those of all other villages, is there a particular rite, incidental to the main ceremony, during which diviners may become possessed.

The offices of priest and diviner deal with the sacred; there is another official, whose role in the Dry Funeral and always is to deal with secular affairs, with organizing and directing the activities of the villagers. His title may be translated as

SECULAR OFFICER. The Kota term, *gotgarn*, means "the man who keeps the community funds," the "purse man." But the general connotation of the term is much more than merely that of a treasurer; it includes managerial functions. In the particular context of the second funeral his main task is to make known to everyone the sequence and timing of the stages of the ceremony. Thus he assembles the meeting to discuss arrangements for the funeral and dispatches messages bearing invitations to other villages. During the days of the ceremony he makes such announcements as are necessary; it is he who gets the processions arranged and moving. He leads off the dancing, except for the one day when the priests and diviners join in. Just behind him in precedence during the ceremony is the

KOILTAL, a minor official whose principal function in the Dry Funeral is the slaughtering of the sacrificial cows. As with the Funeral Boys, one *koiltal* is senior and is from either of the two main clans, the other is from the middle clan. Each *koiltal* has a few ceremonial tasks, one of which is to chop off the horns of the cow he has sacrificed and to place them before a certain stone.

Thus far the roles described have specific incumbents. To them may be added the wives of these incumbents who play no active part but who take precedence (in the same order as their husbands) in processions or in bowing to the relics, before all other women but after all other men.

There are other roles which are not formalized. In ritual matters the secular officer often follows directions given by one or two of the elder men. They hold no formal office but are so well versed in ritual because of long experience and personal interest that the secular officer and all the villagers generally follow their guidance. Still other roles are taken by groups of individuals. Thus the VILLAGERS of the community in which the funeral is being given, participate in the mourning restrictions to the extent that no one in the village eats after sunset during the funeral days. All families contribute to the expenses of the funeral feast. The secular officer collects a fixed sum, two rupees or so, from each household, and each contributes pots for cooking the funeral meal. When this feast is being prepared, most of the adults of the village are busily engaged in preparations for it, leaving the dancing, the wearing of fine clothes, the leisurely chat to the

VISITING KOTA VILLAGERS. For them the ceremony is a festive occasion. The rich food prepared is not the least of the attractions, and when strong drink is available, it flows freely. At two junctures in the ceremony, representatives of all the Kota villages must participate together, symbolizing and demonstrating their mutual concern. After the relics are brought into the place of the Dry Funeral, men from each of the six other villages come in, are welcomed as though just arriving, and touch their foreheads to the relics. Threads from the cloak covering each relic are given to them to be thrown on the pyre, perhaps thus symbolizing funeral offerings of cloth. Later, at the feast, one couple from each village must be seated at the head of the line of dining couples, and they are served before the others.

Finally there are other groups who have regular, though minor, parts in the Dry Funeral. These are

NEIGHBORING PEOPLES, other than Kota. On the day of the funeral procession some of the nearby Badagas come to the village. They sit in a group apart and take no active part, but are brought to the ceremony by their traditional association with this Kota village. Those of the Badagas who keep up former traditions of economic and social linkage with Kota families also bring contributions of money or grain or even a buffalo if the mourning household is one associated with their family.

Kurumbas bring the poles used in the ritual and quickly depart. Todas appear regularly only at the village of Kurgoj which has especially close relations with this tribe. Low-caste people, originally from the plains, regularly come to take away the sacrificed cows, a task which the Kota, who traditionally carry off buffalos sacrificed by Badagas and Todas, will not do in their own ceremony.

3

Such is the list of performers. The performance lasts from a Monday or Thursday through eleven days, but in synopsis is simple enough. There are four main acts: the first includes a day of preliminary ritual, followed by a week during which the mourning taboos are observed and there is dancing every night. The chief event of the preliminary day is the memorializing of each of the mourned with a ritual gesture performed by every villager.

The second act takes place on the following Monday, the "Funeral Day." A procession forms, winds out of the village, carrying some belongings of the deceased which are to be burned and supplies for their use in the afterworld. The procession halts at the place of the first cremation, which is in a little ravine a few hundred yards east of the village. There a bit of bone from each body has been hidden. The relics are reverently taken out, touched by the respectful foreheads of the participants and escorted, with considerable ritual accompaniment, across the brook which bounds the place of the second cremation. It is in a copse still farther eastward of the village by some two hundred yards.

There animals are sacrificed; widows and widowers are stripped of their ornaments and pay their last respects to the relics. The pyres are made and then are set alight by the Funeral Boys. The

Boys, the widowers, and the widows must spend the night in the vicinity of the pyres. Many other do so too. Laments are played through the night. Voices of dead ancestors may speak through a woman medium to bring comfort or warning to the living, and some of the younger among the living may seek and find comfort in each other's arms.

The third act, "Rice Day," begins when the morning star is seen. There is dancing and a procession from the cremation grounds back to the village. A specially prepared ritual meal is served to the widowers, widows, and Funeral Boys; this is the first of several steps in transferring them, and the other people as well, from a state of special sensitivity vis-à-vis the supernatural to ordinary station. After more dancing, still at the cremation grounds, all sit down to a lavish feast.

At nightfall each of the Funeral Boys culminates a ritual movement at the pyres by smashing a pot. Triggered by this deed, all run off from the funeral grounds, not looking behind until they reach the village. There the Funeral Boys have yet another rite to perform, in which they symbolically cook millet and then throw away the cooking pot and cooked grain. There is dancing in the village until late that night. Yet another step toward normal degree may be taken by widowers, who may have intercourse with a brother's wife, and by widows, with a brother of the late husband. Both have been continent during the preceding week.

The final act carries over two days, during which the funeral observances are finished off, the visitors leave, and the village resumes its everyday aspect. On the "Dancing Day," the widows and widowers, their jewelry formally restored and their persons formally brought back to normal life, join in the dancing for the first time. In the afternoon a pole is touched to the houses in the village and then thrown away, an act which signifies both terminal purification and completion of the ritual. On the next day, "Singing Day," there is no further ritual or dancing, but no work is done. The women sing and then the visitors take their leave. The village settles down until the next great festival of the annual round.

4

As the hosts come back into their village, they may gather to gossip in the quiet aftermath of the ceremony, as do the guests when they return to their homes. The events of the ritual days are turned over and over in conversation, examined for noteworthy quirk or meaning, discussed in slashing generalities ("the Badagas are spoiling everything") and in small detail ("the pyres needed more firewood"). Personal deviations and ceremonial variations are singled out for comment, and the flow of talk eddies round and about them.

Yet in all this talk of deviation and variation there may also be detected a strong undercurrent of presumption that the ceremony has accomplished its purpose, that the same purpose will again be accomplished by the same set of acts in the years to come. The gossipers well know, indeed they usually harp on the fact, that the rite does not develop in exactly the same way from year to year. But they also tacitly assume or, if questioned, readily state that there is and must be a constant way of doing something about the recurrent fact of death in the community. As the fact does not vary, the response is regular, known, and invariable.

Hence the patterns of the Dry Funeral which have been set forth above are mainly *invariant* patterns. Together they comprise the form of the ceremony. They are what a group of villagers will agree on as a statement of "What we do about death." Each invariant pattern is a prescription for action, a prescription about which there is general agreement within the community. Each is a statement of modal behavior, past and future. Each permits of little variation as the people themselves perceive variation. Most ethnographic statements are such invariant patterns which have been verbalized by members of the group and can be recognized as valid by most of the community. They are the modes of behavior which the people of the group know and which they habitually enact in a particular context and in response to a particular stimulus.

Invariant patterns range widely in magnitude, in the number of activities and actors which they involve. The way in which the

Funeral Boy lights the pyre, by thrusting the burning brand behind him, is an invariant pattern. The roster of roles in the ceremony is invariant in that these roles are fulfilled when the Dry Funeral takes place and the villagers assume that they will continue to be fulfilled on such occasions. Be it noted that no Kota has neatly formulated the cast of characters as given above. That has been the formulation of the ethnographer, but it is no more than an ordering of the testimony of the villagers on the subject and is an ordering which the villagers recognize as valid when it is presented to them.

Invariant patterns differ also in specificity to occasion. Some are specific to the single ceremony, as the manner of lighting the funeral pyre. Others are common to every ritual occasion, occur whenever men have regular and formalized dealings with the supernatural. Such frequently repeated invariant patterns may be called *ritual recurrents*.

Bathing is one such ritual recurrent. Whenever a person is to address the supernatural, he bathes whenever ceremonial participants proceed from one ceremonial state to another, they bathe. People usually bathe by dousing themselves with bowls of water. When this is impractical or when the occasion is not deemed of sufficient significance, they need only sprinkle themselves with water. Even the objects of ceremonial use must be sprinkled and thus symbolically bathed.

The form and order of the ritual taken as a whole, is a more specific invariant, specific to the occasion of mourning. All Kota agree that the spirits of the dead linger about after the first cremation and must be sent off finally by the second funeral. To the villagers, this broad belief and general action cannot and do not change from season to season, from generation to generation.

Yet variations do occur; everyone knows and expects that they will occur. Certain of these variations are provided for in the cultural plan, in the consensus concerning courses of action to be taken. They are foreseen and foreseeable by the villagers as ways of accommodating for variation without disturbing the successful fulfilment of the purposes of the ritual.

A simple, mechanical manner of providing for variations is an *alternative pattern*. For example, there are two auspicious days of the week, Monday and Thursday, and the *Kotanm* day of preliminary ritual may fall on either, depending on which comes first after the new moon is seen. One alternative is as good and as common as the other. Choice of one or the other is determined by lunar and calendrical factors and is determined mechanically, i.e., by simple antecedent circumstances which involve no complex weighting of factors and without range of choice of consequent action. Both alternatives are choices only within an invariant pattern, namely, that the rite must begin on an auspicious day of the week.

Contingent patterns also provide alternatives, but alternatives which are not usual, which are brought into play under uncommon (although expectable) circumstances. Thus, if no deaths have occurred in the year, the Dry Funeral may be postponed until the next year. No contingent alternative exists for further postponement simply because, within living memory, no village has been free of deaths for two whole years.

Another contingent alternative provides that the ceremony may be given a month early if a new priest is to be chosen. The choosing takes place after the Dry Funeral. If a new priest is selected, then he must participate in the great renewal and refurbishment of the God Ceremony. In the usual month between the two rites, there is not time enough for a newly chosen priest to make ready for the God Ceremony, hence the earlier date.

If the antecedent conditions are fulfilled, as when there have been no deaths during the year, then the contingent action (or lack of the usual action in this case) invariably follows — the Dry Funeral is postponed. In the second case, if an attempt is to be made to choose the priest after the Dry Funeral, then the date of the ceremony invariably comes a month early.

These are invariant consequences, once the contingent circumstance is socially recognized, but there may be great controversy as to whether the circumstance warrants a contingent pattern — whether, say, an attempt should be made to choose a priest that year; whether the Dry Funeral should be performed if the only death to be mourned is that of a ten-year-old boy. Such choices are not clearly provided for in the cultural plan, there is no clear agreement on the matter in the village, and it is these questions and problems which are thrashed out and settled in the interpersonal give and take of the village meeting.

The plan does provide regular circumstances for thrashing out such choices. Village councils are *elective patterns* of this kind within which different sequences of action are considered and one or another selected, usually from a known range of choice. Thus the very first act in the whole cycle of the ceremony is the meeting which is held to decide whether the rite is to be staged that year and, if it is, what scale of expenditure is to be set for it. There was considerable debate, as we shall see below, about the scale of expenditure in the particular economy which we are observing. But we must also note that variations occur and choices are made which are not considered worthy of debate or of notice by the villagers.

These are *patterns of neutral variation*. They are free variations in the sense that one physically possible selection is as good as another within the scope of the pattern. But they are neutral and free variations only within certain limits. Thus any boy may be Funeral Boy — it does not matter which the elders choose — but two must be chosen and each must be from the proper section of the village, one from the middle clan, one from the two larger clans. Or, any man can kill the sacrificial buffalo if he has the knack for it. This in contrast with the killing of the sacrificial cows, which can only be done by the proper official. Such neutral variation is really not perceived by the villagers as significant variation at all. They know as well as does the ethnographer that there is variation, but "it doesn't matter and makes no difference." It has no consequences in the ritual or in the society.

There is another kind of known variation within which one choice rather than another does have consequences, but not necessarily immediate or drastic consequences. These are patterns of permitted variation and preferred variants, or *optative patterns*.

Thus it is an invariant pattern that every mourning family must provide a small-scale cot on which the bone relic is placed and then cremated. But the kind of cot which is provided may vary from a flimsy arrangement of old boards hastily knocked together (or even a chair) to a lavishly turned affair requiring long hours of painstaking carpentry. The villagers agree that the cot should be as fine a piece of work as the mourners can provide. Each family should thus show, by the expenditure of labor and wealth, by thus depriving itself for the sake of conspicuous consumption on the pyre, that it highly valued the dead person and deeply mourns his loss.

So the usual answer to a question about the quality of funereal cots is, "We should provide a fine cot." But mitigating circumstances are acknowledged; the death may be that of a child who had not lived long enough to warrant deep and widely shared sorrow at his passing, or the family may be in economic straits. Hence, if the cot is only a few tacked boards or a chair, no adverse ritual or social consequences follow. But if a family provides a very fine cot, even for the death of a young girl, that family becomes known as one which honors and fulfills the group's preferences as well as its mandates, and the members of that family have more prestige, greater capacity for initiating and guiding group action, than they had before. Thus there are consequences, though not immediate ones, of enacting the preferred variants.

As in the case of the cot, so for the whole scale of expenditure in a funeral. A man who, despite all adverse and mitigating circumstances, provides a lavish funeral for a relative, gains group approval and the potential of this approval for his future influence in the group. Conversely, a man who fails to provide a worthy funeral for a relative who was himself a man of esteem and prestige incurs no immediate penalties, supernatural or mundane. But to him is not likely to accrue any quality of prestige. The optative pattern for funeral provisions includes both the permitted but disapproved variant for closest relatives of skimping on a funeral and the preferred variant of setting a rich display.

It may be noted that if a very lavish Dry Funeral is decided on at the preliminary meeting, then various contingent patterns are brought into play. Some are the usual patterns, but in higher degree: many more guests are invited, much more food is provided, finer funeral goods are placed on the pyre. Others are additional to the usual funeral patterns: musicians go out to meet the incoming guests and play them into the village. And in Kurgoĵ village, a whole new ceremonial sequence, of preparing a special pen for the buffaloes to be killed, is added to the ceremony.

Another kind of pattern involving preference may be distinguished, in which one of two possible choices, rather than a range of variation as in optative patterns, is preferable to the other, although circumstances and special considerations may bring about the less preferred choice without adverse or immediate consequence. In contrast with the simple, mechanical alternative noted previously, this preference for one rather than the other of two permitted choices may be termed a *weighted alternative*. Thus on the night of the funeral feast a widower should have intercourse with his brother's wife and a widow with a brother of the deceased husband. That is the traditional practice and is the generally approved behavior, though not all do so. No immediate consequences, ritual or social, ensue from the selection of one rather than the other of the two possibilities.

But there are long-term consequences in the making. Not so long ago there was no alternative, not even a weighted one, at that juncture of the ceremony. All widows and widowers resumed intercourse that night, just as they all still dance on the next day of the ceremony to indicate their restitution to normal status. Some men have become sufficiently imbued with the new notion that such sexual practices are discreditable to discourage this part of the rite within their families. These men do not voice objection to other families fulfilling the practice and it is still the indicated, if no longer the unquestioned, thing to do. Should the disapproval spread more widely in the village, the preferential weighting may shift to the alternative of omitting the practice. Or another variety of weighted alternative may develop in which verbal preference is on one choice, actual behavioral preference on the other. In the example discussed here, verbal preference is for the traditional practice, and behavior choice, according to the testimony of several villagers, is there also.

No alternatives, no range of choice, no variation is permitted for certain elements of the ceremony. These may be termed *compulsive patterns*. They are the parts of the ritual about which the Kotas say, "This is what we must do." A number of such "musts" have appeared in the account of the Dry Funeral. For example, a widow must be carried in the procession, the middle clan must have a separate pyre and Funeral Boy, the priest must not stay the night at the cremation ground.

Strict prohibitions may also be classified as compulsive patterns, compelling abstention from possible action. Thus, at the funeral feast a man must not eat with a woman related to him as mother, either real or classificatory. This compulsive pattern occurs within the context of other regularities, of the compulsive pattern that each of the seven men representing the seven villages must eat with a woman, of the optative pattern that every other man at the feast should also eat with a woman, of the further optative pattern that each woman should, if possible, be the spouse or a cross- cousin of the man (i.e., an actual or a potential marriage-partner), and finally of the rule which follows from the last relationship that whoever the man's dining partner may be, she must not be in the relation of mother to him.

Compulsive patterns are distinguished from other invariant patterns in that the villagers feel compelled to fulfill them when the proper occasion arises. They brook no obstacles or variations in enacting them. In describing them, the villagers stress that variations must not occur, as though the possibility of alternative courses of action were recognized and rejected. Hence these patterns are fulfilled with little variation and if, for some cause external or internal to the group, they cannot be fulfilled to the letter, then the villagers struggle to reinstate the proper form or the closest approximation of it possible. In the case of other invariant patterns, no such struggle is a priori entailed in the prescription for action, and if forces external to the group block the enactment of a pattern previously invariant, there may or may not be strong effort made to overcome the block. Compulsive patterns are in these ways similar to the emotional, or affective, behavior of individuals.

In the Dry Funeral, the roles of widow and widower entail many more compulsive patterns than do any other of the roles specific to the rite. It may be that behavior which is understood as being particularly vulnerable to supernatural forces tends to be set in the more compulsive frame. Certainly the whole conduct of the priest is couched in many more compulsive patterns than hold for any other individual. To give one instance among many, the priest must not stay the night at the cremation grounds; others may or may not.

But not all compulsive patterns relate to supernatural powers. Thus in the dancing of the preliminary week, women may or may not participate, but on the last night some women must dance. This seems to relate more to a notion of totality of social participation which may be phrased as "all, men and women both, have danced," rather than to supernatural vulnerability.

Perhaps the essential criterion of a compulsive pattern is that the people foresee possible alternatives, albeit implicitly, and reject them before they occur. Thus the contrasting alternative to the proper conduct of the priest is the behavior of the ordinary villager, and implicit in the description of priestly ways is the contrast with the ways of laymen.

Such contrasts are not expressed nor readily inferred in descriptions of other kinds of invariant patterns. Hence it is ordinarily assumed rather than insisted on that a proper funeral ceremony will take place. Only when there was an epidemic of relapsing fever in the village and there was some suggestion of omitting the rites, or at least abbreviating them to save precious food, was an alternative raised and compulsively rejected by most of the village folk. In the larger sense, as was previously noted, some sort of funeral ceremony is an invariant characteristic of all societies. The performance became a compulsive invariant in the village when a possible alternative was posed.

Within the present internal system of the Dry Funeral, the alternative of omitting the rite is not a factor, though it may conceivably arise later in the history of the village. For the internal system of this ceremony, as of every other, becomes modified by the play of forces external to it. Some of these forces are from within the society, a result of cultural development and societal maneuvering. Others impinge quite directly from outside the society itself, as the relapsing-fever epidemic or the edicts of government. The processes of modification are constantly going on, certainly in the present century. Patterns are added or lapse; some are changed from one type to another, as from compulsive to optative; roles are altered, usually in slight detail from year to year, until a massive change is apparent.

Thus certain changes in detail have come about during recent years which have not affected the main outline of the rite as described nor its basic purpose, but which appear to the villagers as significant and to the observer as having important potential consequences.

Cow sacrifice has been eliminated from the ceremony in Kolmel village. It is a compulsive prohibition; the alternative as still practiced in some villages is fresh in the consciousness of the Kolmel people. Buffalo-killing for the ceremony has become disapproved, and the trend is in the direction of killing fewer animals or none. Such trends and shifts often involve social conflict and maneuvers, as the following incident from the Dry Funeral of 1949 illustrates.

When, on the very first morning of the ceremony, the men gathered to take the memorial millet, three men stood aloof, refusing to participate in the rite. Some attempt was made by a few elders to persuade them to take part, but to no avail. Only in the evening of that day, when they had had their say before a village assemblage, made their point, and were duly mollified, did they touch a handful of the memorial millet to their foreheads and thus signified their re-established unity with the community and in the rite.

Their grievance had to do with the number of buffaloes to be killed for the funeral feast. It had been decided that three or four animals were to be slaughtered. This was felt as an affront by the three objectors.

They were affronted because at the last previous Dry Funeral, these three were the chief bereaved. To honor their dead, to proclaim their own worth, they wanted to provide several buffaloes for that feast, but the preferential pattern had become one of minimizing animal sacrifice. This preference was also shared by each of the three, save that in the role of bereaved a villager would subordinate the new preference to the traditional option of staging as lavish a funeral as possible for one's kin. But they were only three, not amongst the most influential of the village, and they finally had to slaughter only a single buffalo. But to show that no personal deprivation was intended, the assembled men then agreed to make it a rule, presumably a compulsive pattern in our terms, that only one buffalo should ever thenceforth be slaughtered for the ceremony.

When this next ceremony was to be held, however, there were some ten bereaved households and among them several of the more influential men. For the men of these ten households, as for the three men at the previous ceremony, the obligation and preferences of the role of bereaved overrode the newer preferences for minimizing or eliminating animal slaughter. These mourners were numerous enough and powerful enough to get their way, and the other villagers agreed to allow the killing of several animals. But now the three saw the rule undone which had been made to soothe their injured self-esteem, and they demanded that no more than one beast be killed. Typically enough, they tried to enforce their demands, not by any physical intervention, but by vociferous objections and then withdrawal from the group activity. Withdrawal is often an effective sanction in the village, but the three were too few to carry against the bereaved of that year.

Some gesture of mollification was in order. At the meeting that night, the villagers contributed to a collective fine of twenty-four rupees into the village purse as a kind of self-castigation to indicate that the three deserved some redress. This expiatory gesture satisfied the three objectors well enough so that they rejoined the group in its ceremonial activity.

The gesture indicated that most in the village preferred that buffalo-killing should be minimized, perhaps eliminated, from the ceremony. Each was willing to act on that belief except when he assumed the role of bereaved. Then the newer preference, held by a man in his role as villager, conflicted with the traditional preference held by a man in the role of bereaved.

The conflict had been brought about because of the shift of preference relating to mortuary offerings of buffalo. It is not unlikely that this optative pattern may be totally eliminated by a new compulsive pattern, barring the slaughter of buffalo as the killing of cows has been barred.

Now why should these new options and new compulsions become part of the system of the Dry Funeral at this juncture of Kota history? One factor is the example of their neighbors. The Kota villagers who, in hot argument, now revile the killing of cows and buffaloes as an unclean practice, call as witness the revulsion of Hindus and of some Badagas to such slaughter.

This is an aversion of long standing; only in recent years have the Kota taken their neighbors as exemplars and begun to share that aversion. The displeasure of some of their neighbors at animal-killing has long been known, but was either ignored or resisted. These opinions have now become forces which the Kota cannot ignore or resist and so they have been incorporated into the internal system of the ceremony. This internalization has been completed in respect to cow-killing, not yet in respect to buffalo-killing.

Two other changes in the system of the ceremony at Kolmel have come about in recent years. The exciting chase of the buffaloes, as a preliminary to killing them, has been dropped. The recently acquired dislike of animal slaughter extends to the near-frenzied beating of the animals after they are caught. The ardor of the younger men for the chase has been further undermined by an external prohibition, that of the Government of Madras on alcoholic drinks. Brandy is not now available as it once was on ceremonial occasions, and unfortified by alcohol, the young men are not so zealous to face the slashing long horns of the panicky buffaloes as once they were. Added is the factor that the buffalo herds are now much diminished, and suitably spirited animals for a proper chase are scarce and expensive.

Neither expense nor danger enters into another change in the formerly traditional pursuits of young men during the ceremony. Sexual intercourse was formerly permitted and preferred when villagers stayed the night near the cremation place after the pyre was kindled. There was a general intermingling of sexes, and though incest prohibitions were not broken, a man or woman could range more freely and widely in the matter of sexual partners that night than on any other of the year. Many still stay that night in the meadow and some of the younger people do manage to have intercourse, but most of the elders express strong disapproval of such behavior and apparently try to discourage the traditional practice. From a preferred variant within an optative pattern there has been a change to a generally rejected variant within a pattern that is still, but just barely, an optative one. The reasons for this shift are probably also due to the acceptance of standards from certain Badagas and Hindus, possibly also from the nearby European missions. Whatever the reason, the lapse of both the buffalo chase and the funeral night of sexual adventure has eliminated two events which were of particular attraction to the younger men.

Not so directly caused by felt pressures from outside the group are other changes which have come about in the ceremony. Several details of the ritual have been dropped. For example, there was a special old silver coin, one bearing Arabic script, which the Funeral Boy held down with his thumb in the palm of his hand as he scooped water from the boundary stream to sprinkle over the cots as they were carried into the cremation ground. The coin was lost or mislaid after a recent funeral and was not to be found when needed again. The elder who was directing the ritual — an unofficial task done by a respected man who is versed in ritual affairs — did not try to arrange for a substitute coin as his predecessor as ritual director might have done. Rather he omitted the entire business of sprinkling the cot on the grounds that only the coin which had been lost could be used for that bit of ritual. It is as though there were a general notion in the village that the traditional detail of the ceremony is no longer as imperatively necessary as once it was held to be.

In a similar manner the final purificatory rite of touching the houses with one of the funeral poles has been abandoned. There was some opposition, by the older men, to dropping this whole sequence, but in the end it lapsed. There seems to have been no direct cause for its abandonment other than the general trend to curtail some of the involved detail of ritual. But the rationale given for dropping the pole ritual by one of the men who insisted on doing so sounds a note which is as vital as it ever has been — the desire for sons and the fear of being sonless. This man told that the particular tree from which the pole is fashioned does not, when cut, grow again. "We think it is a bad tree and if we use it to touch the houses, the men in those houses will not have sons, so we have left off using that pole." Whatever the effective reason may be for sloughing this ritual sequence, it is clear that the villagers can eminently justify the omission by reference to the dominant theme of desire for sons.

A few items have been added to the rite. The recently established shrine for Hindu-like deities has its own priest and diviners. The priest of this new shrine now follows the traditional priests in precedence, and the diviners follow the traditional diviners. But this insertion does not at all affect the main development of the ritual; it is merely a new detail which, as a ritual item, has no consequences. But the establishment of a new shrine has had indirect consequences of considerable importance in the function of the ceremony. The founding of this new shrine was the occasion for the splitting of the villagers into two factions, the more conservative "old rule" and the reformist "cropped heads." The reformist group does not participate in ceremonies with the majority faction of more conservative villagers. Hence the ceremony no longer is an expression of village solidarity as it once was, and does not provide the occasion which it once offered for healing breaches in village unison.

Attendance is sparser than it was a decade or two ago. The ceremony is no longer a rally of the whole tribe. Young people do not flock in from other Kota villages as once they did because the Dry Funeral no longer provides as richly of excitement, sex, and food. All may better be gained, on occasion, in town or elsewhere in the region. The older folk of the other Kota villages come in fewer numbers, partly because of other attractions, partly because of the reduced claims of kinship, partly because of growing village differences which have made it difficult for villagers from all seven villages to participate freely in each other's ceremonies.

Thus the people of Kurgoǰ village do not come en masse to the Kolmel Dry Funeral, although close relatives still join with the bereaved in Kolmel. For the Kurgoj folk maintain the traditional ways in undiminished fullness and rigor. They believe that the Kolmel people are no longer good Kota, and Kolmel villagers mutter that the Kurgoǰ people are more like Todas than Kotas in their ceremonies. The full nature of these differences will be considered elsewhere, but one example will indicate how differently the two villages may react.

In tradition-holding Kurgoǰ certain sequences of the ceremony have also been challenged, as in Kolmel. There it was argued that the sequence was superfluous in which the Funeral Boys, after their return from the cremation ground, symbolically cook millet in the village and throw it over the edge of the street. Some said, "We have done all the rites at the funeral ground; why do this in the village?" And to the observer, that sequence does seem an appendage, which has no ready explanation in the internal system of the ceremony. This in contrast with the lapsed pole ritual at Kolmel, which does have justification as the final purifying touch to restore the whole community to normal state. But in Kurgoǰ the ritual sequence thus challenged by one or two skeptics was not abandoned. Rather a justification for it was devised and accepted. "The food offered at the cremation ground is for *all* those in the Motherland, this offering is *only for those* who have recently died." Whatever flaws may have been detected in this explanation, all objections were overridden by the dominating desire in that community to hold fast to the old ways.

If one Kota village so differs from another in the performance of the ceremony, to which does the ethnographic description apply? If the description really represents what a group of villagers will agree on as a statement of "What we do about death," who are the "we"? Are "we" the people of conservative Kurgoj, of more changed Kolmel, or of much changed Aga·l?

The answer which the villager gives to the ethnographer is readily forthcoming. "We" are the seven villages of Kota. True, there are differences, but the main acts of the ceremony are, in the broad sense, similarly performed in all seven places. And even among those who stage the ceremony most perfunctorily, the traditional order is known. The form as followed at Kurgoj, say, is recognized as valid for Kota people. There is still, in the mid-twentieth century, enough social and cultural coherence among the various Kota villages to give effective meaning to the notion "We Kota."

The description, then, is a generalized one for all the villages, although it pertains particularly to Kolmel, the village best known to the ethnographer. Variations and elisions which occur in any one village do not vitiate the broad validity of the description — at least not yet — in Kota eyes. For the villager himself usually generalizes Kota practice thus, stressing similarities and glossing over village differences when he discusses Kota ways with an inquiring non-Kota. But as the ethnographer comes to know more and to probe deeper, as Kotas speak with him more in the manner of one Kota to another, other problems of variation and of description are posed. Granted that the description applies to all seven villages with particular reference to Kolmel, which Kolmel is taken?

Is it the Kolmel village as first observed by the ethnographer, where cow sacrifice was an invariant of the rite? Or is it the Kolmel as later seen, where it was banned? Further, does the description refer to the "old rule" faction or to the "cropped heads" who are usually segregate from the ceremonial as well as social cooperation with the other factions. Indeed, is the description valid for those who are the bereaved and, as we have seen, try in that capacity to maximize buffalo-offering, or is it valid for the same men when they are not bereaved and then would minimize animal slaughter? Here again, a general account is possible and valid. The time period is the "historical present," the adult life experience, over several decades, of the villagers whose testimony has been noted and whose behavior observed. The personnel for whom the description holds good are those who recognize the bulk of the patterns formulated as being Kota patterns, who have enacted them and who assume that they will repeat similar activities on similar occasions in the future.

5

These are the people and such is the time period to which the description of the ceremony applies. We may now consider again the questions which arose at the outset of the ethnographic description: What is the meaning of the Dry Funeral? What does performing it do for these folk? The "meaning" for the Kota is its relation to other parts and periods of their lives, its effect on various of their systems of behavior. Clearly the Dry Funeral relates to more than one part and to several systems, but manifestly it is foremost a part of the relation with the supernatural, of the religious system.

It is manifestly part of the religious system because so the Kota understand it. They, like other peoples, envisage a set of powers beyond mundane experience, which affect human life and which human beings can deal with in certain regular ways. One of these ways is this Dry Funeral, a collective enterprise which brings about certain benefits for the group.

These benefits are mainly those of sending off the lingering spirits of the dead and of restoring all those who have been affected by death to normal status. Proximity to death imperils a person from the supernatural sphere and disables him in the social sphere. Much of the ceremony is directed towards restoring all those who have been so imperiled and disabled to a condition of "purity," of relative safety and normality. Those who are deemed most closely touched by death are the widows and widowers. Their restoration must be accomplished in several stages. The whole village — people and houses — has also been tainted by proximity to death and the village too is cleansed and restored by the ceremony. Indeed the very corpse and spirit of the deceased are not finally pure, able to take their proper place in the cosmos, until with due ritual their relic is recremated.

The accent is heavily on purity, and purity involves relations between person and person as much as it does between person and supernatural. In fact, we have noted that the deities are not importantly brought into the ceremony. At Kolmel they do not possess the diviners on this occasion as they do in other ritual contexts. There is little speculation or concern about the afterworld, the "Motherland," to which the spirits of the dead go. Occasionally these departed spirits may speak through a woman medium during the night at the meadow near the cremation grounds. But even when the voice of such a spirit chides the people for improper behavior, there is no more excited response to this supernatural admonition than some mumbled prayers asking for forgiveness and promising future rectitude. The priests do lead in prayer at several ritual junctures, but there is no beseeeching, no presenting of a case for sinners. The word for deity, *somi*, is mentioned in invocation (as it very frequently is) and then the hope is expressed, "May death decrease and people increase."

The priests are mainly leaders in ritual, able to lead in these sensitive procedures because of their relative isolation from contaminating influences. And when the procedures are most sensitive, in the final stages of the ceremony, a Funeral Boy must lead. His youth rather than style of life, his lack of opportunities for contamination rather than insulation from it, apparently makes him more suitable than are adults for supernatural dealings.

Many of the recurrent elements of the ritual in this and other Kota ceremonies have to do with purity. Bathing as a way of restoring purity and of making transitions has been mentioned. The use of cow dung is purifying: houses are washed with a mixture of cow dung and water before the ceremony; the memorial millet is poured over a patch of ground plastered with cow dung. The right hand is the more pure, and such ritual gestures as sprinkling purifying water or scooping the memorial millet are always made with the right hand, as is very widely true in India. The right side is the superior. Thus the widower bows to the relic over the right side of the cot, the widow over the left. Even the streets of the village have relative purity, the upper street of each clan being purer than the lower street. To the lower street, women come when first returning from the menstrual seclusion house. Hence the memorial millet may be poured only in the upper street and not in the lower. Purity is an important element of all ritual and many social situations; it is a vital factor through most of the religious system.

In the religious system then, the Dry Funeral is a means of restoring the proper relations between mortals and supernaturals, relations which have been disturbed by the transition of the year's deceased from full-fledged mortals to not-quite supernaturals. They are sent off to full supernatural status by the ceremony, whose climax comes with the race back to the village of the living and the departure up to the afterworld of the dead. In all this restoration of men and spirits to their proper places, the supernaturals have little voice and no option. If men perform the ceremony as culturally prescribed, the restoration is fully effected both in this world and in the other.

Restoring order between men and spirits is only one aspect of what performing the ceremony does. It also restores order among men, an order which has been disturbed by the loss of a member and, even more, by the social disabling of those closest to the dead. Because relationships within this society are operated as though they were in precarious balance at best, they are readily disrupted when some of the members are shadowed by such an impurity as that of death.

Most affected is the spouse of the dead person. Widowers and widows undergo more elaborate ritual and must fulfill more compulsive patterns than those in any other ceremonial roles. Other relatives of the deceased's own generation, his siblings, have a less important part in the ceremony; relatives of the descending generation, sons and daughters, still less. Affines have very little formal function, and relatives of the ascending generation, parents, have no official role or any formal function. Insofar as this reflects the relative importance of a person's social bonds, it seems that the greatest significance is placed on kinship bonds with one's own generation, on the marital tie, and on sibling ties; other relationships are of much less formal consequence.

The social restoration of these kin is the manifest meaning of the ceremony in the social system, a meaning which is readily given by the participants and easily perceived by the observer. Thus, before the ceremony, widows and widowers are disbarred from full participation; they may not dance, be merry, move freely among their fellows. During the ceremonial week they undergo a final period of withdrawal and sorrow and then are reinstated to society.

There are still other societal effects which are not as straightforwardly observable but none the less significant. Evidence for them derives from a variety of situations rather than from a simple formulation and a palpable set of acts. Among these is the effect of the ceremony as a reaffirmation of the social order.

A Kota finds reflected in the performance his own place in various social groupings. The reciprocal obligations entailed in these groupings are remembered and reinforced in the joint action. This is so for all the principal social categories — for the family household, the extended kinship set, clan, village, Kota people, Nilgiri tribes.

Thus all in the bereaved household work together to provide funeral goods. During the mourning period all in the household huddle still and sad together, father, wife, brothers, and son of the deceased, sharing grief and responsibility together even though they have unequal roles in the formal ritual.

The close kin of the family come in to share both grief and

responsibility. The dead man's parent's siblings and their children, his wife's parents and siblings come into the village if they live away from it, to console with their presence and contribute to expenses. For all their lack of formal roles these relatives rally to the help of the bereaved household. To them applies the optative pattern that they should contribute to the funeral expenses, but no immediate or drastically adverse consequences ensue if they do not.

These kin attend the ceremony and bow in last obeisance to the relic. This simple and formerly invariant affirmation of kinship has, on some recent occasions, become a matter of compulsive struggle. The more conservative faction has tried to bar kin of reformist bent and from less orthodox villages from bowing at the bier. In other situations the "cropped" are well content to keep apart from the conservatives, but in this they cannot stay away or be kept away without hot argument, sometimes even physical encounter and police intervention.

They cannot stay away because it would mean to them and to all the villagers a severing of kinship ties. The most ardent reformist does not want that, nor can he tolerate it. Such struggles have come to be the social climax of a good many funerals. For some participants the ritual climax is incidental; the main climax for them — the event to which others lead and after which others follow — is the act of bowing to the relic. In the angry disputes which rage about the act may be seen both the function of the ceremony as an affirmation of social relations and the paramount importance of maintaining kinship ties.

Clan membership is also acknowledged and confirmed in the ceremony. Clanship is used as a taxonomic device in several instances: the memorial millet is taken by clan groupings, the cots and funeral goods of fellow clansmen are ranged together in the clan street, Funeral Boy and *koiltal* are selected according to clan considerations, and in the cremation, one pyre is for the middle clan, a second for the other two clans.

Village affiliation is stressed and reinforced. Reinforced because all the villagers, young and old, men and women, are involved together in the preparation — the invitations, the cooking, receiving guests, and all the other activities which must be cooperatively accomplished. Even in recent years, despite the falling off of full participation in the ceremony, a great part of the village is still involved, if only in watching and discussing the work of others busy with the preparations. Even now many of the hostilities among the villagers are at least temporarily overridden in this cooperative enterprise. And the temporary subordination of tension may well make for smoother relations during the rest of the yearly round.

As is true for the village, so for the seven villages of Kota people. Joint participation in the ceremony provides the opportunity for communication and re-establishment of social links. Communication, talking face to face with fellow Kotas, helps demonstrate that they are one's fellows. The dates of the Dry Funerals in the various villages are staggered so that all may have the opportunity to attend the ceremony at every village. The fact of mutual participation is re-emphasized by ritual symbols, as when representatives from each of the other villages are formally welcomed into the ceremony and when representatives of all the villages are formally seated at the head of the line of feasting couples.

Visitors still come, although the stream of arriving guests on the Funeral Day has diminished in the passage of two decades. Even more thinned is the attendance of the other indigenous peoples of the Nilgiris, but some Badagas still attend. In former times, the interdependence of the four tribes was exemplified and re-enacted at the ceremonies. The Badaga associates of the bereaved household invariably came to sit a while in the village and to bring their contributions to the funeral provisions, contributions of grain or of money or — to show particular esteem — of a buffalo. Toda and Kurumba associates also turned up.

Nowadays the Todas come hardly at all, except to Kurgoj; Kurumbas put in a brief appearance. Most of the former Badaga associates do not come, but some still do. These are mostly the Badagas whose families maintain the old relationship with associated Kota families. Their appearance makes plain that they willingly choose to keep up the traditional affiliation. Just because such affiliations have become attenuated, the Badagas who do maintain them may be specially meticulous in the reaffirmation of the relationship.

These experiences in the ceremony annually rehearse the table of social establishment, tacitly reminding the villager of its parts and personnel, how the sections serve and are served by him. There is a complementary effect, one which is augmented by several of the recurrent elements of ritual. It is an effect which reinforces the villager's sense for the social whole, which enhances his feeling of belonging to the community, and so welds the commmunity's cohesion. Thus it is in the recurrent element of the procession.

When the village men go to clear the cremation ground of growth, they do not straggle in desultory fashion to the wood. It is a group enterprise, a procession, not really labor in the ordinary sense at all. The procession begins, as generally any ritual event begins, with signal blasts from the great horns. A band of musicians play a brisk tune and lead the way; immediately after them follow the religious and secular officers in proper order of precedence. The other men come after, two or three abreast as the width of the path will allow. On the return to the village, there is antiphonal shouting as well as music. One part of the parade starts with a shout of, "Hau," and the others echo back, "Ko." Thus with drums and shouting they triumphantly, at least joyously, come back into the village.

Similar processions take place on the "Rice Day," when the company goes from the meadow back to the village to collect pots for the feast. Later in the same day the visitors come back in procession to the feasting place. Another procession is the funereal one, from the village to the cremation ground. Then no joyful shouting resounds and the music is doleful, but the items of the processional pattern are there, signal blasts, music, order of precedence.

Dancing is another ritual recurrent which brings mutual enjoyment and enhances social unison. There is dancing every night of the preliminary week. Mourners are brought to watch, "to forget their grief;" and it is noteworthy that there is no tendency to expand the area of grief, no attempt to halt this pleasure; rather is there an effort to curtail sorrow, to bring the sorrowful out of their concentration on loss by interesting them, even if momentarily, in the pleasing figures of the dance. And in the dance at the end of the ceremony is enacted the final and complete social restoration of the bereaved spouses; by joining with the other villagers in dancing, the widowers and widows display their whole restoration.

Joint activity and enjoyment also occur in the feast, another ritual recurrent, but the symbolic importance of eating together transcends that of the other ritual elements. It is the testament and seal of social unity overriding diversity, of social concord subordinating discord, of mutual aid over antagonism.

As some aspects of the rite reaffirm the component parts of the social order and others reinforce the sense of the social whole, so the performing of other ritual elements lays stress on the proper hierarchical relationship among the people and parts of the whole. One such element is the strict order of precedence in the ceremony. The order may be formulated in this way: all men come before all women, officials and elders before all other men, officials before elders, religious officials before secular officials, priests before diviners.

These are the principal priorities; to them must be added the ranking among officials and among women. At the taking of the memorial millet, the senior priest does so first, closely followed by the junior priest. Then come in order the three diviners, for the elder male god, for the younger male god, and for the goddess. The priest and the diviners of the new shrine follow next and then the *koiltal*. After him comes the secular officer and then two or three of the oldest men in the village. No further order of precedence or seniority is observed. After all the men have completed the rite, the women do so, the wives of officials in the same order as their husbands (though the wives of officials of the new shrine claim no special precedence) and after the eldest two or three women, all the rest.

Over and again in the ceremony this order is followed. It applies
to the dead who are being mourned as well as to the living. When
the relics are solemnly taken out and placed on the cots, the cots
are ranged in the order of precedence which the deceased had when
alive, highest in official rank first, then eldest in age at death. When
one bows to these relics, he does so in his own proper turn in the
rank order, bowing first to the senior relic and down to the junior-
most. If visiting priests and diviners are present, they come after
their local counterparts; the Funeral Boys, taken here as officials,
come after the diviners and before the *koiltal*. Again, when parched
rice is served after the pyre is ablaze, the same order is followed.
Now the widowers and widows are given precedence just before
the Funeral Boys. This is the one occasion in the ceremony when a
woman, the widow, precedes some of the men.

The order of rank and age is followed in determining who is
the senior deceased among those being mourned. His eldest son
then speaks for all the mourning households in asking the assembled men to allow the ceremony to be held. Then at the end of the
rite, it is in front of the house of the senior deceased of each division that each Funeral Boy symbolically cooks millet. The bell
and the blade carried by each Boy are kept in that house until the
next funeral ceremony.

The ritual order of precedence does not necessarily reflect the
realities of power and influence in the commmunity, although it is
not totally irrelevant to it. Thus, in certain contexts at least, the
priests' opinions carry considerable weight in community action.
And elders are usually given the respectful hearing warranted by
their age. But the priest has no universal or necessary influence by
virtue of his office, and elders are not powerful by sole reason
of their gray hair. It may be that the order of precedence, while
not to be literally translated to degrees of influence, does reinforce
the Kota's concept that in any group action there is an order which
establishes the leadership of certain members and the subordination of others.

Social ranking is further demonstrated in the bowing by one
person to another. Thus, when the guests come into the houses

of their hosts, a younger brother arriving from another village will bow to the outstretched hand of the elder brother and to the feet of his parents. Bowing also expresses the subjection of man to the supernatural. Hence, when the procession comes in to clean the cremation place, all bow with foreheads to the ground as is regularly done when coming into the presence of the supernatural. Similarly, at the end of the ceremony, after the funeral pole is touched to the houses and then carried out of the village in procession to be thrown away, all bow to the ground in the direction of the cremation place, thus symbolizing that they take leave of the supernaturals who have been immanent in the ceremony which has thus been concluded.

Apparent both in the bowing among people and in the order of precedence is the division between men and women which recurs through all ritual. In most group activities women follow the men. In dancing, men dance first and women later, after the men have tired a bit. In procession, all men go ahead, then come the women. That is, if they come at all; for no woman goes along in such ritual tasks as the cleaning of the funeral grounds. A woman precedes some men only in special circumstances, as do the widows in the ceremony. And a man bows to a woman only in special circumstances, as when a son bows to his mother's feet after a long absence. The division between the sexes extends to many aspects of the ceremony. Just one example is the tying of the relic in a corner of the cloak on the funeral pyre. Relics of men are tied with one kind of fiber (toirnul), and women with another kind (pobitnur).

These recurrent elements of ritual — the procession, dancing, feasting, the order of precedence, bowing — enable people to act out some of the major patterns of social organization and so presumably to revitalize them regularly. It seems reasonable to suppose that the patterns are thereby reinforced in the sense that stimulus-response psychologists have demonstrated the reinforcements of habits.

There is yet another series of meanings in the ceremony which may be called psychological meanings. They pertain more directly to the feelings and behavior of the individual as individual. Not that their effect can at all be divorced from the social setting, but their incidence falls when the individual is concerned with himself as "I, Kamaten," rather than as "We, Kota."

For example, a Kota woman whose husband has died, leaving her with a half-grown family, tells of her grief and responds to her loss in ways which are familiar in many societies. She withdraws from her ordinary social relations, she seems almost obsessed with the amputation of a part of her life, she appears to be bewildered and at a loss in her new condition. These are familiar responses to grief among a great many peoples of the world. The Kota widow's keening may be culturally stereotyped and much of her specific behavior conventionally assigned to the role of widow, but the ethnographer cannot but understand that there is also a very large component of personal sorrow and disorientation. The effect of the Dry Funeral on her — and on all similarly affected by the death — is to assuage grief and provide personal reorientation. These purposes are not completely fulfilled by the first cremation as Kota culture is constituted. The second funeral provides a definite end-point for poignant expressions of grief and for disorientation. In the ten days of the ceremony, the cutting smart of grief is evoked again, and then perhaps more easily and finally dismissed. Reorientation is accomplished by restoration in full cynosure and approval to normal status.

The healing attribute of the ceremony may have such meaning for a villager at any stage of his adult life, whenever he may happen to be bereaved. There is another psychological meaning which pertains mainly to a particular stage of the male life cycle. It is the meaning for the young men, newly enough arrived at adult physical powers to be delighted to test their strength in danger, and no less eager and delighted to seek sexual experience. For these the buffalo chase and the funeral night were particularly satisfying experiences. With the change in both, the emotional attraction of the ceremony for the young men has diminished, although there still is for them the excitement of seeing and perhaps attaining girls and women from villages other than their own.

99

For some of the men the ceremony provides an avenue to acquiring prestige. Not all men are affected by this motive. But some are, and they find in this and in other ceremonies opportunities for fulfilling the preferential patterns, as in lavish giving, which yield approbation and result in personal influence.

There is yet another kind of psychological meaning which applies not to stages or conditions of individual lives, but rather to certain kinds of personalities. Thus Ka·kn, a man who for many years before he died acted as ceremonial director, was a person who delighted in ritual. When he described a ceremony, his gratification in the neatness and precision of ritual shone through his recounting of the detail. He held no office, but he told the officials what was to be done next. His authority in ritual matters, based on long interest, was unquestioned. To a personality like Ka·kn's, which finds special satisfaction in the neat ordering of group action within a definite compass, the ceremony probably brought personal satisfaction beyond that felt by his fellows.

6

These are some of the meanings of the ceremony for the Kota. It remains to consider briefly the meaning of this discussion as a whole for methods of anthropological analysis. Some gains in the clarification of useful concepts may be forthcoming.

The form of a ceremony, we may summarize, consists of the invariant patterns. These are modes of behavior which are replicated and replicable, which can be observed by the ethnographer and verbally described to him. This form may conveniently be understood in two parts, roles and action — as indeed the participants readily so describe it. It would be gratuitous to note, if accounts of ceremonies did not so often confusingly scramble the two, that a role is a set of behavior patterns modally enacted by a specific participant in the ceremony, and the action is the sequence of behavior, the plot, which is performed by the group.

Invariant patterns are those which are constant over a certain space (in this case the seven Kota villages) and through a certain time period (the adult experience of the active participants). They

are constant in the sense that they are so perceived by the participants and have constant consequences according to the evidence
available to the observer. They are the ways which "we Kota"
have followed in living memory. They make up the stable, reliable
form with which the recurrent problem of death is met. But the
stability of form does not exclude variation.

Variation is of two main types, accounted and unaccounted.
Accounted variations are those which the people foresee, at least
as possibilities, and make accommodation for in the form of the
ceremony. These variations are incorporated within invariant patterns, made part of the stable internal system of the ceremony. The
seven kinds of accounted variants which were distinguished, as
the alternative and contingent patterns, are simply Kota ways of
interpreting and dealing with possible or permitted variations.
The patterns called compulsive may be interpreted as means of
handling potential variation by rigidly excluding variation.

Unaccounted variations are those for which the people have no
a priori manner of accommodation within the plan of the ceremony. They are modifications of form which occur when unanticipated pressures bar repetition of the full traditional form. Whatever accommodation is then made is improvised, and while the
analyst may be able to formulate regularities of improvised responses, they appear irregular to the participants.

The incidence of such pressures may be external or internal to
the group. One external pressure was the relapsing-fever epidemic
of 1924, which wiped out the religious officials. Another has been
the governmental prohibition of strong drink. Internal changes
may be set in motion by external forces, but the pressure for change
comes from members of the group. The abolition of cow sacrifice
is an internal change, although those Kota who brought it about
were undoubtedly influenced by a whole range of social and economic forces arising outside the group.

Among these forces were those set in motion by the advent of
trade goods and of caste Hindus to the plateau. Badagas could
then buy their tools in town bazaars and so were freed from dependence on Kota craftsmanship. They also learned from caste Hindus

of a greater social disdain than they had formerly entertained for those who practiced such crafts and customs as did the Kota. The change in the economic situation enabled the Badaga to break off the traditional relations between the two peoples, and that in the social outlook induced many of them to do so. The Kota themselves were not untouched by these forces, and the economic jolt forced them to reorient their views of themselves. In the process of reorientation, they have sloughed off certain ceremonial practices, among them cow sacrifice. Thus one effect of the coming of new goods and peoples has been this internal, previously unaccounted change in the form of the Dry Funeral. In this matter the form has become invariant again. To the extent to which this chain of reaction can be put in general rather than particular terms, it can be said that one meaning of the advent of new goods and peoples has been change in ceremonial. But the term *meaning* has been confined in this discussion to regular influences among systems of action within Kota culture and society.

Meaning refers both to explicit and implicit relationships. The Kota, as we have noted, can explicitly tell what the meaning, i.e., the purpose, of the Dry Funeral is — to send off the spirits of the dead. In order to accomplish this purpose, activities are performed which require actors from various social groupings and patterns of action from various contexts of life, economic, esthetic, religious. All these are assembled and ordered into the particular system of action called the Dry Funeral.

This action has regular effects on other systems. These effects are not readily stated by the people, nor are they directly apparent to the observer. Yet they are not the less significant in the lives of the Kota and in the analysis of the observer for being implicit. We have discussed such implicit meanings of the Dry Funeral as those which help maintain the group's coherence and order, and which contribute to personal coherence and order.

These comments on form, variation, and meaning may clear the way for further explication both of the nature of Kota culture and society and of the methods for demonstrating such analytic concepts as that of implicit meaning.

by ALLAN R. HOLMBERG

Adventures in Culture Change

Today there are few aboriginal cultures of the world which have
not been profoundly affected by the influences of Western society.
Especially the effects of the modern technological revolution have
been deeply felt in the most remote corners of the world. Because
of this, modern anthropologists, concerned with problems of culture change, have been afforded (or they have sought) few opportunities to observe at first hand situations in which there has
previously been little or no contact between an isolated aboriginal
group and representatives of the Western world. Here it is proposed to discuss an instance in which just such an opportunity
arose.

During the course of an ethnological investigation among the
Siriono Indians of Eastern Bolivia in 1941–1942 I, in company
with a Bolivian companion and a number of semiacculturated
Siriono, encountered in August of 1942, after wandering some
fifteen days through the swamp jungles southeast of the village
El Carmen, a band of Siriono who had had so little contact with the
outside world that about the only items of Western technology
found among them were two machetes worn to the size of pocket
knives.[1] Having devoted several months previously to a study of
the native language and culture at a Bolivian Government Indian

---

[1] These machetes, insofar as we were able to determine later, had been
acquired many years earlier by robbing rubber tappers who worked for an
English firm which found it uneconomic to continue operations in this area
after 1928.

My Bolivian companion, a faithful one, was Luis Silva Sánchez, who at the

School called Casarabe — situated about thirty miles east of Trinidad, capital of the Department of the Beni — and having adjusted myself to the seminomadic conditions of forest life, I followed these Indians around for a while, finally settling with them on the banks of the Rio Blanco at a site which we founded and named Tibaera, the Indian word for a palm tree which grew in great abundance there. It was while I was in residence at Tibaera, from October 1942 to April 1943, that I was presented with favorable opportunities to initiate a number of "experiments" in culture change which brief subsequent visits to the area enabled me to check on from time to time.[2] This paper, therefore, is devoted to a consideration of a few of the changes introduced at that time and of some of the effects resulting therefrom.

Under aboriginal conditions, the Siriono are a seminomadic people who, in terms of technology at least, may be classified among the most handicapped peoples of the world. They live with a bare minimum of what the late Professor Malinowski called "material apparatus." In fact, the most effective tools with which they wrest but a meager living from their environment consist of a cumbersome bow and arrow and a crude digging stick, the former being used exclusively by men and the latter principally by women. While they practice agriculture — small amounts of maize, manioc, camotes, and tobacco are planted in natural clearings in the forest — they live principally by hunting, fishing, and collecting. Having neither stone nor steel tools — little stone is found in the environment — they are unable to clear any large amounts of land

time this study was made was employed as an explorer for a Bolivian Government indigenous school located at Casarabe, Beni, Bolivia.

I am grateful to the Social Science Research Council which sponsored my work among the Siriono. For more complete details about the people the reader is referred to my monograph entitled *Nomads of the Long Bow*, Smithsonian Institution, Institute of Social Anthropology, Publication No. 10, Washington, 1950.

[2] These are not to be regarded as "experiments" in the true scientific sense. For this reason I have employed the more esthetic term "adventures" in the title of the paper. At the time this work was done I had much less sophistication and training in experimental method than I now have and, besides, my central problem dictated use of the observational method. While some attempt was made to manipulate subjects, I realize that my lack of controls does not allow me to dignify my ventures by the scientific term "experiment."

for agriculture; and because they occupy a relatively harsh environment, much of which is inundated for about four or five months of the rainy season, from December to May, the major problem with which they have to contend is that of supplying sufficient food for survival. Since the solution of this problem is impeded in part, at least, by a technological insufficiency, the setting struck me as an excellent one in which to initiate technological change and observe its effect on the native economy and other aspects of culture.

It should be made clear at the outset, however, that on first contact with this band of Siriono I was in no position to assume the role of an innovator. We were traveling as light as possible at the time, and besides, my central problem required that I make observations on the native culture as it functioned under aboriginal conditions. Thus it was only after such observations had been made and the band had voluntarily returned with us to Tibaera (we had previously established ourselves there with remnants of another group of Siriono who had escaped from bondage[3] several months before) that I was able to initiate what attempts I made at innovation. It should be stated for the record, however, that my Bolivian companion and I had taken with us a few basic items of Western technology upon which our own survival depended. These included a rifle and shotgun, a number of machetes, fishhooks, hammocks, mosquito nets, several changes of clothing, and a few aluminum cooking utensils. In addition, I carried a camera, notebooks, and a few common remedies such as quinine, aspirin, and injections of emetine hydrochloride. The only supplies of food we carried with us were salt, sugar, and coffee. Unfortunately our supplies of sugar and salt were accidentally lost during the first few days of our trip so that about all we had to remind us of our former diet during a sojourn of about a month was coffee, of which we had taken an abundant supply and for which the Indians had not yet acquired an appetite.

[3] It was the general practice of Mestizo farmers in this area to lure Indian groups in from the forest on the promise of food and tools and then force them to work in their fields. Through threats and punishments many were thus kept in servitude.

I mention these matters in passing to indicate that at the time of first contact and for about two months thereafter our influence on the band was minimal, for we needed what supplies we possessed to take care of ourselves. Nevertheless, the desire on the part of the Indians for a superior technology was immediately felt. We had been with the band for little more than a few minutes before we were bombarded with requests for tools, especially machetes. These we did not have, but I had brought with me several boxes of cotton thread,[4] which were distributed to the Indians by way of compensation. It was at this time that the idea of future experiment first presented itself to me.

Shortly after returning to Tibaera, therefore (I had established by this time that the Siriono under aboriginal conditions do face a life of extreme impoverishment), I made a journey of several days down the Rio Blanco by canoe in quest of some basic items of technology to introduce. Limited by matters of budget, however, as is so often the case in field work, I was only able to afford to purchase a few machetes and axes together with a small supply of such seeds as rice and watermelon, which the Siriono did not then plant under aboriginal conditions. These, together with trade goods and food, I brought back with me to Tibaera. The machetes and axes, of which I had only six each, I presented to members of the band who I thought were the most influential and with whom I had had greatest contact. They were distributed in this manner because I felt that my own residence among the Siriono depended on maintaining rapport with at least the persons of most prestige in the group, particularly the chief and some of his immediate kinsmen. In order to temper the disappointment (in some cases, hostility) of those who did not receive tools, I made gifts to them of such trade goods as beads, necklaces, cloth, thread, pocket knives, and salt. Since it was not yet the season for agriculture, the seeds were withheld for future planting.

The introduction of these few tools alone represented a drastic change in the technological system of the people who received

[4] This is an excellent trade item in the Tropical Forest Area of South America, where fine cotton thread is highly prized for arrow making.

them; they progressed overnight from a technology of the pre-Stone Age to one of the Iron Age. As might be expected, of course, repercussions of this change were immediately apparent, especially on the economic life. Whereas formerly, for example, a person spent as much as half a day in extracting a palm cabbage, a Siriono staple, with a digging stick, he could remove more than a half dozen in a similar period with an axe. For the people possessing tools, therefore, the production of palm heart ceased to be a serious economic problem. To take another example, the Siriono are extremely fond of wild honey, the only sweet they possess. They seldom become satiated with it, however, for lack of an efficient means of extracting it. Wild bees generally build their hives in dead, hollow trees still standing in the forest, and in order to extract the honey the hole through which the bees enter the hive must be enlarged sufficiently to permit the entrance of the hand. Under aboriginal conditions firebrands and digging sticks are employed for this purpose, but often an entire day af labor is rewarded by only a few handfuls of honey. Actually, by aboriginal methods but a small proportion of the exploitable wild honey is removed from the environment each year. By using an axe, however, a hive of wild honey could be removed — and much more efficiently — in less than an hour's time. Since the introduction of axes corresponded with the season for gathering wild honey, the production of this food also increased enormously.

The same may be said with respect to most economic activities. Wild fruits were more easily harvested, the inaccessible ones by cutting down the trees; wood for bows and arrows and house-building was more readily extracted; slain animals were more rapidly cut up; mobility through swamp and jungle was greatly increased; wooden utensils and tools were better and more rapidly constructed. In short, the productive capacity of the families receiving tools more than doubled at once.

With respect to the social effects of these innovations, only a few remarks can be made. In general, the economic benefits were not enjoyed by all members of the band. Native ideas of personal property and patterns of food distribution were, at first at least,

rigidly adhered to. Among the Siriono feelings of food deprivation are extremely high, and they are reluctant to share products
outside of the extended family. Actually, the machetes and axes
were jealously guarded and the fruits of their production confined
principally to the families who possessed them. Because of this,
complaints were bitter, and demands for tools — demands which
I could not fulfill — were constant.

Another consequence of the limited introduction of more efficient tools was a noticeable rise in in-group hostility. One of the
first effects of the increased production of wild honey, for example,
was an increase in the supply of native beer and in the number and
duration of drinking bouts. This in turn led to a more frequent
expression of aggression, since drinking feasts are the principal
occasions when both verbal and physical aggression are expressed
among the men. Under aboriginal conditions these drinking feasts
seldom lead to long-lasting hostilities because the supply of native
beer is limited by the arduous labor involved in the extraction of
honey. But with improved techniques it was possible to hold these
feasts with greater frequency and greater intensity. On one occasion, in fact — and this was a direct result of the increased production of native beer — the aggressions expressed at a drinking bout
of considerable intensity resulted in such a strong hostility
among the members of two extended families that the unity of the
band itself was threatened. Needless to say, this was an effect which
I had not anticipated at the time the tools were introduced.

Perhaps the most significant consequence of the introduction of
steel tools, however, was that it paved the way for an expansion
of agriculture — and hence an ensuring of the food supply — hitherto unknown among the Siriono. Attempts to improve agricultural
methods and to introduce new plants met with a variety of responses. I had originally suggested to the men who received steel
tools that they might most fruitfully employ them to intensify
agriculture. But since it was the dry season, the best one for hunting and fishing, three of the men were away from camp so much
of the time that little heed was paid to my advice. With another
three, however, I was able to establish workable relations. These

were Eantandu, a chief, and two of his brothers-in-law, Enia and Mbiku. Changes in agriculture were initiated largely through them. The pattern followed was that of disrupting as little as possible native agricultural practices, such as that of each man planting for himself,[5] and of fitting the changes as nearly as possible into the existing culture pattern. The procedure consisted first in convincing each of the men to clear a sizable plot of good land for himself. When this was done and the brush was thoroughly dried, the plots were burned over. Then shortly after the first rains came in late November each man was encouraged to seed his land with maize, manioc, and other native products. For lack of better tools, this was done largely with the digging stick; however, the methods of planting were considerably improved. In addition, each man was asked to reserve a piece of land for dry rice farming, which my Bolivian companion and I introduced at Tibaera. Finally, Eantandu alone was encouraged to seed a small patch of watermelon.

All of the agricultural labor connected with the experiment was performed by the men themselves or by their wives. But not voluntarily, nor without reward. Often during the course of the work, I or my Bolivian companion had to supply the families with meat, which we could obtain only by hunting and fishing ourselves, sometimes at night; otherwise they would have spent almost all of their days in the forest, and our attempts would doubtless have failed. Then too, some such encouragement was necessary because of a logical suspicion on the part of the Siriono that we intended to profit by the results of their labor, as had been the case in all previous instances of contact with whites.

Since the season was favorable and the land was new, the crops thrived far beyond expectations. After being weeded and hoed a number of times (again largely with digging sticks), the resulting harvest was — to the Siriono at least — prodigious. Suddenly Eantandu, Enia, and Mbiku found themselves with more food than they had ever possesssed before at one time in their lives. From

[5] My Bolivian companion and I made attempts at cooperative gardening with members of both bands at Tibaera but with little effect, for individualism runs high among the Siriono.

this small patch alone, Eantandu harvested more than a hundred watermelons. These he ate in such quantity that on two occasions he became violently ill with indigestion. During a week or so of harvest, Eantandu, Enia, and Mbiku laid away what might normally be regarded as a six months' supply of rice and maize. Others, planting by aboriginal methods, had harvested much smaller yields of maize for themselves, supplies which were almost exhausted by the time I left the band a month later. During this month Eantandu, Enia, and Mbiku had only occasionally shared the results of their bountiful harvest and then only begrudgingly in exchange for meat or other products they happened to be in need of at the moment. Everyone, however, had managed at least to taste rice and watermelons and to acquire seeds which they were reserving for later planting. Two years later the Siriono to a man were growing these crops on the banks of Lago Huachi, some twenty miles east of Tibaera. In the meantime they had acquired more steel tools through trade with the whites, and the nomadic pattern of life had been greatly reduced.[6]

Hand in hand with experiments in agriculture, attempts were made to introduce some domestic animals. These were made through one man alone, Chief Eantandu. Under aboriginal conditions the Siriono possess no domestic animals, not even the dog. This is not surprising; their seminomadic pattern of life is hardly consistent with animal husbandry. Even the dog would be of little use to them in hunting in a tangled jungle where the meat supply is mostly shot in trees and where it is not sufficient to feed even themselves, to say nothing of others. Moreover, the Siriono responded with great fear to the dog. Since the footprint of a dog is very similar to that of a jaguar, the two animals were equated under one term (yakwa) and the suspicions and fears of one were generalized to include the other. Consequently Eantandu expressed grave doubts as to the utility of the dog, which I attempted to introduce. Actually his suspicions were well founded. Even though well-trained in some types of hunting, the dog proved to be a burden

---

[6] This was in part due to a wild rubber boom which hit this area after the United States entered World War II.

to him. He scared more game away than he hunted; he robbed food from camp; he frightened women and children; he even bit a child or two. In short, he was not adaptable to the existing culture pattern. This was brought home to me on many occasions but especially once when I was absent from camp for about five days. I returned to find the dog almost dead of starvation. Consequently, on leaving the Siriono, I left the mongrel with my Bolivian companion, and on my visit of a couple of years later found that the Indians were still doing nicely without the animal.

Attempts to introduce domestic fowl were somewhat more successful. Returning from a trip down the river, I brought with me several roosters and a number of hens which I had planned to use as a provision for meat and eggs for myself and as an experiment in culture change among the Siriono. With this latter idea in mind, I presented a pair of hens and a rooster to Eantandu with an explanation of the benefits he might expect providing he took proper care of his brood. In this case it was not even necessary for him to feed and water the chickens since there was plenty of food around camp in the form of insects, rotten wild fruits, grubs, and worms, and the supply of water in the river was unlimited. In spite of this, the first attempt failed. Within three days after receiving the fowls, Eantandu, feeling the pinch of bad luck in hunting, butchered them. He explained to me that his wives — he had two at this time — had urged him to do so because his children were hungry. Needless to say, I gave him no more at the moment.

Meanwhile I had a number of hens setting myself which, within the expected time, hatched out more than twenty chicks. While they were growing to maturity — we had constructed a rude chicken house of bamboo to shelter the brood[7] — Eantandu began to regret his previous lack of foresight and asked me if I would give him a few more hens and a rooster to begin the experiment anew. This I agreed to do, but only after he had constructed a chicken house and after he had promised to take good care of his chickens. On this occasion the experiment produced different results. Within

[7] This is necessary in the jungle to protect the fowl from jaguars and vampire bats, which are very abundant in this area.

five months his flock had grown to the size of my own, and he was able to enjoy the fruits of their production whenever pickings in the forest were slim. Up to this time, however, his good fortune had been shared with no one.

After leaving Tibaera in April 1943, I did not see Eantandu again for more than two years. During the interim one of his wives had been killed by a falling tree, and the band had undergone numerous unpleasant encounters with whites. The pattern of chicken-raising, however, still persisted with Eantandu and had by this time diffused to three or four of his kinsmen as well.

Another item of Western technology which served as the basis for experiment while I was living among the Siriono was the shotgun. Although no attempt was made by me to introduce the use of firearms to the Indians generally, this weapon did serve as a means of confirming a hypothesis as to the relation between prestige and hunting in Siriono society. While living with the Indians in the forest and at Tibaera, I was daily impressed, of course, by the importance of hunting and food-producing activities. I had also observed that the men who hunted the most game were generally the most respected. But in no way were these observations more neatly confirmed than in an experimental situation which arose while living at Tibaera. Among the Indians living there was a young man named Enia, who was regarded by everyone as a poor hunter. Part of the reason for this was that he had resided on a Bolivian *estancia* at an age when he would normally have been acquiring the techniques of hunting with the bow and arrow had he been living under aboriginal conditions. As an adult he rejoined his band and married the sister of the chief. But he had never been able to develop his skill in hunting, although he made every effort to do so. Actually, when I first knew him, he was very unhappy about his lack of hunting ability, for he was being constantly insulted at drinking feasts and was almost daily ridiculed by his wife for returning from the forest empty-handed. Once he had possessed two wives, one of whom he lost. His brother-in-law, the chief, made no bones about telling me (and Enia) that he was not much good.

This situation struck me as an excellent one in which to introduce a more efficient technology. Having firearms myself, I began to take Enia with me on the hunt and gradually taught him the use of the shotgun, which he soon learned to manipulate very well by himself. As a result of this, his meat production jumped enormously and his prestige began to rise. In addition to this he was one of the participants in the successful agricultural experiment so that when I left the band he was enjoying exceptionally high status, as exemplified by the fact that he had acquired a second wife and was insulting others at drinking feasts instead of being insulted by them. When I left the band, taking the shotgun with me, I feared for the status of Enia, but on a visit by plane to Lago Huachi, on the banks of which remnants of his band of Siriono were camping a couple of years later, I found that he had again latched himself onto "white" civilization and was working on a plantation of wild rubber, apparently doing quite well. What has happened to him since, I do not know.

After the war, however, the working of wild rubber became a losing game. The plantation probably fell into disrepair. In any case the Indians left. Recent letters[8] indicate that they are now living with my former Bolivian companion, Silva — by whom they are probably being exploited — about halfway between Missions of Guarayos and the village of El Carmen. For the most part they abandoned their old way of life, shifting from a largely nomadic to a largely settled existence based on agriculture. Today I am frequently disturbed by the fact that I had a hand in initiating some of the changes which probably ultimately overwhelmed them and over which neither I nor they had control. Indeed, when I contemplate what I did, I am not infrequently filled with strong feelings of guilt. Maybe they should have been left as they were.

[8] From Don René Rousseau of Baures, Beni, Bolivia.

CULTURAL ANTHROPOLOGY

by ERWIN H. ACKERKNECHT

On the Comparative Method
in Anthropology

W ITHIN a hundred years the comparative method has in anthropology, especially in cultural anthropology, descended from a dominant position to a point where it is in general either not practiced or even condemned explicitly. Criticism of the comparative method seems to have started in the 1890s when Franz Boas published his ideas on the *Limitations of the Comparative Method*.[1] Similar arguments were voiced by Sir G. Lawrence Gomme (1908), Graebner, and others. The 1934 edition of Haddon's *History of Anthropology*, echoing this period, still contains a condemnation of the comparative method (p. 142). This attack on the comparative method coincided with the decline of the evolutionary school, so closely identified with the comparative method, and the rise of the historical school in cultural anthropology. The historical school still used a modified comparative method on a large scale. Complete disregard of the comparative method became fashionable only in the era of functionalism, especially with Malinowski, Margaret Mead, and some others. The comparative method has never been abandoned to the same degree in other branches of anthropology — physical anthropology, linguistics, or archaeology. Even in cultural anthropology there are signs of a renaissance of the comparative method. One of the most encouraging is the appearance of G. P. Murdock's *Social Structure*.

[1] Boas, 1896, pp. 901ff; Boas, 1938, pp. 3, 669, 678.

S. F. Nadel, though he starts his remarkable *Foundations of Social Anthropology* (1951) with the typically Malinowskian statement that anthropology is the "biography of simple societies" (p. 6), finds later anthropology "wedded to the comparative method" (p. 193) and the field of comparative sociology to be the typical field of social inquiry (p. 227).

In this paper I have chosen to discuss the comparative method because I feel that anthropology, limited in its methods by the nature of its material, can ill afford to give up a method, unless the method is proved to be without value. And this has never been done in the case of the comparative method. In my own work I have found the comparative method of definite value. The enormous collecting of ethnographical evidence during the last hundred years, continued faithfully in our own time, makes sense only in view of an eventual comparative use of this material. A continuation of the tragicomic attempts to avoid this admittedly frightening task by all sorts of shortcuts would actually imply a declaration of bankruptcy on the part of anthropology.

The great popularity of the comparative method during the nineteenth century in both anthropologies (cultural and physical), and for that matter in many other disciplines — A. Harnack stated rightly in 1917: "During the 19th century the comparative method became the ruler of science" (p. 6) — can be understood today only through another, now largely forgotten phenomenon of the period: *the immense popularity of comparative anatomy* in general and its influence on anthropology in particular.[2] To avoid misunderstandings, I should like to state immediately that comparative anatomy was certainly not the only influence in anthropology's formative years. I am well aware of the influence, for example, of certain philosophies, of practical issues like slavery or national emancipation, or of tendencies like Gall's phrenology and Quetelet's social physics. Yet in the field of methodology the influence of comparative anatomy can hardly be overestimated.

[2] See Rothacker, 1947, p. 88, for the influence of the comparative anatomy of Cuvier and Goethe on other sciences; *ibid.*, p. 92, for an interesting passage from Dilthey on the influence of Cuvier.

From Linné, through Buffon, Daubenton, Hunter, Owen, and Cuvier, to Darwin, with whom it reached its climax and in whose hands it became one of the basic theories of modern science, comparative anatomy was the "glamor science" of the day, very much what physics has become today. This is partly due to the technology of the period, when man still depended on animals not only for food but for such other basic needs as clothing, lighting, and transportation.[3] While the influence of Darwin is still acknowledged, the hardly less powerful impact of Cuvier and his techniques on his time is no longer realized. Yet it was tremendous. Cuvier practically created paleontology and stimulated such sciences as geology and prehistoric archaeology, which became important formative influences on anthropology. Two of the founders of modern linguistics, Jacob Grimm and Fr. Schlegel, were in their methods directly inspired by Cuvier and his collections.[4] Under the same influence Grimm developed comparative mythology and folklore. A third of the great early linguists, W. von Humboldt, was particularly impressed by the comparative anatomy of Cuvier's German counterpart Goethe, who had stated that "natural history is basically comparison."[5] It is well known to what extent Comte used the work of Blainville, the comparative embryologist and successor of Cuvier, and how much he insisted on the comparative method. Spencer was equally indebted to comparative anatomy. In these circumstances it is quite understandable that anthropology underwent the same influences. It is impossible to list here all the radiations of Cuvier's comparative anatomy, but its impact on architecture through Semper[6] and on literature through Balzac[7] may at least be mentioned.

We are aware of the fact that the comparative method was applied by such ingenious precursors of cultural anthropology as Lafitau (1670–1740) and Charles de Brosses (1709–1777) without

[3] Lawrence, 1822, p. 37.
[4] Rothacker, 1947, p. 94.
[5] Muehlmann, n.d., p. 69.
[6] Rothacker, 1947, p. 105.
[7] E.g., Balzac, 1859, Preface. Or Balzac's aphorism on the first page of "La Recherche de l'Absolu"; "L'Archéologie est à la nature sociale ce que l'Anatomie comparée est à la nature organisée."

visible influences from an embryonic comparative anatomy.[8] The
evolutionary idea was more clearly expressed by early social scientists like Voltaire and Condorcet in their field than by contemporary biologists. In general, basic biological ideas like that of evolution or mutual aid in animals seem to result from social stimuli
even among biologists.[9] Goethe frankly admitted such stimuli.[10]
The catalytic effect of Malthus on Darwin is well known. It remains
nevertheless true that when the comparative method started to
play a conspicuous role in the growing anthropology of the late
eighteenth and early nineteenth centuries, earlier forerunners in
the social field were unknown or forgotten, and for better or worse,
often the worse, the method was borrowed from and shaped by
comparative anatomy, by now a full-fledged and respectable, even
powerful science. While the methods and techniques of physics
seemed not translatable into anthropology, those of biology seemed
applicable.

Such a borrowing appeared all the more natural as physical and
cultural anthropology had not yet separated. The writings of
Blumenbach (1798), G. Forster (1783), Meinert (1794), Pritchard
(1836), Desmoulins (1826), and W. Edwards (1829), even when
their primary aim is the elucidation of biological problems,
abound with linguistic, psychological, cultural (especially religious), and historical materials and problems. (A belated echo of
this period is Deniker's treatise of 1900.) The same picture is offered
by the early ethnological societies (those of W. Edwards in Paris
in 1839 and of Pritchard in London in 1842; see also Pritchard's
presidential address to the latter). The majority of these early
"undifferentiated" anthropologists or ethnologists were comparative anatomists and had been trained as physicians.[11] The medical
and anatomical background of the early anthropologists is per-

[8] Muehlmann, n.d., pp. 41ff.
[9] Nordenskjöld, 1935, pp. 441, 446, 458ff.
[10] Merz, n.d., II, 217.
[11] The same, by the way, holds good for economics, where many of the authors
of the early classics, were trained physicians like Conringius, Petty, Quesnay,
and Villermé. Trained physicians continued to play an important role in both
anthropologies. This is easily understood in the case of physical anthropology,
where we remember such names as Serres, Virchow, Broca, Rokitansky, von

haps one reason why physical anthropology crystallized before cultural anthropology.

A more important reason may be that well into the nineteenth century the idea prevailed that social science was only a department of natural science. Not only in seventeenth-century philosophers like Bacon, Descartes, and Leibnitz and, understandably enough, in eighteenth-century physician-philosophers like Vicq d'Azur or Cabanis (or a little later Fodéré, Virey, and others) does the idea appear, but in the early social scientists themselves, like Volney, Destut de Tracy, and H. Saint Simon.[12] Only Comte emancipated social science from this tutelage, which would almost be bound to give physical anthropology an earlier start.

Around the middle of the nineteenth century physical and cultural anthropology became separate disciplines. Though the two were still largely cultivated in common societies and journals, most anthropologists were no longer working simultaneously in both fields, but only in one. This specialization was dictated by certain objective necessities (too large materials, necessity to learn special techniques, etc.). It was favored by the fact that the results of one line of inquiry had very little bearing in their details upon the other. It became possible through the growing notion of independent social science.

In spite of the separation the comparative method retained its influence in cultural anthropology. It even became *the* method, as physical and cultural anthropology both turned evolutionist, and as evolution was the crowning result of all previous endeavors in comparative anatomy. As a matter of fact, it was so powerful that even the biological antievolutionists used the comparative method. Pitt-Rivers' comparative work on material culture, begun in 1851, and inaugurating a whole new line of research and museology, is comparative anatomy in the most literal sense of the word. One need not probe very deeply into the anthropological classics

Luschan, Hrdlicka, E. Fischer, G. E. Smith, Weidenreich, and Vallois. It is less well realized that many well-known cultural anthropologists or field workers like Bastian, Ehrenreich, v. d. Steinen, Livingstone, Rivers, Seligman, Crevaux, Rivet, and W. Matthews had also a medical background.

[12] Merz, n.d., Vol. IV, Chap. 10; Ackerknecht, 1948, p. 143.

of the second half of the nineteenth century to discover the not always fortunate influences of comparative anatomy. We mention only one such classic, that in which E. B. Tylor, probably the greatest of the early anthropologists, introduced his *Primitive Culture* with the demand: "A first step in the study of civilization is to dissect it into details, and to classify those in their proper group. . . . What this task is like may be almost perfectly illustrated by comparing these dates of culture with the species of animals and plants as studied by the naturalist. To the ethnologist the bow and arrow is a species, the habit of flattening the child's skull is a species, the practice of reckoning by ten is a species" (I, 7–8, N.Y., reprint 1920). Tylor's famous "survivals" are but first cousins of Darwin's "atavisms."

The wave of scientific criticism that seriously jeopardized biological Darwinism and nearly eliminated cultural evolutionism around 1900 brought discredit also upon the comparative method. Cultural evolutionism was far more vulnerable than biological evolutionism, insofar as the former had claimed a parallelism in evolution which the latter had never assumed. The archaeological foundations of cultural evolutionism were different from and weaker than the paleontological foundations of Darwinism. Cultural evolutionism had no embryology to support its argument.

Yet, the historical school, the successor of the evolutionary school, did still use a modified comparative method. It is in this context interesting that Boas in 1938 still called for a "cultural morphology founded on comparative studies of similar forms in different parts of the world" (p. 675). Only the functionalist school of Malinowski broke completely with the comparative method in a move which in future times might not be regarded as the climax of anthropological theory.[13] Malinowski felt able to tell us about the crime, sex life, myth, trade, magic, etc. of "savages" on the basis of "functional" observations of one single tribe. Malinowski's method is a far worse misunderstanding of the tendencies in biological science than that from which the evolutionists suffered.

[13] Bidney, 1953, p. 698, has pointed towards some of the less-known reasons for abandoning the comparative method.

In biology comparative anatomy was overshadowed in importance by physiology when it became possible to replace serial comparative observation by conclusive experiments on single animals. This turn in biology towards the laboratory is symbolized by Claude Bernard, one of its greatest practitioners and theoreticians. Even biological evolutionism was able partly to turn from comparison toward laboratory experiments via experimental genetics. Malinowski turned from the comparison of series toward analysis of single societies *without the possibility of using the experiment*.[14] By a sleight of hand, observations of single societies were elevated to the rank of generalities. His anthropological pseudophysiology has therefore at best been inconclusive.

We may gain a more balanced outlook on the comparative method if we look at the results of the evolutionary school, which was always comparative but in its greatest representatives far less dogmatically evolutionary than its opponents make it appear to be,[15] and at the results of its successors. That the comparative method was followed for decades with such devotion and enthusiasm was, after all, not merely an effect of borrowing or copying or adapting to a cultural climate, as outlined above; the method was followed because *valid results could be obtained by it*. We might today feel little sympathy for the work of such comparationists as Spencer, Frazer, Westermarck, or Hutton Webster. Our position is already different when it comes to Bastian, Ratzel, Morgan, Wundt, or Waitz. And can anybody deny the value of the contributions made, for example, by Tylor, Maine, van Gennep, H. Schurtz, Ed. Hahn, M. Mauss, A. L. Kroeber, or Clark Wissler (who called anthropology "the comparative point of view")? What would anthropology be today without these contributions? Can anybody deny the value of the results obtained in linguistics and archaeology by the comparative method?

I have dealt with the comparative method historically, although I know that in a culture where the new is somewhat rashly identi-

[14] Nadel, 1951, p. 22, rightly emphasizes these "natural limits" of cultural anthropology (which to a minor degree exist also in physical anthropology) created through the impossibility of using the laboratory experiment.
[15] Lowie, 1937, pp. 27ff, 51ff, 72ff, 90ff; Muehlmann, n.d., 111ff.

fied with the good, and the old with the bad, this may discredit a method which I want to recommend. I have done so not only because I am personally a hybrid between history and anthropology, but above all because I feel that the erstwhile prevalence of the comparative method as well as many of its earlier shortcomings, due to an all too mechanical and superficial application of some notions of contemporary anatomy, can be best understood through history. Often one finds anatomical notions like homology and analogy used in the literature in such a way that one wonders whether the author bothered to study the meaning of these terms when borrowing them from comparative anatomy. No real student of comparative anatomy could have come up with the gruesome notions of species quoted above from Tylor. The pseudo "species" of Tylor can, of course, be studied comparatively; not, however, as "species" but only as "organs," "tissues," "functions," etc. of social species. (As to realistic notions of "species" in cultural anthropology, we should like to refer to the excellent paper of G. P. Murdock in *Anthropology Today*, pp. 467ff.)

The expression of evolutionism has lost much of its former horrors for cultural anthropologists. We have even neoevolutionists today like J. Steward. It might therefore seem superfluous (but still useful) to state that the comparative method is not necessarily evolutionary, either in the social sciences or in biology. The anti-evolutionists in the latter field were just as much comparationists as their adversaries. In a certain sense there is not just one comparative method; there are several. Comparison has been made and will be made according either to form or according to function, quantitatively or qualitatively, morphologically or statistically, etc. Some of these different approaches have been combined. What approach is used will depend on the object and problem of the inquiry — and on the inquirer.

The comparative method is, of course, not a magic method that will solve all problems. It is just one of several legitimate methods, among which I certainly would not discount the functionalistic one either. Like every method it has its limitations. If anthropology returns to the comparative method, it will certainly not forget what it has learned meanwhile in general and what it has learned about the limitations of the method in particular.[16] It will return only in that spiral-like movement, so characteristic of the progress of scientific thought, arriving after half a century at the same point, but on a higher level. It will know better what and how to compare than it knew fifty years ago.

One of the great advantages of the comparative method will be that in a field where the controlled experiment is impossible, it provides at least some kind of control. As Nadel puts it, the artificial induction of variations in phenomena is replaced by the observation of variable phenomena (p. 222).

A revival of the comparative method will eventually bring to good use the rich stores of observation that now gather dust in oblivion, and bring back some discipline of thought to a science that perhaps too often recently has shown an inclination toward impressionistic snap judgments for the sake of rapid "applicability." This is a regrettable phenomenon rather frequently observed in the history of young sciences. In whatever form the comparative method may reappear, it will express the growing desire and need in cultural anthropology to find regularities and common denominators behind the apparent diversity and uniqueness of cultural phenomena.

The usefulness of the comparative method seems so obvious, the compulsion to use it in anthropology is so strong, that its marks are observed even in "functionalist" thinkers like Ruth Benedict, who nevertheless opened remarkable new vistas in the field of comparative psychopathology. I have had strong hesitations in submitting what in a way may be nothing but truisms. I have found my justification in the fact that the comparative method, in spite of its obvious usefulness, has been abandoned. The only reasonable solution of the problem, in my opinion, consists, not in abandoning, but in using and improving it.

[16] Nadel, 1951, p. 237.

by ROBERT F. SPENCER

The Humanities in Cultural
Anthropology

For some years now, the battle has been waged between anthropologists themselves and between anthropology and its sister sciences as to the proper place of anthropology in the pyramid of social versus natural sciences. Interesting though such post-Comtean alignments may be, and however much they serve to effect an over-all view of the interrelationships between the various scientific disciplines, they never seem sufficiently inclusive. Moreover, from the point of view of the anthropologist, the broad claims of his field are not given proper justice. The niche accorded to anthropology under a rubric "science" appears to fail to present the broader implications of the study of man. There are today those anthropologists who rather shy away from any philosophical premises which the field is belatedly attempting to devise. And there are, on the other hand, those who take refuge in the social role of the scientist and who thus would apply a rigid yardstick to the variables of human behavior. These and other considerations make it important that anthropology take stock of itself, widen its methods, and find new areas for study which will in some measure aid in answering the question of where anthropology belongs in a gamut of scholarly disciplines.

In a sense the anthropologist loses himself in words when he seeks to envision himself as operating with the same detachment as does the biologist or physicist. And should he seek to ally his work with that of the psychologist, he is placed in the predicament that he lacks controls analogous to those which can be created in the laboratory situation. One may say, with Lévy-Strauss, that the field situation is a laboratory experience, but it is evident that some vastly different kinds of circumstances obtrude themselves. In this whole-hearted identification with science, anthropology apparently faces a difficulty and a threat. Clearly the tendency toward a stultifying quantification of human behavioral data is growing. When the anthropologist begins to compile statistics on behavioral situations and to plot his discoveries on graphs, he may be exceedingly faithful to the recording of social phenomena, but he has effectively dulled the awareness he might have of the force of culture which moves behind society. Is this, then, the future of anthropology? It is to be hoped that even if the men of the primitive world are engulfed in twentieth-century technology, the anthropologist will find grist for his mill in human situations other than the primitive and so remain faithful to the great traditions of the study of cultures.

When, in 1947, the late Ruth Benedict retired as president of the American Anthropological Association, her term of office was climaxed by an address which pointedly called attention to some of the significant interrelationships between anthropology and the humanities. And indeed, at the time of her premature death, her own research efforts were being directed toward applications of anthropological method and point of view to materials which scholarly tradition had always regarded as being encompassed by the humanities. It is not possible to single out any one professional anthropologist who has taken Benedict's remarks or research efforts sufficiently seriously either to apply them or to find in them a rich and virtually untapped source of data for new investigations. It is not, of course, that anthropologists are ignorant of the humanist traditions; as educated persons in contemporary society, they have frequently considerably more than a smattering of knowledge of the forces which have shaped Western man, at least, if not man in the other great world civilizations. And there are those anthropologists who have utilized data derived from the area of what might be called the humanities — some, indeed, have done so with signal success — but the points of view in their researches have most often involved applications of specific scientific or historical methods. Although some have sought to employ what will be called here a method of the humanities, the attachment to concepts drawn from natural science has made such attempts tentative and groping. The wealth of the humanities, in short, has been all but ignored.

Before reviewing what anthropologists have done with the humanities and before raising the question of what else it is that they might do, it may be well to recall that the concept "humanities" is an extremely broad one. From the point of view of the contemporary university or college curriculum, the humanities become almost universal in scope, at least insofar as they apply to the civilization of the West, embracing sometimes such diverse and broad fields as the history of philosophy and science, not to mention the social, religious, artistic, literary, or musical history of Western nations from classic or medieval times to the present. In a sense, the humanities, as taught in the American university, offer a kind of catch-all; what is not science or social science falls into the domain of the arts. Unquestionably this academic preoccupation with refinement, with "culture" in the narrower sense, is in itself a reflection of the classic and neoclassic traditions of Western history. As Kroeber remarks, humanists claimed a position of privilege.[1] It is through the humanists that the values of scholarship came to have meaning, and it is in the realm of the humanities that the search for "truth" began. But unlike the scientist, the humanist has not been obliged to eschew judgments tinged with value. He has been free, in fact, to make capital of them. It is he who has become the final arbiter of the greatness or baseness of human endeavor. He is free to show the worth of Goethe's *Götz von Berlichingen*, while at the same time he may deplore *Clavigo*. And what is more, because of his role as critic, the word of the humanist finds general acceptance.

Benedict finds no problem in the subjectivism of the humanities. In offering a definition, she resorts to the concept *humanitas* itself:

[1] Tax, 1953, p. 359.

"what man is, his powers, his relations to his fellows and to nature, and the knowledge of these human powers and man's responsibility" (1948, p. 585). It is put in another way by Matthew Arnold, who in defining criticism offers likewise a wholly acceptable formulation of the humanities as such: "a disinterested endeavor to learn and propagate the best that is known and thought in the world." Both definitions are entirely compatible with a broad view of the humanities. It may be agreed, on the one hand, that there is the serious attempt on the part of the humanist tradition to understand man in his secular rather than in his theological relations, and on the other, that there is the inevitable corollary that the greatness of man must be recognized by his works. But here a caution is in order: the humanities do not directly concern what has been called the philosophy of humanism. While it may not be amiss to evaluate progress in terms of humanity, it does not follow that the humanist, with his predominantly historical preoccupation, has the means at hand to promote human progress. The distinction is an important one. While the humanist does not employ the methods of science, his attitude remains one of criticism, not of amelioration.

The premises of the humanist become clear when it is reflected that through them the attempt is made to appreciate and evaluate man and his works. As Kroeber remarks: ". . . the phenomena of man's culture, his products and values, or at least certain of them, have, by general consent, been left to the humanities" (*loc. cit.*). But Kroeber goes on to say that, while the humanists dealt with the human spirit, in the sense of the *Geisteswissenschaften*, humanity was essentially treated as being beyond the laws of nature. This criticism does hold true in view of the failure of the humanists to present a systematic and integrated methodology. In general, there has been concern on the part of the humanists with segments of culture, not with cultural systems. No humanist has apparently successfully reconciled his critical or esthetic judgments with the total human picture, claiming, indeed, as Kroeber remarks, exemption from the necessity of doing so. If, for these reasons, the humanities fail to offer a meaningfully coherent system, then presumably anthropology, concerned with man in nature and with the concept of the culture whole, has much to offer the humanist. But by the same token, because anthropology and the humanities interest themselves in the same kinds of phenomena, the intimacy which can exist between them should be given its proper place, and the benefits to be derived by anthropology from close association should no longer be ignored. As Benedict notes: ". . . to my mind, the very nature of the problems posed and discussed in the humanities is closer, chapter by chapter, to those in anthropology than are the investigations carried on in most of the social sciences" (1948, p. 585).

In the consideration of the role of anthropology in relation to the humanities, it is all too easy to fall afoul of statements as to what anthropology is or purports to be. The old argument as to whether anthropology is history or science or both seems rather unimportant if it be agreed that the proper task of cultural anthropology is the understanding of cultures. No one will deny that the anthropologist operates empirically, and that there is clearly an historical bias to the field. While this is also true of the humanities, there is the claim in anthropology of an attachment to the methods of science. Like the historian, the anthropologist is in search of evidence demonstrating "descriptive integration," as Evans-Pritchard (1951, pp. 60–61) and Kroeber put it. To this end, cultural anthropology, not to mention the other and perhaps more scientifically oriented branches of the field, becomes highly eclectic in methodology. Certainly in line with the goal of understanding cultural behavior, whether holistically, comparatively, or in diachronic or synchronic terms, anthropology must remain an empirical discipline and utilize all methods which come to hand. The task of analyzing, comprehending, and depicting cultures as growths and wholes creates a dependence on the findings of various of the natural sciences as well as those of history and the humanities.[2]

For present purposes, and to avoid a beclouding of the issue, it can be stated that cultural anthropology does use the methods

[2] Redfield, 1953, p. 729.

of the established sciences. Certainly the initial steps of the scientific method — the propounding of hypotheses — are followed out. But the great variability of human data with which the field has to deal creates the tremendous eclecticism which leads Evans-Pritchard to define anthropology as a branch of the humanities (1951, p. 7). And further, in order to reach conclusions based on the testing of the hypotheses set forth, anthropology inevitably uses data which do not conform to mensurable or proven fact. One area in which this holds particularly true lies in the use by anthropologists of materials drawn from the realm of the humanities. In short, anthropology has the difficult task of somehow reconciling a scientific approach with data which do not lend themselves to scientific scrutiny.

But even if one agrees with Evans-Pritchard — or, indeed, with Voegelin, who ascribes the same status to linguistics — that anthropology is a branch of the humanities, a definition of the latter must indeed be made so broad that the traditional humanist may well take exception to it. In the accepted sense, or in terms of the definitions given above, the humanities concern themselves with such cultural products as "great" ideas and values, in the sense of Hutchins and Adler, and with criticism and esthetic judgment. If, however, it is accepted that the anthropologist attempts to obtain the same kinds of perspective, even though, as among primitive peoples, he may be handicapped by lack of historical depth, it is apparent that the methods of the two broad fields are only superficially diverse. It is quite evident that there have been anthropologists to whom these aspects have been of vital concern. Without looking for a rationale, but simply accepting the fact that there was common cause between anthropology and the humanities, Edward Sapir lent his sensitive perceptions to cultural data. Not only do many of his writings and interests reflect a major preoccupation with the arts, but it was he who so aptly demonstrated that there is no great gulf fixed between culture," in the Gallic sense of refinement, and culture in more objectively conceived anthropological terms (1924, pp. 401–407). He easily bridges the gap by showing that every culture has its sense of refinement, known to few or many, as the case may be, which has meaning and force in the perpetuation of the total cultural entity. It is on the basis of the depth of awareness of the reality and meaning of its own traditions that Sapir judges a culture to be "genuine"; when this sharpness of realization of the arts meaningful to the group becomes blunted, a spurious situation is held to result.

It can readily be seen that such insights lead to a good many tremendously vital formulations by anthropologists, most of which form the foundations of much of the work in the field today. Not only Sapir's many contributions, but also Benedict's early venture into humanistic materials, provided by Spengler and Dilthey, in the resolution of her concept of "patterns," have led to such important conceptualizations as Kluckhohn's "overt versus covert" cultures, Whorf's analyses of linguistic phenomena, or Morris Opler's significant elicitation of cultural "themes," to mention only a few.[3] It is evident that no humanist, in the accepted sense of the word, would deny that in these efforts, in vastly differing cultures, are seen attempts to derive the stuff of which the humanities are made; indeed, it would appear that many humanists are reaching out to such anthropological formulations in order to benefit by the insights which they provide. If it is possible to resolve the premises on which a given group operates — its sense of good and evil, its view of the world and the nature of man, its compactness or looseness — it is then possible to comprehend the more meaningfully the artifacts of its total culture. Clearly, too, the methods of eliciting such basic premises, the motivating points of view and propositions in a culture, cannot be conceived in objective terms but depend wholly on what amounts to the intuition and experiential background of the investigator. In "getting the feel" of the culture with which he is working, the field anthropologist employs the same kinds of perception utilized by the literary critic or the artist. Just as the humanist tries to see the whys of the *Don Quijote*, to drink in its flavor, and to appreciate and evaluate the total world of Cervantes, so the anthropologist tries to immerse himself in the shamanistic séance or folktale and to fathom their implications.

[3] Kluckhohn, 1941; Whorf, 1941; Opler, 1945, 1946.

It might be argued that the anthropologist must and does strive for a greater degree of objectivity in his pursuit of facts relating to other cultures. This would again be in keeping with the assumption of the role of scientist. In fact and practice, however, the anthropologist, working in new situations, has only his critical judgments and his own intuitive perceptions and sensibilities on which to rely. On this level of the analysis of the individual culture, it is of course not to be implied that the anthropologist in the field, confronted with new human situations, becomes a creature of temperament. He is not a creator; his role is essentially that of the critic and he attempts to weigh and evaluate the evidence which his respondents and observations give him. If the problem is to see the functional interrelationships within a culture, then the elicitation of formal and informal patterns making up the total *Gestalt* is wholly legitimate. Ideally, the anthropologist in the field remains objective but open to nuance and suggestion, following the lead offered by new situations. Ideally, too, he comes provided with a background, a knowledge which may have permitted the formulation of a particular hypothesis to be tested. And it is at this point that many cultural anthropologists are in a quandary.

The more orthodox of the natural scientists — physicists, chemists, biologists — have no qualms about admitting to the importance of the "hunch." As an initial step in scientific inquiry, in the statement of problem, there is candor about the fact that from the guess may proceed the discovery. Many social scientists, however, not excluding anthropologists, have become so jealous of the "scientific" label, and so defensive of their role as scientists, that the very word "intuition" has been thrown into the lexical dustbin. As the present paper is being written, social scientists are producing a veritable rash of so-called value studies. These are subject to no particular criticism. In their way they succeed in testing, in ostensibly objectively conceived terms, the intuitive judgments of those somewhat more daring. And it seems obvious, too, that one does not ask of an informant from another culture, "What are your values?" These are elicited only with increasing depth of knowledge of the culture. A case in point is provided by Morris

Opler's extremely significant contribution of the concept of cultural themes. However much Cohen and others may condemn them — that here is nothing new, that they lack scientific foundation, that another observer might produce a different set — it cannot be denied that Opler brings together an interpretation which makes the hitherto colorless facets of ethnological description of Lipan Apache culture have vibrant life and meaning.[4] The penchant for objectivity in terms of strict adherence to the scientific method has had some unfortunate results. Nowhere, perhaps, is this more apparent than in contemporary studies of so-called national character.

It is quite evident that there is such a thing as a national culture, character, or flavor in each of the various nations making up the world today. If there is no unity of language or of ethnic groupings, then there are at least the series of common understandings brought about by the legalistic structure of the state. Because of their intimate relation to problems of modern living, few areas of study seem to hold more promise. Those who have been engaged in appraising peoples as nations up to now either have been professional anthropologists or have had a definite orientation drawn from the anthropological literature. But here again the sense of need for — conceptually, at least — a tested objectifying mechanism has obtruded itself. It is not regarded as sufficient to formulate the atmosphere, the ethos, of the national culture under consideration, to describe what is there, and to derive a sense of appreciation of it. On the contrary, such studies must have predictive value. In another guise the search for laws in human behavior is being resumed. It is the psychoanalytic element in studies of national character which has made them palatable and which has perhaps occasioned their popular appeal. In the manner of Kardiner, it is possible to make such startling, and at first blush, quite satisfying, correlations as between ruthless aggressiveness or withdrawn passivity and infantile traumata such as weaning or toilet training. No one, of course, has satisfactorily demonstrated as yet the priority; it seems to boil down to nothing more than such tautologies

[4] Opler, 1945, 1946; Cohen, 1946, pp. 41–42, etc.

as "aggression is aggression." As Mandelbaum points out in his recent statement of concern over the trend, anthropology, if it is to be used to evaluate national cultures, has an historical as well as functional side (1953, p. 176). And if it be added that the insights gained from the total range of the findings of the humanities might also be used, the study of national character assumes considerable purpose and meaning.

Again, no one was more emphatically aware of this than Ruth Benedict. Because the presence of written traditions in the world's nations admits a diachronic rather than a synchronic view, the materials of the humanities lend themselves more readily to use and interpretation than do comparable data from nonliterate peoples. In appraising some selected national cultures, Benedict leaned heavily on literature as an expression of the total cultural spirit. In her best known work in this field, however, she combined, perhaps unfortunately for her study and its ultimate success, a view drawn from the humanities with a questionable psychoanalytic appraisal. It seems that so violent a controversy was aroused over the latter that the worth of the former was ignored. Reference is made here, of course, to the *Chrysanthemum and the Sword* (1946), Benedict's descriptive analysis of Japanese national character. She might well have avoided the challenge to this study by employing only data drawn from the humanities of Japan. Had she, for example, followed up her analysis of the tale of the Forty-Seven Rōnin with one of the behavior of the characters in such a drama as Shikamatsu's *The Love Suicides*, or had she given greater weight to the seeming incongruity of the rich Buddhist literature of the Tokugawa age, her work on the general social structure of Japan, and the solution to the problem of why the Japanese behave as they do, would not have needed the questionable support of the imperfectly understood infantile trauma of parental rejection. In short, the national character of Japan, of any modern nation, or indeed, the ethos of any cultural grouping can be resolved by the anthropologist who is trained to perceive the interrelationships between discrete data, the bulk of which may be drawn from the field commonly called the humanities.

The question how far the anthropologist may invade the field of the humanities may justly be asked. In the final analysis, and because cultural anthropology possesses so high a degree of eclecticism, the answer would appear to depend on the background and interests of the individual investigator. In the concern with the national culture, the anthropologist does not depart either from his purpose of observing a whole culture in action or from the empirical methods which he employs in examining a somewhat less complex group. As with a primitive culture, there is preoccupation with the *Stimmung*, the prevailing mood, as it were, which lies behind overt behavior. The humanist, versed in a single culture or in some special aspect of a single culture, lacks the anthropologist's goal of perceiving the integration of the parts. His view of the esthetic implications of various facets of a national culture can nevertheless give to the anthropologist a remarkable depth of perspective.[5] It is suggested that an example of the application of humanistic materials to a specific national culture be given, not, it must be understood, for the purpose of offering a full appraisal, but rather in order to determine how the humanities may contribute to method in anthropology. For several reasons, the choice is made here of Ireland, and more specifically, of Catholic Ireland, or modern Eire.

As a marginal culture, one which lies at the remotest edge of Europe, Ireland comes to assume certain particular characteristics. There is perhaps no European nation, except possibly Poland, which has been so harassed and torn over so long a period. But despite attempts, from Tudor times until fairly recently, to suppress Irish nationalism, the Irish language, the Irish folk spirit, in short, the whole of Irish national culture, the nation has possessed a remarkable resiliency. It has successfully reasserted itself after each blow, and perhaps because of its unfortunate history, has developed an intensity of national feeling scarcely equaled by any other nation. The anthropologist has at hand means by which he can interpret the history and culture of Ireland. It is possible to give historical perspective to Ireland in terms of cul-

[5] Tax, 1953, p. 154 (Haas).

tural diffusion, of integration of culture elements, and to observe the variations which the Irish have developed on the general cultural theme of the Western world. Unquestionably, to see Ireland in its historical role, as a medieval culture center, as an entity in the British political sphere, and as a culture area marginal to Britain and France, is a necessary prerequisite to the understanding of its national character. But while it might be said that Ireland's marginal position might be a factor in the promotion of national feeling, this still does not provide a means of gauging the depth or intensity of the Irish ethos. There is something in Irish culture which differs in quality either from the rest of Western Europe, or from such closely related peoples as the Welsh, the Scots, or the Bretons.

The principal expression of the Irish spirit has been in literature, not only in Gaelic, but particularly in the works of the Anglo-Irish writers of the nineteenth and twentieth centuries. It is in this latter phase, away from the age of Swift and Steele, that Irish literature loses its cosmopolitan character and becomes intensely local in its manifestations. The literary revival of this period, as it is commonly called, involved an amazing number of creative literary artists, writing in English, it is true, but concerning themselves virtually exclusively with Irish matters. The versatile Yeats comes at once to mind as a leader in the Irish literary renaissance, the dramatic artistry of Synge and Colum, and the startling success of the Abbey Theater being further reflections of it. Even the expatriate Shaw betrays his intimate preoccupation with his homeland and its problems in his *John Bull's Other Island* and many other works. Authors too many to mention have written an infinite number of pieces reflecting the recent Irish intellectual movement. It may be argued that such a development is artificial, that the Irish intellectuals have placed emphasis on literature and have displayed indifference to other arts. The plastic arts and music, for example, are accorded little recognition, and Ireland has no composers or painters of importance. But the Irish intellectuals, humanists themselves, have in their creativity reached down into the Irish folk spirit, which their works intimately reveal.

To the casual observer, a striking aspect of Irish national culture is its stark individualism. This can be evaluated not only in the works of the near-contemporary writers, but also in the particular twist which the Irish gave to the Romantic movement. On the one hand, the bias of Roman Catholicism made for the rejection of many of the implications of Romanticism, but on the other, the movement appears to have lent added support to the patterns of Irish individualism. The Catholic Romanticism of Ireland, so distinctive and so unusual as compared with Continental developments, produced equally unusual Irish politicians. The unhappy Wolfe Tone or the dominant Daniel O'Connell would have been impossible in any but the setting of Irish culture.

Historically, therefore, the humanities provide a means by which the whole concept of the national culture can be evaluated. How the approach that might be used by an anthropologist in this connection differs from that employed by a more orthodox literary or political historian is a question that at once arises. Each will be empirical in his methods and approach and each will require much the same kinds of data. Here again, however, the anthropologist, trained to see the parts in relation to the whole, can be more inclusive in his appraisal. He cannot, and should not, deal with criticism in the same sense as the literary or artistic critic, but he can supplement these fields by determining the extent to which these phenomena, as cultural phenomena, are outgrowths of culture pattern and social system. In his role as culture historian, this is exactly what the anthropologist does. With respect to Ireland, this approach seems somewhat more promising than to attempt an explanation of Irish aggressive individualism in terms of a drunken father and a shift from mother's milk to potatoes. Not that such individualism should not or cannot be explained; with Sapir it may be agreed that there is an interaction between intellectual movement and *Volksgeist*. It remains to bring the two together to complete a view of the culture whole.

There is actually somewhat more, however, to the analysis of national character, or indeed, of the character of a whole civilization, such as of the West in general, of India, or of China. If, as has been seen, the Irish intellectuals, not to mention the whole tone of Irish culture, were influenced at one point by the European Romantic movement, the anthropologist must for the moment become an historical philosopher in order properly to gauge the effects of this development. No one has pointed this out as effectively as F. S. C. Northrup. In his appraisal of modern Mexico, for example, he demonstrates the interrelationships between native culture, Thomistic theology, and positivism (1947, Chaps. 2, 3). As compared with the Mexican development, he lays great stress on the influence of Locke in the development of the culture of the contemporary United States.[6] The Lockean ideals of freedom and property, of the functions of government, and their interpretations by Hamilton, Jefferson, and others, serve to shape the existing United States culture. Yet, obviously, these are the tasks of the philosopher — to determine the import of the system. By common consent, the anthropologist chooses to ignore the historical figure, whether thinker, statesman, or militarist, and to assume that a culture is the product of innumerable diverse and intangible threads. The heritage of interest in the primitive culture, where it is usually impossible to determine the future effects of an individual action, apparently makes this so.[7] While it is evident that the great man is the product of his culture and that his greatness, in whatever form, takes a turn compatible with his cultural setting, it is likewise evident that there may be alternative developments. Mexico and the United States, while sharing in the same general cultural heritage, are not different solely because one is oriented primarily toward Roman Catholic and the other toward Protestant traditions. Idea systems grounded in the culture of the West but evolving through the systematization of selected ideas may produce vastly differing results. One has only to consider the Western world today, divided and apparently irreconcilable because of differences in point of view predicated on philosophical systems.

But Northrup and others who have utilized idea systems as a

[6] Kirk, 1953; Commager, 1950; Northrup, 1947.
[7] Cf. White, 1949, pp. 190–281.

key to a realization of culture are not anthropologists. Important though a basic philosophy may be in fixing the cultural behavior of a group, it remains for the anthropologist to demonstrate the culture in action, to show how behavior is actualized in the face of the system. In a primitive society, with a small and relatively stable population, this is less difficult to do. Here the anthropologist becomes his own philosopher and reconstructs what may be a wholly unverbalized system. On this level the anthropologist is establishing himself as a humanist. But in respect to more inclusive units, nations with a highly complex social and technological structure, with a long history, there is no shorthand way to the realization of national character, any more than a brief stay in the ethnographical field can equip one for the perception of the subtleties and shadings which every culture has to offer. But if the study of the national culture in its historical depth is desirable, then the combined approaches of several disciplines are required. If the anthropologist may, in all modesty, claim for himself the task of associating the parts, it is from the work of the humanist that the bulk of his data will come.

But the national character approach is not the only one in which anthropology and the humanities find common applications. Granted that the materials of the humanities, the criticisms and judgments of the humanists, may be of immeasurable aid in this connection, it remains for anthropology to undertake comparative studies. Both fields concern themselves with culture history. Here the emphasis shifts in response to the question as to the nature of the forces which have shaped either institutions or whole cultures. An essential difference in point of view between the humanities and anthropology appears not so much in method and technique as in the choice of materials for study. More than the humanist, perhaps, the anthropologist has attempted to resolve the problem of variability of patterning in human behavior and has, in consequence, interested himself less in the esthetic component as such. But there are those historians and humanists who have come very close to the anthropological view, or have anticipated it, in their treatment of human situations. Burckhardt's

Renaissance, for example, a classic in the humanities, is at the same time a vivid prelude to the anthropological approach to culture, while Spengler, and to a degree, Toynbee, not to mention the numerous scholars who have concerned themselves with the problem of the meaning of civilization, parallel the interest of modern cultural anthropology. However eclectic in method, anthropology knows fairly well what it wants in the study of cultures. Through comparative analyses, the field has been able to offer contrasts and perspectives on the societies of the world. When the spatial and synchronic interests of the anthropologist are brought together with the diachronic and evaluative treatment of the humanists, a mutual undertaking of great value can begin.

The earlier traditions in anthropology of studies of cultural diffusion have not entirely fallen by the way. In general, the field retains its interest in the invention, spread, and effects of virtually any culture trait or complex. Thus the beginnings and diffusion of printing, the cultural effects of the spread of Islam, of the horse among the Plains Indians, or of canoe and adze types through the Pacific world have all provided problems for analysis. Except, however, for folklore studies and the detailed investigations of certain religious movements — Islam, the Ghost Dance, Wallis's analysis of various messianic movements — the anthropologist has steered fairly clear of applying his methods to nonmaterial phenomena. Some new areas, it is true, are being pioneered. Examples are seen in Kroeber's use (1944) of data from the realm of the conventional humanities in order to determine to what extent various human creations — art, drama, philosophy, music, and the like — are related and clustered in time and space. There is also Kroeber's interest in style patterning, while in a recent study (1951) he attempts to discover the patterning and functions of the novel as a literary form in the cultures of Asia and Europe. All such approaches are extremely valuable, lending new perspectives to problems of cultural continuity. But innumerable other problems remain for investigation.

Because of its interest in the comparison of cultures, anthropology has been led to the realization of the culture whole, the ways in which the elements composing a culture form an integrated total unit. Those tutored in the humanities have not shared this interest, being content either to appraise an art form as such, or to treat it historically but outside the context of the culture whole. Among many contemporary critics, however, there is a convergence of interest with the anthropologist. The realization now exists that Shakespeare's dramas are to be understood in terms of Elizabethan England and its society, that the *Sturm und Drang* era which produced Goethe's *Werther* was not only a period of literary revolution. It has remained for the philosopher or for the artist himself to demonstrate the relationship between the theory underlying human action and its esthetic expression.[8] But no anthropologist, using a view of culture, has attempted to appraise the differences in integration of aspects of eighteenth-century intellectualism among the differing peoples of Europe. Indeed, it is a humanist (Pearce, 1953) and not an anthropologist who recently evaluated the American Indian from an unusual point of view: the European ideas which were held about the Indian and the effects of such attitudes in American history. It thus appears that although there are some anthropologists who have been concerned, for example, with the place of Neo-Confucianism in the cultures of China and Japan, or with analogous movements in India and Southeast Asia, the rich intellectual background of the European cultures has been left to the humanists and unexplored by anthropology. In line with the traditions of the humanities, it has not been necessary to demonstrate the ultimate relationships between phenomena, a reflection of the failure of the humanities to systematize. But if there is a correlation between cultural integration and human productivity, it is one which anthropology is prepared methodologically to evaluate. As Benedict notes, anthropology suffers when it fails to take cognizance of the work of the great humanists (1948, p. 593).

But it must also be granted that the anthropologist is not a humanist in the academic or Renaissance sense of the term. As observed above, he becomes too inclusive in his interests, too uni-

[8] Cf. Northrup, 1947, pp. 161–164.

versal in scope, to do more than become acquainted with the work of the orthodox humanists. It is the insight which the humanists provide, the critical perceptions and awareness, which can have meaning to the anthropologist. A step in this direction has already been taken by Lowie (1945, 1948) in combining anthropological and humanistic approaches and bringing them to bear on the social and intellectual development of the Germans. No other anthropologist seems to have been so successful as a social historian. And on the whole, the study of man has chosen to neglect the social historical portraits. Trevelyan's history of Britain is an ignored example. His treatment is amazingly inclusive, ranging from farm life and land laws to ecclesiastical music and the drama from Chaucerian to Victorian times, and gives an invaluable panoramic survey. And there are innumerable others germane to the problem.[9] Just as the anthropologist attempts to elicit the flavor of a contemporary culture, so also could he lend his perspectives to an historic one. Humanistic data could well be employed to depict the nature of the culture of France of Louis XIV, or of any other chosen epoch in world history.

No anthropologist today will argue that by finding a better defined interest in the documented accounts of human achievements, of the values of human products, he is being unfaithful to his field. If in respect to a primitive culture the goal is understanding of the nature of cultural integration, more elaborate cultural manifestations, those with a prolonged history, can be subjected to the same yardstick. Further, the latter provides additional insight into the former. When Goldschmidt (1951) treated the cultures of northwestern California in the light of contemporary capitalistic theory, he successfully defined some new and hitherto unrealized aspects of these cultures. By the same reasoning, and following Arnold's definition, there seems nothing amiss in evaluating, in humanistic terms, not only the products of various primitive cultures, but the whole cultures in themselves. The success or failure of a culture with respect to the kinds of satisfactions it accords its members can obviously be gauged only in subjective

[9] Cf. Trevelyan, 1942; Kany, 1932; Bryson, 1938.

terms, a point which indicates why anthropologists find themselves in such a dilemma when they attempt to solve "human rights" problems. Sapir could, without flinching, find wholly balanced, successful, and satisfying cultures in the Athens of Pericles or the England of Elizabeth I (1924, p. 418). Here his criterion was largely one of degree of cultural participation. Similar judgments by anthropologists are constantly being made, largely on the same basis. Nor are they subject to challenge.

But anthropology retains its unfortunate diffidence with respect to the data and approaches of the humanist. There is clearly a reluctance to deal in such terms as artistic truth, beauty, greatness, since it is argued that all such abstractions are relative and defined by cultural context. There is again no disagreement with this point. For centuries, however, the humanists have been dealing with just such concepts. However much they may have failed to offer a systematization of their ideas, they nevertheless provide the means by which such views may be evaluated. When ideal patterns and values are made to conform to quantitative design, the whole import of the cultural setting is lost. When anthropology begins to ask why it is that a culture may choose realism in art at one phase of its history and rigid conventionalism at another, it will have gone further along the road toward understanding the nature of culture. The anthropologist thus may safely employ the subjective insights and approaches of the conventionally defined humanities in his resolution of human problems. In the last analysis, those cultural anthropologists who have been most successful have been less the scientist and more the humanist.

by RALPH LINTON

The Problem
of Universal Values

THE study of values has assumed much more than academic interest for the modern world. With the rapid improvement in means
of communication which has taken place during the last century
and the resulting increase in cross-cultural contacts, the potentialities for conflict have become greater than ever before. It is obvious
that unless the various nations which compose the modern world
can come to some sort of agreement as to what things are important
and desirable, we are headed for catastrophe. Moreover, the very
ease of communication which may produce such a catastrophe
ensures its inclusiveness. In the Dark Ages which would result
from a world war of atomic bombs and bacteria there would be no
region sufficiently isolated to escape destruction and carry on the
torch of enlightenment. The peoples of the world must find common areas of understanding or die.

As students of human behavior in all its aspects, anthropologists
might be expected to take a prominent part in solving the problems which the present situation has created. However, they have
consistently avoided judgments regarding what things are universally desired or valued. Their principal contribution to date
has been the development of the concept of cultural relativity.
Through their comparative studies they have been able to demonstrate that different societies have successfully achieved the same
ends by employing widely different means. From this they have

concluded that the really scientific attitude toward cultural differences is the one summed up in the old saying: "Well, some do and some don't." While such tolerance is a necessary first step to international understanding, its contribution is essentially negative. Any sort of successful cooperation must be built on a realization that, no matter how various societies may go about it, all of them prize and desire certain things and should be willing to work together to get them.

No matter how much one may stress the right of every society to adhere to its own ways, the fact remains that some of the culturally approved practices of any society are likely to arouse strongly negative emotional reactions in the members of some other society. The European feels that the Muslim practice of eating with the fingers is repulsive, while the Muslim is equally revolted at the thought of using forks and spoons which may be ceremonially unclean. In spite of thorough training in cultural relativity, the present writer has never been able to observe the common Latin country practice of picking chickens alive with real equanimity. It is difficult to overcome such reactions and, the more of them the culture of another society arouses, the more difficult it is for the outsider to feel at home among its members. The assumption that continuous contact with the members of another society and increased familiarity with its culture will automatically result in increased liking is a victory of optimism over experience. Anyone who has had numerous cross-cultural contacts can testify that there are societies continued contact with which merely results in increasing dislike. If the world's societies are to reach a state of adjustment in which they can cooperate toward common ends, these ends must be so clearly defined that the societies' members can understand them and be willing to overcome some measure of mutual distaste in order to see them achieved. This, in turn, involves a recognition of universal values which can be used as a basis for determining which ends will be universally acceptable. Thanks to their long experience in comparative culture studies, the anthropologists should be able to make a real contribution toward this. They are in a particularly good position to recognize basic similarities as well as differences, and it is to be hoped that their current preoccupation with the latter is only a passing phase in the development of the science.

Philosophers have been involved with the problems of value for centuries, and scientists have been willing to leave these problems to them. Now that the importance of values is increasingly recognized in all the sciences which have to do with man, the philosophers' conclusions are not proving as useful as might be hoped. The philosophic approaches have leaned heavily upon supernatural sanctions or upon vaguely defined concepts such as the good, the true, and the beautiful. While their conclusions have been developed over centuries, they have been developed in the absence of the conceptual tools provided by modern social science and psychology. None of the great philosophic authorities on values were familiar with the modern concepts of culture or culture process, and none of them possessed our modern knowledge of the role of learning in personality development and in the establishment of group personality norms. Moreover, the philosophers' conclusions are often phrased in a language which the scientist finds it difficult to translate into his own. It would seem that the time is now ripe for an attack on the problem by the scientific method of cross-cultural comparison.[1]

The first requirement for a scientific approach to the problem of values in culture is some agreement as to what is meant by the term *value*. Like many other words in the English language, *value* carries multiple meanings depending upon its context. Even if we ignore its technical usages in such fields as economics, mathematics, and art, several meanings remain. The element common to these seems to be best expressed by the superficially humorous definition: "A value is anything of any value," i.e., anything regarded favorably. A value is thus anything capable of influencing the individual's decisions in choice situations or, going one step further back and as a necessary preliminary to such influence, any-

---

[1] An excellent summary of the current anthropological views of the subject will be found in Kluckhohn's article on values in Parsons and Shils, *Toward a General Theory of Action* (Harvard University Press, 1952).

thing capable of producing an emotional response. Under this definition there are, of course, individual values as well as those which are cultural, i.e., shared and transmitted by the members of a particular society. However, in a search for universals the individual values, insofar as they are individual, may be ignored. They are transitory, like the persons who hold them, and unless they come to be shared by other individuals, have little influence on the social-cultural continuum.

For our present purposes we will define a value as: *anything capable of producing similar choice responses in several of a society's members.* It may be noted that this fails to bring in the factor of favorable response implicit in the ordinary use of the term. However, any consideration of values as dynamic elements in culture soon reveals that there are, in all cultures, numerous acts, objects, and concepts toward which the members of the society have strong negative attitudes. These attitudes are frequently much stronger than one would anticipate from a mere antithesis between the thing toward which the attitude is held and its opposite. Thus in our own society at the present time the hysterical opposition to communism and the persecution of individuals in which it is reflected certainly are not matched by an equally strong emotional attachment to the liberties assured by our democratic system of government or by an equally intense respect and admiration for those who are attempting to maintain them in the face of the present attack upon them.

One hesitates to employ the term *negative values,* yet in any attempt to understand the operation of cultures one must recognize the functional significance of negative as well as positive attitudes. The members of a society will work quite as hard to *avoid* certain things as to *obtain* others. In a brief discussion of the concept of cultural values for which the writer was responsible some years ago [2] he suggested that the situation might be clarified by substituting for the single term *value* the more precise term *value-attitude system.* Under this terminology a value may be regarded

[2] Ralph Linton, *Cultural Background of Personality* (New York: Appleton-Century-Crofts, 1946).

as anything toward which the members of a society normally have a definite attitude, whether favorable or unfavorable. Since the question of positive versus negative attitudes is not particularly significant for the present discussion, we will use the single term *value* for systems of both sorts.

To understand the relation of values to the operation of a society, one must recognize that values are an integral part of any society's culture and that, with regard to their origin, transmission, and integration, they follow the same rules as other culture elements. The normal society consists of an organized, self-perpetuating group of individuals which persists far beyond the life span of any one of its component members. Its persistence is made possible by the presence of a culture, i.e., an organized series of ideas and behavior patterns which are transmitted from generation to generation within the society. The culture as a whole provides techniques by which the members of the society can both satisfy their individual needs and cooperate toward common ends. The latter involves an elaborate system of specialized activities and reciprocal behaviors which together constitute the social system. The needs of individuals and of the society are shaped and the possible ways of satisfying them delimited by the milieu in which the society operates. At any given point in time this milieu is a product of the interaction of the society's external environment, both natural and social, and the content of its current culture.

All societies and cultures are not only continuums but continuums in a constant state of change and internal readjustment. The milieu is always unstable, presenting the society with new problems, and the culture itself is always changing under the pressure of internal as well as external forces. Individuals develop new solutions to old problems and new patterns are borrowed from other societies while each new element introduced into the culture produces disharmonies which take time to adjust. The only really stable factors in the cultural-social continuum are the needs of individuals as these stem from the physical-psychological qualities of our species and the social imperatives, i.e., the problems posed by organized group living per se, problems which must be solved if the society is to survive.

In this situation of constant flux, the society's main guide in meeting new problems and in deciding which of the new behavior patterns brought to its attention shall be accepted and integrated into the culture is its system of values. It is this system which guides its members' choices among the possible alternatives which are always present. From what we now know of psychological mechanisms we may assume that any pattern of behavior which is consistently effective, i.e., rewarded, will be given preference over other less consistently effective patterns in situations involving choice. It will also acquire the emotional associations which make it a value. However, human beings constantly generalize from one situation to another, while their use of language provides them with a highly effective tool for organizing such generalizations and expressing them as abstract concepts. Both behavior patterns and concepts are transmitted from individual to individual within the society and thus come to form part of the culture and to function as elements in the milieu within which culture change takes place.

Most value concepts find expression in more than one pattern of overt behavior, while, conversely, all but the simplest patterns of overt behavior involve more than one conceptual value. However, the number and the functional importance of the behavior patterns in which different values are involved vary greatly even within a single culture. Thus in our own society such a conceptual value as national survival is related to innumerable behavior patterns, while a conceptual value such as amusement is related to a much smaller number. The relative importance of the same conceptual value may also differ profoundly in different cultures. Thus the importance of esthetic activities relative to economic production was quite different in ancient Greek culture from what it is in modern America.

From the foregoing it can be seen that the values recognized by any society fall at once into two classes: *instrumental* and *conceptual*. The distinction can best be illustrated by an example.

Nearly all societies have a conceptual value of modesty which is reflected in specific patterns of coverage for various parts of the body under various circumstances. Insistence that the genitals of both sexes should be kept covered in public is as nearly universal as any culturally determined pattern of behavior.[3] The objects used for this purpose vary greatly, ranging from *tanga* and pubic tassels to robes and trousers. However, the custom of wearing a garment of a particular type is always a focus for attitudes and emotions and constitutes in itself a value of the instrumental type. Thus some years ago the head of a great Christian denomination refused to receive the late Mahatma Gandhi because the latter insisted on wearing a loin cloth instead of trousers. Both the parties involved would certainly have agreed on the conceptual value of modesty, yet for each the behavior pattern by which this was instrumented in his own culture had acquired meanings and attitudes which made it a value in its own right. To the prelate, trousers were a symbol of both respect and respectability. To Gandhi, the loin cloth was less a garment than an expression of the struggle for Indian independence. Trousers, as the garb of the politically dominant European, had acquired strong negative associations. He no doubt felt that to don them for his reception would be an act of obeisance to the British Raj.

While instrumental values are, in nearly all cases, concise and easily recognizable, conceptual values are much less so. Some of those whose influence can be detected in the greatest variety of behavior patterns may not even be conscious or verbalized. They belong to what Kluckhohn has called the implicit category of culture elements. Every culture includes a number of values which are so abstract and so generalized in their expression that they carry little emotional effect in themselves, although they lie at the base of the whole cultural structure. In general, the more concrete and conscious a value, the easier it is to attach emotion to it. For this reason the instrumental values of a society tend to carry higher emotional effect than the conceptual values. They constitute a sort of sensitive surface layer highly susceptible to

[3] Exceptions: African Nilotics, Amazonian Indians, and some Melanesians.

external influences, and interference with them brings a more rapid response from the society's members than does the less obvious contravention of deeper-lying conceptual values.

Instrumental values are also much more susceptible to change than conceptual ones. In studying the history of particular societies, one is struck again and again by the persistence of particular conceptual value systems. Such systems not only determine what elements will be accepted or rejected in situations of free choice but also serve as guides in the reinterpretation of elements forced upon the society. This process of reinterpretation is nowhere better illustrated than in the modifications which various proselytizing religions have undergone in their diffusion. Originally pacifistic, Christianity became a warrior's creed in militaristic Europe. The simple, clear-cut creed of Islam was transformed in Persia into Sufi, mysticism, while Buddhism, after its initial denial of the efficacy of worship, became the most highly ritualized of all the great religions.

It is obvious that instrumental values are exceedingly variable. They constitute the area of value study to which the concept of cultural relativity is most completely applicable. If universal values exist, they must be sought for at the level of the deepest and most generalized conceptual values, those which stand in closest relation to the individual needs and social imperatives shared by the whole of mankind. A comparative study of cultures would seem to indicate that there are a considerable number of such values, but their identification is rendered difficult by their generality. Most of them are so fundamental and are taken so completely for granted by the people who accept them that they are likely to be overlooked.

In any attempt to list conceptual values, the mere order of precedence given to them in enumeration would seem to reflect judgments as to their relative importance, but the writer wishes to disown any such implications immediately. The values which seem to be universal are listed in a certain order only because it is impossible to present them in anything but a linear form.

Since in popular thinking the relation between values and

religion is a particularly close one, supernatural values may be taken as the starting point in our search for universals. Practically all cultures believe in the existence of what we would call supernatural beings, entities which cannot be perceived by our senses at ordinary times, yet which are able in some way, usually undefined, to influence the course of nature and thus to aid or injure men. These entities are usually conceived of as essentially human in their motives and emotions, a quite natural projection of the worshiper's experience.

Some cultures, but by no means all, have also developed a concept of an impersonal force called variously *orenda, wakan, mana,* and so forth. This belief is frequently regarded as primitive, but it is more just to consider it as a philosophical *tour de force* by which all unusual ability for accomplishment is reduced to a single common denominator. It becomes the equivalent in the field of the supernatural of such a concept as energy in the field of mechanics. *Mana,* to use its most familiar name, must be distinguished from the concept of natural law, as held by modern mechanics and materialists, in that it is manipulatable. All peoples who hold the *mana* belief also believe in the existence of individuals, both human and supernatural, who are able to concentrate and utilize this force. The attitudes toward such wonder-workers are basically the same as that toward deities or individuals with miraculous power in societies which do not have the *mana* concept. Since attempts to acquire and manipulate *mana* have always been limited to a comparatively small number of cultures and have been the first victims of the rise of modern mechanistic concepts, we can eliminate them from further consideration.

Closely related to the belief in beings able to affect the lives of men is a belief in persistence after death. This belief is held by practically all societies and finds a rational explanation in the inability of the individual to imagine either himself or those who are closely associated with him as nonexistent. However, the concepts held by various societies regarding the after-life are fully as varied as their concepts of the supernatural in general. The future life is normally conceived of in terms of familiar experience. The formal Christian concepts of heaven can be traced to the royal courts of the Near Eastern region in which this religion originated. One may suspect that to most West European and American Christians they seem highly unreal, or, if taken seriously, disappointing. According to whether the trend of a culture is optimistic or pessimistic, the future life is thought of as either an endless bank holiday or an endless rainy Sunday. Extremes of either pleasure or pain are seldom anticipated. Ethical factors are much less frequently involved in determining the condition of individuals after death than the average Christian would anticipate. In general, the commonest punishment for antisocial behavior is exclusion from the company of ancestors or deities, based on the logical premise that if an individual makes himself a nuisance in earthly society, post-mortem society will not want to be bothered with him.

The behaviors enjoined by different societies for dealing with the supernatural are even more varied than the beliefs. It is obvious that the approach will differ according to whether the operator believes he is dealing with beings or with an impersonal force. In the former case, approaches are patterned upon the individual's experience with other individuals either more or less powerful than himself. In the latter, they are patterned upon his experience with the manipulation of familiar objects and forces and are correspondingly mechanistic.

The distinction between approaches to the supernatural based on the assumption that the operator is dealing with beings and those based on the assumption that he is dealing with forces has much in common with the long-established distinction between religion and magic, yet the two formulations are by no means identical. Tylor suggested as the essential difference between religion and magic that in religion the operator approaches the supernatural powers as a suppliant, uncertain of the outcome, while in magic he approaches them with a belief in his own ability to control the outcome. However, the attempt to control impersonal force is always fraught with danger and with all sorts of possibilities of failure. The operator may make a technical error or another operator may block his efforts. In dealing with super-natural beings the attitudes of human dependence and dominance may blend into each other in curious ways. Thus, if the worshiper is dependent upon the deity, the deity is also dependent upon him for the satisfactions which the deity derives from worship and sacrifice. In later Egypt, magicians frequently selected some obscure and long forgotten deity and worshiped him on the principle that, as the only person feeding the god, the magician could be assured of the full exercise of the god's powers on his behalf.

By no means all supernatural beings are regarded as more powerful than their human manipulators. In the belief of many societies there are minor spirits who can be captured and enslaved or otherwise compelled to perform the acts which the priest or magician demands of them. There are also a surprising number of cases in which the worshiper's patience becomes exhausted and he turns from petition to compulsion. The same being may have prayers and offerings made to him on one occasion and on another be subjected to threats and punishment. Such techniques are per-fectly intelligible in view of the ordinary experience of interper-sonal relations in which more powerful individuals have to be placated, less powerful ones can be coerced, and the same indi-vidual successfully subjected to one or another treatment according to the circumstances.

Even the rituals performed in those religions in which the wor-shipers' purpose is to placate an all-powerful deity vary greatly from one society to another. Where the Christian and Muslim deity is satisfied by prayer, reading of holy books, and attendance at formal services, Zeus demanded hecatombs of oxen, and Huitzi-lopochtli bleeding human hearts. Because of the high emotional effect involved in dealing with the supernatural, the techniques prescribed by any culture acquire high value in their own right. One has only to recollect the martyrs who have suffered at the hands of fellow Christians for minor behavioral deviations such as insistence on complete baptism instead of sprinkling, or for using a different position of the fingers in signing the Cross.

It should be noted that there are numerous societies in which the favor of supernatural beings is not to be gained by ethical behavior. This is not limited to those cases in which the supernatural being is dominated by the operator. Even where the being occupies a dominant position, the relation between him and his worshiper is frequently conceived of as something quite apart from the worshiper's relation with other human beings. So long as the worshiper performs the appropriate rites, and, so to speak, maintains his half of the reciprocal relation between himself and the being, his behavior in society is considered no concern of his supernatural vis-à-vis. In some cases this attitude reaches great lengths. Thus in Polynesia, in accordance with a generalized pattern of occupational specialization which extended even to supernatural beings, there were deities to whom one might appeal successfully for aid in each and every type of antisocial behavior. More familiar examples would be the classical Mercury, god of thieves, or Magdalene, the patron saint of medieval prostitutes.

It may be noted that until one reaches the level of monotheistic civilizations, the only category of supernatural beings who are uniformly insistent upon ethical behavior on the part of their worshipers is that of ancestral spirits. The individual's childhood experience of parents in their dual capacity of disciplinarians and protectors seems to carry over directly in so-called ancestor worship, and, while the shades feel a deep interest in the welfare of their descendants, they are also quick to censure and even punish deviations from good behavior.

The only universal features which can be derived from such a wide variety of beliefs are those of man's universal sense of inadequacy in the face of many situations and his belief that there are beings whose powers exceed his own and who will give him the aid which he so vitally needs, if he can learn the correct methods of approaching them. To this may be added the well-nigh universal belief that the individual's personality is not extinguished in death.

This is a slender foundation upon which to build mutual understanding, especially when the small but powerful group which now dominates much of the world's population denies the existence of supernatural beings and has atheism as an article of faith implemented by high emotional effect. This last would seem to negate what has been said previously regarding the universality of supernaturalism, but one must evoke once more the fact of the social-cultural continuum. It remains to be demonstrated that societies can exist for any length of time without deities or that the average individual can endure the innumerable frustrations and griefs of even normal life without the anticipation of post-mortem satisfactions.

The values associated with the operation and perpetuation of societies are more numerous than those associated with the super-natural and also show less variety. This is no doubt due to their more intimate connection with the physiological needs of human beings and the practical aspects of organizing groups of individuals for their mutual advantage. The problems presented by these are more numerous than those involved in dealing with the supernat-ural, but the possible solutions for each problem are much less numerous. Thus the possible methods for developing and con-trolling the exchange of products and services or for rearing children are strictly limited in number, while there seems to be no limit to the variety of beliefs and rituals which will serve to satisfy man's desire for help from supernatural powers and reassure him in time of crises.

Social values which are universally present are of the utmost interest, since societies rather than individuals are the units in the human struggle for survival. They also establish the limits within which many values are operative. Thus nearly all instru-mental values which have to do with the interaction of individuals apply only to interaction with other members of the same society. At the primitive level the individual's tribe represents for him the limits of humanity and the same individual who will exert him-self to any lengths in behalf of a fellow tribesman may regard the nontribesman as fair game to be exploited by any possible means, or even as a legitimate source of meat.

One of the most significant trends in the evolution of human culture has been toward the expansion of societies to include more and more individuals of increasingly diverse racial and cultural backgrounds. The great proselytizing religions, such as Christianity and Islam, have been particularly active in furthering this trend. At the same time, this extension has been accomplished largely by the inclusion and mutual adjustments of subsocieties whose members feel a closer tie with each other than with the members of the larger group. An excellent example of this would be the criminal subsocieties which function within the broader frame of all modern civilized nations and may even be international in their affiliations. Such groups have their own value systems and their own rules of behavior by which they abide in dealing with other members of the criminal subsociety. Their relation with the other subsocieties within the larger units is generally a parasitic one, yet they have a recognized position and even potentialities for social service under special circumstances. Thus gangsters performed a very real function under prohibition.

Societies normally include a number of individuals of both sexes and at all age levels. This fact provides the starting point for differentiation of activities. Even the simplest societies distinguish between men's work and women's work, while the trend toward specialization culminates in modern mechanized society with its innumerable skilled occupations. The well-being of the society thus depends upon an exchange of goods produced by specialists and of services performed by them. As a result, all societies attach high value to reciprocity and to fair dealing. The latter statement may be questioned by those who have had uncomfortable experiences in our own system. However, in all societies, shrewdness and deceit are considered as legitimate in certain areas, usually those which are of not too vital importance for social well-being. The mutual recognition that the rule of *caveat emptor* holds in such areas endows dealing in them with a certain sporting element. Thus the old-time Yankee who deceived another man in a horse trade without resorting to a direct falsehood was admired by his society, while an attempt to pass a bad check would result in social ostracism.

The existence of reciprocity between different subsocieties within the larger unit, particularly by members of different classes, may be doubted by those trained in Marxist doctrines. However, one must recognize that even such a seemingly exploitive system as the feudal actually represented reciprocity on a large scale between noble and peasant. The feudal system emerged in a period of violence and confusion, when the trained soldier who became the feudal lord protected the peasant in return for his economic contribution. Indeed, without this contribution the soldier would have been unable to purchase the expensive equipment which the current military techniques entailed or to get the long practice required for its efficient use. In the same way, during the early phases of the capitalist system, the owner, who was normally also a manager, not only provided the capital required to obtain the machines which increased the workers' output, but also organized production processes and attended to the marketing of the product. That his returns were disproportionately large relative to his services cannot be doubted, but in the social-cultural continuum such inequalities tend to right themselves. A feudal system which has been outmoded by the growth of new technology and tactics is swept away by revolution, and we can see how, in the capitalist system, ownership is passing from single individuals or families to large numbers of stockholders, management is passing from owner to trained technician, while the relation between management and organized labor is shifting increasingly from exploitation to cooperation.

Management, in the sense of leadership and direction, is probably as old as social life. The differentiated activities of a simple society's members and a more or less equitable sharing of the advantages derived from them can be carried on without any formal type of direction or conscious techniques for enforcing reciprocity. However, most group activities, such as land-clearing, drive hunts, or seine fishing, require a high degree of coordinated effort, while the whole society needs leadership in emergencies. All societies recognize and obey leaders under certain conditions, although different individuals may assume the leadership in different situations. Thus many American Indian tribes had a war chief and a peace chief, the functions of each being clearly delimited.

The rewards which go with leadership differ greatly from one society to another and frequently do not involve economic advantage. Thus the head of a Plains Indian band levied no contributions upon his followers, though at the same time he was expected to keep open house and to maintain his followers' allegiance by frequent gifts. Even in medieval Europe a king was expected to meet his expenses from his personal estates, and any attempt to levy taxes on his feudal lords was hotly resented. That individuals are still eager to become leaders under such circumstances shows the efficacy of the psychological rewards to be derived from prestige and power.

The need for leadership and the universality of the power drive, no matter how it may be culturally camouflaged, are responsible for the fact that there are no genuinely equalitarian societies. Every human group recognizes that certain individuals or categories of individuals are socially more important than others. The so-called equalitarian societies are those in which the individual is able to find his own level in the prestige series without initial handicaps. However, in aristocratic societies the value of individual mobility involved in the democratic system is replaced and to some degree compensated for by values of social responsibility and skilled performance in the aristocratic role. Where the status of aristocrat is hereditary, it uniformly carries obligations both toward inferiors and toward the group as a whole, and involves elaborate patterns of behavior. One of the least desirable features of our own system is that which accords high status to the man of wealth, no matter how acquired, while imposing no social obligations upon him.

The values just discussed relate to the functioning of the society. However, the need for the society's preservation is even more vital. If the social-cultural continuum is to be perpetuated, there must be a constant increment of new individuals to replace those who drop out and, equally important, these individuals must be trained in the behaviors and indoctrinated in the attitudes necessary for the performance of particular roles in the operation of the society as a whole. The family is unquestionably the most efficient institution for meeting these social imperatives. It not only produces children but it trains them in the way that they should go. For this reason one finds that in all societies the family has become a focus for strong emotional attitudes.

Families are essentially of two types, conjugal and consanguine: those like our own (conjugal), in which the functional group is primarily the close, biologically determined unit of parents and offspring, and those in which the functional unit is primarily a group of siblings of the same sex and their offspring (consanguine), with their spouses always regarded as somewhat marginal. However, even in families of the latter type, the desirability of continuing matings, i.e., marriages, is recognized. Families of this type tend to be extensive and a constant turnover in spouses is as disconcerting and as injurious to efficiency as a constant turnover of labor in any other organized work group. Moreover, long before the days of modern psychology, it was recognized that the child needs affection and emotional security for its proper personality development. This is more likely to be provided by the child's own biological parents than by a succession of less emotionally involved caretakers.

The desire for permanence of matings has given rise to two quite distinct lines of approach, each with its own associated value system. In one of these, premarital chastity is valued, largely, it seems, from the anticipation that an individual who enters marriage without previous sex experience will be deterred by timidity from experimenting with other partners, the chance of new and disruptive attachments thus being reduced. This attitude is most frequently found in societies where marriages are arranged for the sons and daughters by the family elders. From this conceptual value has developed such rites as the tests of the bride's virginity, common in Muslim countries, or the idea held by our not very remote ancestors that a woman who had lost her virginity was permanently ruined and unfitted for marriage, even if she had been violated against her will. Where this particular configuration of values exists, it is usually supplemented by economic sanctions for marriage: such things as the dowry and the more widespread and frequently misunderstood bride-price. By giving both the partners and their affiliated kin groups an economic interest in the maintenance of the union, these sanctions act as a strong deterrent to separation.

In the other type, reliance for the continuity of the marriage rests primarily on the physical and emotional adjustment of the partners. Under these circumstances there may be strong insistence on postmarital faithfulness, but the attitude toward premarital experimentation is one of tolerance, if not actual encouragement. It is thought that partners are most likely to be faithful when they are sexually congenial and when their curiosity about other possible partners has been satisfied. Our own situation in this respect is a curious one, since our society reprehends premarital experimentation, the arrangement of marriage by elders, and economic sanctions — i.e., all the techniques for preserving marriage which have proved effective. Under the circumstances, it is not surprising that so many of our partnerships end up in the divorce courts.

The roles of individuals within the family are everywhere culturally prescribed. Parents, or in the case of strong consanguine family organization, members of the parents' generation in the kin group to which the child belongs, are expected to assume responsibility for the child's physical care and training. Conversely, the child is expected to render them respect and obedience, at least until it becomes adult, and to care for them in old age. The failure on either side to live up to these obligations is severely reprehended. Wives are, in general, expected to be submissive to husbands. In the marital relationship husbands are normally dominant, in spite of the claims made by certain earnest feminists. Needless to say, the exceptions to this rule fall into two groups: those in which a particular wife establishes dominance over a particular husband without cultural sanction, or those in which, owing to consanguine family organization, the husband is not regarded as a family member. In such cases the dominant role, both in respect to the woman and her children, is assumed by one of her brothers. The reasons for this are presumably to be found in physical factors, the male of our species being in general larger, stronger, and more active than the female, while the latter suffers from the additional disabilities connected with pregnancy and nursing. Each of the practices in which these factors of familial interaction are reflected becomes an instrumental value for the particular society, while such concepts as parental responsibility, filial obedience, and wifely submission are conceptual values which find incidental expression in great numbers of behavioral practices.

On the border line between the value systems which relate primarily to social imperatives and those which relate to individual needs lies the whole area of property concepts. It may be stated at once that no society has been able to maintain a completely communistic arrangement for more than a few generations. Moreover, the attempts to do so have not occurred among primitive peoples but among highly civilized ones where communities of disillusioned individuals have attempted to escape in this way from the conflicts and inequalities of an overinclusive system of individual ownership. The property concept probably originates in the sort of individual identification with particular places and objects which may be observed even in animals. Objects which the individual has made or which he uses consistently acquire a whole series of associations which give them values over and above those resulting from their practical potentialities. Among even the simplest and most primitive groups we find well-developed concepts of both personal and group property. Personal property is usually limited to tools and weapons, clothing, and similar objects of immediate utility. While there may be an easygoing attitude toward the loan of such objects, this in no way negates the fact of private ownership. Group property, aside from particular objects which acquire value from their function as symbols of the group, is mainly territorial. Each band or tribe has its range within which its members are free to hunt or exploit natural resources, but which is forbidden to members of other social units. This again is in line with the behavior of most gregarious animals.

Between the claims of the group as exemplified in these patterns of communal ownership and free exploitation and those of the individual as they may be extended over particular natural resources or means of production, there is an inevitable conflict which every society has had to solve. The solutions which various societies have chosen have depended upon whether priority was given to the interests of the entire group or to those of individuals. Where the groups involved are small enough and sufficiently localized so that there are frequent face-to-face contacts between members, the potential antisocial consequences of extreme extensions of individual ownership do not arise. They are neutralized by social pressures. The wealthy man finds it more rewarding to be admired and praised for his generosity than to continue hoarding, subjected to the disfavor of the group and to the spectacle of individuals suffering from want with whom he inevitably feels a considerable identification. Only the absentee landlord or slaveholder and the modern corporation manager are immune to these social pressures, and it is under them that the potential evils of private ownership have found fullest expression.

Another set of values, lying on the border line between the social and individual categories, comprises those which have to do with knowledge. Since organized social life depends upon individual learning, it is obvious that much knowledge has a primarily social function. No individual can operate successfully in any status unless he knows the associated roles. However, few people are content to cease learning at the point where their knowledge would suffice for adequate social integration. Curiosity and extreme teachability are characteristic of our species, and every individual tends to accumulate a quantity of information which is of no practical importance. The accumulation of this information and the drawing of conclusions from it become sources of emotional satisfaction not unlike that derived from skill in a game. They also may provide an escape from the immediate pressures of reality. Most readers have encountered persons who have followed some abstract line of study for sheer love of the intellectual exercise. Thus the writer has known a journeyman printer in Chicago who had taught himself to read and write the Malagasy language, an advertising man in a department store who had made himself one of the foremost American Tibetan scholars, and a bank clerk who was a nationally recognized authority on early American genealogies.

The attitudes of societies toward such accumulation of "unprofitable" knowledge vary profoundly. In general, the individuals who possess it are regarded with a mixture of admiration and contempt. The scholar is everywhere officially honored and unofficially starved. It is only in the few societies which support institutions of higher learning that he is able to use his accumulation of esoteric knowledge as a source of income. To these might perhaps be added Imperial China, where scholarship of a particular type was rewarded by official preferment and by assignment to political office. However, even here, pure scholarship brought no great financial reward. To be profitable, it had to be combined with good social connections and a considerable measure of shrewdness and political skill.

Impractical, "useless" knowledge of the sort just discussed is only one aspect of the need for escape from reality which underlies considerable areas of human behavior and which has not as yet been successfully explained by the behavioristic psychologists. There is no known society which does not have games of the sort in which the individual sets up purely artificial obstacles and gets satisfaction from overcoming them. Neither is there any known society which lacks literature, with its potentialities for emotional satisfaction through vicarious participation in the adventures of fictional characters. While this is only one of any literature's multiple functions, its importance is not to be discounted. Lastly, every known society has various forms of esthetic expression: music, the dance, and graphic arts. These serve to relieve the monotony of daily existence and to evoke pleasurable sensations, although why they should do the latter is still an unsolved problem.

The concrete expressions of the esthetic urge, if one may so term the human need to create beauty, are extraordinarily varied. In order to realize this, one need only contrast the music of different peoples, with its varied tonal scales and use of melody and rhythm, or the even more diverse expressions of graphic art. Whether there is some denominator common to all the expressions of a single type is one of the most important problems confronting the student of esthetics. It is obvious that appreciation of any particular art form is to some degree a result of learning and habituation. Thus, to a European, most African art is repulsive at first contact. It is only after he has become accustomed to the medium that he can appreciate its qualities and derive esthetic satisfaction from it. The real problem is whether behind such diverse objects as a Poro mask, the Venus de Milo, and a Peruvian jar there are common factors of form, dynamic interrelation of parts, harmony of color, and so forth, which may appear in different combinations but are responsible for the esthetic effect. It seems that we have here an area in which modern psychological techniques could be brought to bear on a problem which philosophers have discussed for centuries without coming to agreement.

This discussion of values has been of necessity brief and incomplete. Nevertheless, the writer hopes that the existence of universal values has been demonstrated and it has been made clear that these are to be found at the conceptual rather than in the instrumental level. When one turns from the discussion of such values in the abstract to a consideration of their possible utility as a basis for mutual understanding between societies, a number of new problems present themselves. It has already been noted that the conceptual values which have widest influence within a culture are frequently unverbalized. The emotional reactions to them are thus vague and diffuse. The values whose contravention brings the sharpest and most immediate response are those at the instrumental level. Thus two societies which share the same basic conceptual value may fail to realize the fact because of their different ways of implementing it. The best answer to situations of this sort would seem to be to bring the conceptual values into consciousness, a difficult task.

An even more serious difficulty arises from the varying degrees of importance which different societies attach to the same conceptual values. All societies arrange the values to which they subscribe in a hierarchy which determines the reactions of individuals and of the society as a whole in situations involving choice. Concepts like business honesty, truth, or chastity may stand high in the value hierarchy of one society and low in that of another. Such differences not only make for misunderstanding but also for mutual recriminations on moral grounds and for feelings of contempt and hostility.

Of particular significance in the present world situation is the relative importance accorded in different societies to individuality and conformity. Numerous conflicts between the desires of individuals and what the society conceives of as the well-being of the group are inevitable. Every society must make some allowance for both, but the point at which one or the other is given systematic precedence will vary greatly. The white pioneer American and most of the Indian tribes with which he came in contact represented a climax of individualism, and the Indians were in no small degree its victims. Since discipline of any sort except self-discipline violated one of their most fundamental values, it was impossible for them to organize effective defense against white invaders. During the last century here in America, the individualism of the pioneer has been giving place steadily to a higher degree of social control and of integration of the individual into the group. Even the most enthusiastic individualist must admit that in many respects this has been advantageous. Thus few persons would question that a man suffering from smallpox should be prevented from traveling about freely, attending public assemblies, and in general distributing the virus of the disease, although in the first half of the nineteenth century quarantine was hotly resented as an invasion of individual rights. One of the most pressing problems for modern Americans is how far the trend toward increasing socialization should be allowed to continue and how far our conceptual values can be modified in adjustment to it. The conditions which made pioneer individualism possible have passed, and in a modern society the attempt to reinstate these values in their original functional vigor can only lead to confusion. At the same time these values have survived as ideal patterns of our society, and the conflict between these ideals and their frequent and inevitable negation in practice becomes a source of irritation and misunderstanding.

At a time when we have been thrown, largely without our own volition, into a position of world dominance, it is also important for us to recognize that most societies do not attach the same high value to individual initiative and freedom of choice which we accord them. The completely free individual is of necessity an insecure individual and one upon whom the necessity of choice constantly devolves. There are large sections of the world's population that have become habituated to obedience and to relying upon the presumably superior intelligence and ability of hereditary ruling groups. Whatever the deficiencies of these systems may be, they provide the individuals who live under them with a feeling of security. They believe that if they obey, they will be taken care of. It is exceedingly difficult for such groups to accept the responsibilities involved in democratic patterns of government or to accord respect and allegiance to individuals whom they themselves have selected. The attempt to "sell" such groups the democratic ideal calls for much skill, especially when, thanks to modern techniques of communication, they are constantly being reminded of the defects which it shows in operation here in the United States.

The values on which there is most complete agreement are those which have to do with the satisfaction of the primary needs of individuals. Whatever their other values may be, all men desire the three wishes of the Irish fairy tale, health, wealth, and happiness. To the people of the world's backward areas the first two are represented by an opportunity to acquire and put into effect the technological and scientific knowledge already available in America and Western Europe. That these do not necessarily produce happiness we have abundant evidence, but this is something which the backward people will have to find out for themselves.

PREHISTORY, LINGUISTICS
ETHNOGEOGRAPHY

by LLOYD A. WILFORD

Archaeological Method in the
Eastern United States

TAYLOR'S CRITICISM

THE most comprehensive study to date of the methodology of American archaeology is Walter W. Taylor's *A Study of Archaeology* (1948). Drawing upon his own field experience and upon the ideas of historians, anthropologists, and archaeologists, Taylor had obviously given much careful thought to his subject. He has produced a work of high merit, which has been both informative and challenging to his fellow workers.

Noting the inconsistency in defining archaeology as a branch of anthropology whereas its aim is commonly said to be the reconstruction of history, Taylor considers the relation of the three disciplines. He reviews the history of archaeology and finds reasons why archaeologists studying the American Indian cultures and the Paleolithic cultures of Europe consider themselves to be working in the field of anthropology, whereas archaeological research in the Bronze and Iron Age cultures of the Near East and in the cultures of Classic Greece and Rome is usually conducted under the banner of history, or even of art, the classics, or philology. He defines history (more specifically, historiography) and anthropology and notes that "cultural anthropology, like historiography, is one of the so-called historical disciplines" (p. 37), which "are characterized by four steps or levels in the procedure by which they seek to attain their objectives." The levels are given as: "*first*, the definition of problem in terms of a conceptual scheme;

171

second, a gathering, analysis, and criticism of empirical data; *third*, the ordering of these data in a chronological sequence; and *fourth*, the search for and, to the extent that it is possible, the establishment of the reciprocal relationships within this series" (p. 32). He designates the fourth level as that of "integration and synthesis, of context and so-called historical reconstruction," the level of historiography.

As to the relation of anthropology to history in terms of procedure, he finds that the level of cultural anthropology is one step higher than the level of synthesis and context. "When the archaeologist collects his data, constructs his cultural contexts, and on the basis of these contexts proceeds to make a comparative study of the nature and workings of culture, in its formal, functional, and/or developmental aspects, then he is 'doing' cultural anthropology and can be considered an anthropologist who works in cultural materials" (p. 43). Archaeology as such is said to be neither history nor anthropology, but a method and a specialized technique for the gathering of cultural information (p. 44). The necessity for the archaeological method and its specialized technique is due to the nature of the material from which cultural information is to be derived by the archaeologist as contrasted with the cultural behavior observed by and the oral information given to the ethnographer, and with the written records from which the historiographer gathers his cultural data. In other words, archaeology ends with the third level of procedure where it has provided the data from which a synthesis and context may be made. If the archaeologist attains the fourth and fifth levels of procedure, he does so as historiographer and anthropologist respectively and not as archaeologist.

It is to the attainment of the fourth level of procedure that Taylor devotes much of his attention. The published reports of several of the most prominent American archaeologists are reviewed, and the serious indictment is made that each of them has failed to attain the fourth level of procedure, but has stopped short with the third step. He believes that the failure is due to too much concern with the comparative or taxonomic approach, which is primarily an attempt to determine the significance of specific cultural items with regard to relationships *outside* the cultural unit being investigated. Instead of seeking to construct as full a cultural picture as possible for the particular manifestation, this approach applies itself mainly, if not wholly, to those phenomena which have comparative significance *outside* of the site or component. . . . The conjunctive approach, on the other hand, has as its primary goal the elucidation of cultural conjunctives, the associations and relationships, the "affinities," *within* the manifestation under investigation. It aims at drawing the completest possible picture of past human life in terms of its human and geographical environment. It is chiefly interested in the relation of item to item, trait to trait, complex to complex (to use Linton's concepts) *within* the culture unit represented and only subsequently in the taxonomic relation of these phenomena to similar ones outside of it. It is an integral part of this major aim to make every effort to interpret the concrete, empirical findings of archaeology in terms of culture itself, of cultural behavior, and of the non-material results of cultural behavior whereby the materialistic and "lifeless" data may be given life and depth. Such objectives should help not only to bring about the construction of fuller cultural contexts but also to provide material for the study of culture itself, i.e., for anthropology on a fifth level of procedure. [Pp. 95–96.]

He finds that American archaeologists devote too much of their attention to the descriptive and quantitative aspects of their empirical categories (the elements, constituent parts, attributes, specifications, designs, affinities, etc. of a manifestation or of a group of manifestations having certain specified similarities) which can be observed directly; and that fearful of not being objective, they are unwilling to construct cultural categories (use, function, and/or the technique of manufacture) or culture categories (the culture-idea objectified or the meaning made manifest) which cannot be observed directly, but must be inferred from the observable manifestations (p. 116). Yet, as noted above, his conjunctive approach requires the use of the cultural and culture categories in the construction of the synthesis and context, as well as in the further study of culture itself. The place he reserves for the admittedly empirical and descriptive, his empirical category, is his second level of procedure. This is the spot in an archaeological report where such headings as Objects of Shell or Bone Artifacts have their proper place (p. 195). But on the fourth level his headings would be those of cultural categories, such as Food, Dress, or Hunting (p. 114).

While Taylor is clearly correct in his insistence on the inclusion of a synthesis and context in terms of cultural categories in archaeological reports, particularly in those dealing with rich sites or with aggregates such as an aspect or phase, it is not so clear that such a context has much practical value in reporting the type of sites so frequently encountered in eastern North America. Most of the readers of any archaeologist's reports are his fellow archaeologists or anthropologists, as shown in the list of subscribers to *American Antiquity*. Such readers are accustomed to draw their own inferences from empirical data and in fact do so more or less automatically on reading the empirical data. When one has read the description of the ten or twenty stemmed flint points, the bone harpoon or two, and the possible copper or bone gorge, and has duly noted the inventory of animal bones and bivalve shells, presented in the empirical data from a single site, he has already mentally formed his own construct of the food quest, and finds the author's construct under the cultural rubrics of Hunting and Fishing to be useless repetition.

Worse still, many sites do yield just such an assembly as the above, and to read and reread the same cultural inferences in report after report may become boring to one who has read the report of the empirical data on which the inferences are based. For example, in the volume *Indians Before Columbus* (Martin, Quimby, and Collier, 1947), where a great many cultures of eastern North America are discussed, and where the cultural category Livelihood is always presented, such statements as "Livelihood — These Indians subsisted by hunting, fishing and food-collecting" (p. 299), or "Livelihood — The Candy Creek people made their living by hunting, fishing and food-gathering. Possibly they practiced some agriculture" (p. 348), are to be found many times in these same words or with slight variation. The example is not given by way of criticism but to indicate the necessarily repetitious character of constructs involving the cultures of the Archaic and Woodland patterns.

In this particular example, owing to the necessity of not unduly lengthening the volume, the authors have saved much repetitious material by giving only the cultural categories without the empirical data on which they are based. This treatment, however, has the disadvantage that the reader not only is not given the opportunity to judge of the validity of the inferences drawn by the authors, but he cannot visualize with any assurance the empirical data from which the inferences were made. To quote these authors again, it is said of the Lamoka culture that "Each village probably consisted of a group of rectangular bark houses. Hearth and refuse pits were scattered throughout the houses" (p. 240). One might guess that the inference of rectangular houses was drawn from the visual evidence of post molds in a rectangular pattern found at one or more of the sites. Yet one might legitimately surmise that the presence of houses was inferred from the nearly universal desire of mankind for shelter from the elements, and that the rectangular shape and the bark covering were inferred from the house types of historically known groups in a stage of culture comparable to that of the Lamoka villagers. The lack of empirical data is not so serious here, as the reader may consult the original monograph, but certainly in a primary source, if either the empirical data or the cultural construct must be omitted for the sake of brevity, the former should be retained.

Because of his interest in seeking the cultural and chronological relationships of the site under investigation with other sites and groupings of sites, the American archaeologist is branded by Taylor as working and writing in the field of "comparative chronicle" (p. 67) and is denied the right to call himself an anthropologist because he has failed to attain the fifth level of procedure.

DIFFUSION

The study of culture is not limited to the comparison of one cultural synthesis and context with another or with many others.

One of the active fields in anthropological research is that of the dynamics and processes of culture, the discovery, invention, diffusion, and integration of culture traits and trait complexes. In this field American archaeologists have been very much concerned. It is true that one approach to the study of cultural processes is the method of comparing cultural constructs as wholes, noting points of difference in the cultural content, and investigating the factors responsible for the acceptance of a trait by one group and its rejection by another. Another approach is to study the origins and spread of specific traits from one society to another, such as Kroeber's classic study of the spread of the alphabet (1948, p. 508).

It is to the latter approach that American archaeologists have devoted much of their efforts. In the study of the cultural manifestations of a single site, the origins of the traits found there are always a matter of concern. Since the probability that a trait has been derived from the outside is greater than the probability that the site represents the birthplace of the trait,[1] attention is directed outward to find other sites where the trait is found in much the same form. This attention is responsible for the compilation of trait lists and for the comparisons between cultures and groupings of cultures on the basis of the presence or absence of the listed traits.

There has been an increasing tendency to confine studies to local areas, particularly to areas included within the boundaries of a single state, because so much research now is being sponsored by state institutions. In seeking manifestations more or less closely related to the one being studied, it is inevitable that comparisons should first be made with reported sites in the immediate area or state, then with those in neighboring areas.

But there has long been an interest in the much broader picture of the relation of the cultures of America to those of Asia, in the relation of the cultures of the eastern United States to those of the Southwest and of Meso-America, and in the possible relationships between Meso-America and Asia that might have indirectly affected the eastern United States. Accepting Asia as the homeland

[1] Linton, 1936, p. 325.

of the earliest immigrants to America and the Bering Strait or an Alaskan land bridge as the most likely point of entry directed attention to the probable traits brought by the migrants. Such generalized traits as warm clothing, knowledge of and use of fire, a probable house type or shelter, and hunting and fishing implements were accepted as imposed by the climate. The domesticated dog was judged to be very early because of his widespread distribution in America. These traits, augmented and modified with the passage of time, are believed to have formed the basis of the cultures known in eastern North America as comprising the Archaic pattern, preagricultural and preceramic.

Though the richness of the cultures of the Mexican and Mayan areas was known in the eighteenth century, there seems to have been little or no early speculation as to the role these areas may have played as a source of traits found in the United States. In 1833 Josiah Priest had remarked on the similarity of the pyramids of the Ohio Valley and of Mexico (1835, p. 276). At the end of the century Holmes, in speaking of the pottery of the Lower Mississippi Valley, wrote: "With respect to the origin of this particular group we may surmise that it developed largely from the preceramic art of the region, although we must allow that exotic ideas probably crept in now and then to modify and improve it. That exotic features did migrate by one agency or another from Mexico is amply attested by various elements of form and technic found in the ceramic as well as in the other arts" (1903, p. 81). His statement doubtless reflects the theory current in his day — that the aboriginal cultures were largely indigenous, though affected by some traits introduced from the south.

A very definite change in this point of view occurred with the acceptance of Meso-America as the area in which agriculture was developed in the New World and from which it diffused without essential modification to the United States.[2] At once a parallel between New World history and Old World history became manifest. In each hemisphere, in an area located on both sides of the isthmus joining the continents, primitive man had accomplished

[2] Wissler, 1922, p. 25.

the domestication of plants (and of animals in the Old World), and by becoming a food-producer had made possible a rapid accumulation and proliferation of culture traits, leading to ever higher stages of civilization. As traits diffusing from the Egyptian-Mesopotamian center were seen to have ultimately reached the Atlantic and Pacific shores of Eurasia, so traits from the Meso-American center were seen as diffusing to the parts of North and South America outside the center. There was a more active concern with similarities in the culture traits of Meso-America and the United States, and interest in the archaeology of northern Mexico and of the Caribbean Islands was stimulated by the thought that these areas were likely routes of diffusion.

The history of the eastern United States subsequent to the introduction of agriculture is seen as falling into three major episodes and is so represented in the midwestern taxonomic system, which undertakes to classify all the cultures of the area. The Early Woodland period has incipient agriculture, the most widespread evidence of which is not charred corn, hoes, or storage pits, but the presence of simple tubular tobacco pipes. Pottery of simple jar forms is found in most of the area, though bowl forms and even tetrapodal vessels found in the Gulf States have been ascribed to the period, and its appearance is considered roughly coeval with that of corn. The bow is added to the spear-thrower, and simple burial mounds are found in parts of the area.

The second period is dominated by the brilliant Hopewellian culture of the Ohio Valley, best known for the size and complexity of its great burial mounds, the richness of the offerings to the dead, and the art forms in copper, mica, and polished stone. Perhaps more notable is the evidence of widespread trade and commerce at this time, with the Ohio area as a center of diffusion exerting strong influences over a wide area. There is little evidence of much greater reliance on agriculture, though pipes are elaborated to works of art. Pottery in general shows little improvement other than in the designs of the better wares.

The third episode is the rise of the Middle Mississippi cultures with a high development of agriculture, fortified towns centered in truncated earthen pyramids surmounted by public buildings, a wide variety of new pottery forms including effigies, stirrup spouts, double spouts, and bottle forms, and with new decorative techniques such as painting, engraving, and modeled appendages. Also present were many new art forms such as monolithic axes, ceremonial clubs, large human figures, and circular palettes of polished stone; pendants and plates of copper with symbolic designs formed by *repoussé* or cut-out background; and shell gorgets elaborately engraved with symbols, portraits, and scenes showing close similarities to Meso-American types. Most of the new art forms are now classed as objects and symbols pertaining to a religious cult, the so-called Southern Death Cult.

The southeastern quarter of the United States was the intensive center of the Middle Mississippi culture and from it culture traits diffused outward into the peripheral areas. They included the greater emphasis on agriculture and some of the pottery and art forms, but did not include some of the salient features such as temple mounds and most of the objects referred to the Death Cult. The cultures of the peripheral areas have been designated as Upper Mississippi in the area north of the center, a belt extending from Minnesota and Iowa to New York, and as Plains Mississippi in the area to the west. Beyond these were areas where cultures were still on the Woodland level (the Late Woodland); farther out were cultures lacking pottery and agriculture, essentially on the Archaic level.

In view of the acceptance of the leading role played by Meso-America in the development of cultures beyond the Archaic level in the Western Hemisphere, it might be pertinent to inquire what particular culture traits are believed by archaeologists to have reached the eastern United States from that source. Agriculture and the raising and smoking of tobacco are closely associated in the Early Woodland. Pottery, customarily linked with agriculture, was seen as accompanying the latter in its northward spread. But the bow is a hunter's weapon, and was known to have been used in Eurasia in the Mesolithic period and to have been more highly developed to the north and northwest than to the south.

Diffusion from Asia, not Meso-America, is indicated. The burial mounds of the Early Woodland horizon have no specific counterpart in Meso-America and may well have developed locally. When McKern (1937) and Fewkes (1937) questioned the derivation of Woodland pottery from Mexico, presenting instead the hypothesis of an Asiatic origin, the only important Woodland traits widely accepted as of Meso-American origin were reduced to agriculture, including the growing of tobacco and the use of tobacco in smoking, and the manufacture of tobacco pipes.

In the succeeding Hopewellian horizon there are no new traits for which an Asiatic or Meso-American origin need be postulated, and even the brilliant Ohio Hopewell can logically be seen as a local development from older Archaic and Woodland elements. But in the Mississippi horizon so many of the distinctive traits of the period show general or specific resemblances to their Meso-American counterparts that diffusion from the south cannot be doubted. The southeastern United States becomes peripheral to the Meso-American cultural sphere to such an extent that Newell and Krieger have been able to attempt the dating of the Davis site in eastern Texas by fitting it into the sequences established for the Mexican and Mayan areas on the basis of pottery affiliations (1949, p. 224).

In considering the diffusion of traits into the eastern United States from regions outside the area, the American Southwest, the Plateau area, and Canada should be mentioned as possible places of origin or of transmission of traits. The semisubterranean earth lodge of the Plains may very well derive from the Southwestern pit house. In fairly late times Pueblo groups are known to have dwelt east of the Rockies for short periods, and the Southwest was the principal source of supply for horses. But in general the influence of the Southwest appears to have been slight and limited to the western edge of the area. In the Archaic cultures of New York the presence of ground slate knives, including the ulo as well as stemmed blades, seems to point to a connection with the Canadian Dorset culture. Yet, in a recent paper on this subject (1952) Hoffman concludes that the spread of these objects was probably from south to north rather than the reverse. Canada is, of course, the area through which any elements derived from Asia reached the eastern United States. Some of its southern regions share in the cultures of the adjoining areas to the south, but for the most part Canada's cultures were Archaic or Eskimo during the prehistoric period.

The problems of diffusion into the area of the eastern United States from the outside, while by no means solved, are simpler than the problems of diffusion within the area. The presence of pottery may be taken as forming a boundary between the Archaic and Woodland cultures, although some sites where pottery appears are classed as predominantly Archaic rather than Woodland. The position of the Mississippi cultures is fairly clear, for they have many traits that distinguish them from Woodland and Hopewellian manifestations. Divisions within the Mississippi pattern are clearly enough marked to delimit the localized variants and their sequences within the intensive center, and to indicate the manner of spread into the peripheral areas. The distinctiveness of the cultures of the Mississippi patterns is due to the rich inventory of cultural remains; to the large village sites; to the better preservation of such village features as mounds, house floor plans, outlines of fortifications, and other features; in part due to the relative lateness of the cultures; and to the distinctive traits and the wide variety of the pottery, permitting segregation of types on both a real and temporal basis.

The most difficult problems within the area center in the relations of the manifestations of the Woodland pattern among themselves, in the relation of the Woodland cultures to all of the various manifestations associated with the Hopewell culture, and in the relations within the Hopewellian group. Woodland cultures believed to antedate the Hopewell horizon are called Early Woodland, and are considered one of the sources from which the Hopewell culture rose. Some cultures ascribed to the Early Woodland period, in particular the Adena culture, which are typologically closer to Hopewell than are the simpler Woodland manifestations, are classed in the Hopewellian group and believed to represent developmental stages of the classic Hopewell. Woodland cultures contemporary with Hopewell are called Middle Woodland, and those following it are known as Late Woodland cultures. Because of the evidence of wide trade relations exhibited in the Ohio Hopewell, one expects to find cultural influences from the Ohio center diffusing to both the Middle and Late Woodland cultures. But in fact it is often difficult to recognize the Hopewellian influences within the Woodland cultures or to know which of the latter are earlier, which are contemporary, and which are later than Hopewell; so the direction of the diffusion is not certain. It follows that any estimate of the time required for the spread of Hopewellian influences to any specific area of Woodland culture — the culture lag — is very precarious.

One of the bases of this difficulty is that in contrast to the number and variety of types exhibited in the Mississippi cultures, Woodland types are relatively few in number and therefore show much uniformity over wide areas. Stemmed arrowheads, side and end scrapers, knives, and drills are the most common artifacts other than pottery, but are too much alike to be of much value in defining any one culture unit. The pottery usually has one of two surface treatments — plain (smooth) or cord-wrapped paddle impressions — and decoration is commonly limited to dentate stamping, stamping with a cord-wrapped stick, punctates, and incised lines. Burials are usually in mounds, below the surface, on the surface and/or in the mound fill, and may be primary, secondary, or cremations, but all of these may be found at a single site. It is difficult to segregate a Woodland manifestation as a distinct unit unless it has some distinctive trait or unless it conspicuously lacks one or more of the common traits. Thus eastern New York and New England are distinctive in lacking burial mounds; the Laurel pottery of Minnesota lacks stamping with a cord-wrapped stick; and the Blackduck pottery of Minnesota lacks dentate stamping. But the Mille Lacs aspect of Minnesota, which has all of the common traits in chipped stone objects, pottery decoration, and burial, is difficult to define.

The Hopewellian culture, too, has the basic Woodland traits

enumerated above, though it has many additional traits which differentiate it. Much of the pottery cannot be distinguished from Woodland. Some vessels do have distinctive designs, but the methods of decoration such as plain or rocker dentate stamping and incised lines are also Woodland. Hopewellian mounds are much more elaborate than Woodland mounds and have some features, such as a multi-roomed charnel house covered by a mound, not found in Woodland mounds. But such Hopewellian burial practices as burning of bodies or of bones in place, deposits of cremated bones and ashes, and primary and secondary burials are Woodland traits also.

Among the many distinctive objects of the Hopewellian culture, those most commonly found at a distance from the Ohio center include copper-covered ear spools and breastplates, polished stone gorgets, and platform pipes. The presence of such objects in burial mounds in Wisconsin, New York, and the Kansas City area has had much to do with classification of the mounds as Hopewell. The alternative suggestion that the mounds be classed as Woodland showing strong Hopewellian influences has not been made. Yet it is reasonable to expect that there would be mounds of the Middle Woodland period that are truly border-line cases, where the Hopewellian influence is not expressed in such distinctive objects, or where the number of distinctive objects is relatively small. It is to be noted that as regards such an object as the platform pipe, the frequency of distribution between the three named peripheral areas and Ohio as contrasted with the distribution beyond the peripheral areas clearly points the direction of diffusion. Within the narrower limits of the area immediately surrounding the Ohio Hopewell manifestations, the pattern of distribution of Hopewellian traits is less obvious, and the temporal relation of Adena to Hopewell is in dispute.

CHRONOLOGY

Valuable though the patterns of type distributions may be in determining the direction of diffusion and thereby indicating the relative age of the donor and receptor cultures, they are all too often inadequate for the purpose. But if the temporal relations between sites or cultures can be known by any method of obtaining relative or absolute chronology, the problems of diffusion between them are much simplified. Knowledge of the chronological position of any culture relative to other cultures, i.e., its place in history, is essential to any historical reconstruction. Chronology is as important to the archaeologist as to the historian, and problems of chronology hold a very important place, if not first place, in the interests of American archaeologists.

Two methods of obtaining relative chronology that are particularly the archaeologist's own, i.e., not dependent upon other disciplines, are the study of the horizontal and vertical distributions of types — patterns of distribution and stratigraphy — and of these the latter is the more valuable. Unfortunately for archaeology in the eastern United States, stratified sites are not common there. One type of stratified site is that in which two or even more groups of people with distinctive cultures have sequentially occupied a single site. The reason this type of site is rare may be the sparsity of population or the many available camp sites and habitation sites. A good supply of water and of fuel was the important factor in the selection of habitation sites, and this well-wooded area with its many streams and lakes had an abundance of such locations. The relative lack of sites with components of two or more cultures has been a serious handicap. In 1920 Shetrone concluded, on the evidence then available, that the Hopewellian, Fort Ancient, and Stone Grave cultures in Ohio were contemporary, that the Ohio Algonquian (read Woodland) was earlier than, contemporary with, and later than these, and that the Adena was a subculture of the Hopewellian and probably earlier (p. 169). Griffin in 1951 stated that the temporal relation between Adena and Hopewell had not been demonstrated stratigraphically in the central Ohio Valley (1951a, p. 26).

Another type of stratified habitation site is one in which only one culture is represented but in which the occupation has continued over a temporal span sufficiently long for typological changes to have developed between the earliest and latest periods of occupation. But sites of this kind are also uncommon, particularly among the cultures of the Woodland pattern. One factor militating against long-continued occupation of one site is that hunting and food-gathering were always important in the economy of the Woodland cultures, favoring frequent removals to less exploited areas. A second factor is that the meager inventory of Woodland traits, such as the limited number of decorative elements in the pottery, does not permit much latitude in typological change. The four common decorative elements previously mentioned are found in all three Woodland periods. Nowhere is there a site where one could demonstrate a long series of sequent culture periods, based on modifications of pottery types and associated artifacts, in the manner of Kidder at Pecos Pueblo or of Gladwin and Haury at Snaketown.

Stratigraphy may be found in mounds, both burial mounds and temple mounds. In the former it may take the form of intrusive burials in a pre-existing mound. The Ohio culture known as "Intrusive Mound" is so named because burials of this manifestation were often found as intrusions in Hopewell Mounds, and are therefore known to be later than Hopewell. A burial mound fill may contain potsherds and artifacts alien to the culture of the builders of the mound, indicating that the builders took earth from a habitation site occupied by an earlier group. Or a mound fill may significantly lack the pottery types of a habitation site in its immediate vicinity, indicating that the former preceded the latter. The best-known example of this form of stratigraphy is that of the Fort Ancient site of Ohio where the habitation site is of the Fort Ancient culture and the earthworks are Hopewellian.[3] The temple mounds of the Mississippi pattern are commonly cumulative and lend themselves to stratigraphic study as readily as a habitation site.

Though stratified sites of the Woodland and Hopewellian cultures are not numerous, a relatively small number may indicate the proper chronological order of a larger number of related sites. This is because certain manifestations can be considered contem-

[3] Martin, Quimby, and Collier, 1947, pp. 284, 285.

porary by virtue of the close relationship of their cultural inventories or of the presence in each of one or more unusual artifact or pottery types. The determination of the position of any one of these manifestations relative to a noncontemporary manifestation may be projected to the others. As an illustration, a distinctive object, called by Martin, Quimby, and Collier "a hafted engraver, consisting of one, sometimes two, beaver incisors hafted transversely in an antler tine" (p. 279) is present in the Intrusive Mound culture of Ohio and is also present in the Red River aspect of Minnesota and in the Point Peninsula culture of New York (p. 253). Stratigraphic evidence that the Intrusive Mound culture is post-Hopewellian is evidence that the Red River and Point Peninsula cultures are also post-Hopewellian. With continued research it may be expected that sequences in addition to those now known may be stratigraphically demonstrated, and that each demonstration may have repercussions beyond the immediate area of discovery.

A feature that is definitely a part of the methodology of the eastern United States is the regional conference. A conference is primarily a pooling of the knowledge and ideas of its members regarding typological and chronological relationships of the cultural units manifested in the region. From them have derived and developed the classifications which have been established. The Plains Conference meets annually, and has been a principal factor in developing a Plains chronology. The Southeastern Conference was of prime importance in determining the basic classifications of that region. The Midwestern Conference in 1936 adopted a taxonomic system to apply to the entire area of the eastern United States, and continues to meet at irregular intervals. The taxonomic system adopted in 1936 incorporated the classifications already established and provided a framework within which new units might be added.

Various criticisms of the system have been made, but it has not lacked for defenders, and is at present basic to interpretations of all cultural relationships and groupings. It has been said that it does not provide for chronological relationships, yet the sequence

expressed in the names of such major categories as Archaic, Woodland, Hopewell, and Mississippi is as implicitly chronological to
the eastern archaeologists as is the sequence of Pioneer, Colonial,
Sedentary, and Classic to the southwestern archaeologists. A recent usage in which Woodland manifestations are designated as
of Early, Middle, and Late Woodland periods makes the temporal
relationship explicit, but is not a part of the taxonomic relationship system because there is no inference that Early Woodland
cultures comprise a related group distinguished from Middle
Woodland cultures as a group.

In the sequence of Archaic, Woodland, Hopewell, and Mississippi there is implied not only a chronological system but also a
value system, with each category having a richer material content
than its predecessor. It is possible that the system of values has
unwittingly affected judgments as to the temporal position of any
manifestation. Has the superiority of the southwestern cultures
been a factor in ascribing to them too great a priority in time over
the eastern cultures, resulting in a too late dating of the latter?
Is there a tendency to estimate the age of a site with an assemblage
of Archaic traits as earlier than it is? An archaeologist excavating
a Mississippi site may feel that the inhabitants of the site were
culturally superior to those of a Woodland site he had excavated
earlier. Yet the French explorers of the late seventeenth century
who, in the Lake Superior–Upper Mississippi region, met Chippewa of Archaic culture, Dakota of Woodland culture, and Iowa
of Upper Mississippi culture, do not seem to have been aware of
any considerable degree of cultural superiority or inferiority
among them. Value differences in the three categories are indeed
present, but the archaeologist is warned not to be overimpressed
by labels he has himself assigned.

In 1919 (pp. 52–54) Holmes listed the "category of data available to the Americanist in determining measurable periods of
time as well as relative antiquity" under the following groupings:
historical, traditional (mnemonic), biological, cultural, geological,
paleontological, mineralogical, geographical, and astronomical.
Except for the cultural and traditional, which fall within the dis-

ciplines of anthropology and archaeology, the groupings represent the disciplines to which archaeologists may look for aid in chronological determinations. But the archaeologist does not always rely on a colleague in another discipline, and this is notably true in the field of history. For the historical approach holds an important place in archaeological methodology. It is the method of working from the known to the unknown by locating an historic site and attempting to relate its cultural content to sites in the prehistoric horizon; or to identify a site with an historically known group by relating it to the traits described for the group; or to ascribe a site containing contact materials to the people known to have lived in the area during the contact period. Many publications summarizing the cultures and culture sequences of an area, such as a state, contain a chapter on the history of the area, as, for example, Strong's Nebraska study (1935, pp. 7–29). The historical research is done by the archaeologists themselves, who feel that an adequate grasp of the known facts pertaining to the Indian population of an area is essential to archaeological research.

Two of the disciplines listed by Holmes which have indeed proved of great value to the archaeologist are geology and paleontology. But these fields require so much technical knowledge that for the most part the archaeologist has been obliged to call for assistance from the glacial geologist and the vertebrate paleontologist. The two techniques for determining absolute chronology, which Holmes could not possibly have foreseen, dendrochronology and radiocarbon dating, are the outstanding developments in archaeological dating since his time.

Dendrochronology was developed in the Southwest by A. E. Douglass, a physicist and astronomer, in studying sun spots; but aware of the tremendous value of his discovery to archaeology, he devoted himself to dating sites in the Southwest. In spite of the fact that different climatic conditions made Mr. Douglass's master chart valueless east of the Rocky Mountains, dendrochronological studies have been undertaken in the area. Mr. George Will has constructed a chart enabling him to date certain earth-lodge villages in the Upper Missouri Basin; the University of Chicago constructed a chart which permitted the dating of the Kinsaid site in Illinois; and steps are in progress to attempt the dating of the recently excavated sites on the Missouri River. The dendrochronological method has been turned over to the archaeologists, but it requires so much time that it calls for the services of a specialist in each local area.

Radiocarbon dating is the invention of another physicist, W. F. Libby. In the development of his method he received materials from archaeologists, as did Mr. Douglass, and also from geologists, botanists, and others; for the much longer time span that can be dated by the method makes it of interest to several disciplines. Use of the method requires trained personnel and a well-equipped laboratory, but its value is such that at least three laboratories are already functioning or in the planning stage.

The effect of tree-ring datings in the Southwest was in general to shorten the interval estimated to have elapsed from the beginning of Basket Maker III to the present. But radiocarbon datings east of the Rockies have greatly lengthened the times of beginning previously ascribed to the Woodland, Hopewellian, and Mississippi Horizons. Martin, Quimby, and Collier have given these as A.D. 500, A.D. 900, and A.D. 1300 respectively (1947, pp. 233–238). But the radiocarbon method gives a date of about 1000 B.C to an Early Woodland site in New York, which contained pottery and was typologically linked with another site containing corncobs.[4] Ohio and Illinois Hopewell dates cover roughly the first four centuries B.C.[5] A date of A.D. 400 is given to a Middle Mississippi manifestation at the Davis site in Texas.[6] Even more unexpected was the placement of the Adena and Tchefuncte cultures, formerly believed to antedate Hopewell, and of the Marksville culture, formerly considered a southern contemporary variant of Hopewell, as of about the same time period, roughly A.D. 440 to 790. Griffin believes that this placement is so contrary to archaeological concepts that there is a likelihood of error due to the selection of the

[4] Ritchie, 1951, pp. 131–133.
[5] Griffin, 1951a, p. 28.
[6] Krieger, 1951, p. 144.

samples or to changes in the condition of specimens secured years ago (1951a, pp. 28, 29). His doubts reflect the difficulties previously mentioned in determining the developmental and chronological relationships within and between the cultures of the Woodland and Hopewellian groups. In some respects the radiocarbon sequences do less violence to typological relationships than does the older scheme. The tetrapodal vessels of the Tchefuncte culture are quite alien to the conoidal based vessels typical of the northern wares of the Woodland period (Early). But legged vessels were very common in the Mexican area, and dates placing their appearance in Louisiana at about the time Meso-American influences in pottery were making themselves felt in eastern Texas are consistent with the view that the tetrapodal vessels were also received from that source. Together, the Texas and Tchefuncte dates may indicate the beginning of an era in which diffusion from the South was bringing to the Southeast traits important in the development of the Middle Mississippi cultures.

The very great aid archaeologists have received from dendrochronology and radiocarbon dating and solving their problems of chronology has increased their awareness of the benefits to be derived from closer cooperation with experts in other disciplines. In March 1950 a conference on archaeological methods was held in which archaeologists and associated technical experts participated.[7] The paper which Anna O. Shepard hailed as "the keynote of the conference"[8] was Frederick Johnson's "Collaboration among Scientific Fields with Special Reference to Archaeology."[9] Johnson's ideas mark a decided advance over those of Holmes of thirty-seven years earlier. He looks to other disciplines for assistance not only in chronological determinations but in the interpretation of all cultural data. His association of experts is not solely to aid the archaeologist but mutually to benefit all the experts involved, and he believes that the collaboration should extend to all stages of the inquiry. With the ever growing tendency toward specializa-

[7] Griffin, 1951b, p. 1.
[8] Shepard, 1953, p. 273.
[9] Johnson, 1951.

tion it may safely be predicted that interdisciplinary collaboration will assume an ever larger role in the methodology of archaeology.

As the temporal relationships between cultural manifestations become clearer by reason of the accumulating archaeological data and the chronological determinations made with the assistance of other sciences, the archaeologist of eastern North America need not be so preoccupied with questions of chronology and of direction of diffusion. He will find himself in a much better position to make the kind of historical constructions and culture studies so rightly urged by Mr. Taylor.

by JOSEPH H. GREENBERG

A Quantitative Approach to the
Morphological Typology of Language

O NE of the steps which any science must take if it is to realize
the potentialities of the scientific method is to advance beyond
mere description to comparison and classification of the objects
it studies. That linguistics has taken this step is indicated by the
very existence of a subject matter called "comparative linguistics,"
one which is, moreover, of respected standing among the sciences
dealing with man. However, the methods of comparative linguistics represent but one of two fundamental methods by which
languages may be compared. The second method, which may be
called the typological, is the subject of the present paper. It has
had a more checkered career than the historic-genetic method
which characterizes comparative linguistics. It is important to
distinguish as clearly as possible the differences between the two
methods. Each is legitimate in its own sphere, but a confusion
between the two methods, as when typological criteria are employed to establish genetic relationships, has had harmful effects
in the past.

The genetic-historical method classifies languages into "families" which have a common historic origin. A familiar example is
the descent of the modern forms of Romance speech, French,
Spanish, Portuguese, Italian, Rumanian, etc., from an original
unified Latin as the result of changes of the same speech form in
distinct areas. When this diversification has not been so remote

in time as to remove all evidential traces, comparison will reveal characteristic resemblances among languages which have such a common origin. What is chiefly relevant for such comparisons is the resemblance between individual forms in language, both with respect to sound and meaning. For example, English *nose* and German *Nase* have similar sounds and both have virtually identical meanings, "nose"; English *hound* and German *Hund*, "dog," are similar in sound and similar though not identical in meaning. Any language consists of thousands of forms with both sound and meaning, the relation between the two being arbitrary. In principle, any sound whatever can express any meaning whatever. Therefore, if two languages agree in a considerable number of such items, as do German and English, and if — a problem not discussed here — the resemblances cannot be explained by borrowing, we necessarily draw a conclusion of common historic origin. Such genetic classifications are not arbitrary, in the sense that there is no room for the establishment of varied criteria leading to different results. This is because such classifications reflect historic events, which must either have happened or not have happened. Either the speakers of German and English speak a language transmitted from an original unified proto-Germanic speech community or they do not. The analogy here to biological classification is extremely close as, indeed, the use of such terms as *family, related,* and *genetic* might suggest. Just as in biology we classify species in the same genus or high unit because the resemblances are such as to suggest a hypothesis of common descent, so with genetic hypotheses in language.

One can, however, compare languages which cannot be shown to be related genetically and this either with respect to some features of sound only or meaning only. The two following examples will serve at once to illustrate this possibility and to show that, in this way, legitimate scientific problems arise. All languages must express comparison — the fact, for example, that one thing is larger than another. If we compare all the languages of the world in this respect, we discover that the number of methods is limited — e.g., a special, inflected form of the adjective (English *greater*), the use of a preposition meaning *from* (Semitic), the use of a verb meaning *surpasses* (as widely used in Africa) — and that of these some are far more frequent than others and have definite geographical distributions which disregard genetic boundaries. All these are surely data of real interest which require an explanation. The phenomenon just discussed is semantic. In the area of sound patterns, the independent appearance of a system of fine vowels with two degrees of length — a, a·, e, e·, i, i·, o, o·, u, u·— in classical Latin, Hausa in West Africa, Yokuts, an Indian language of California, and doubtless elsewhere — is surely worthy of attention. Indeed, such phenomena have been studied by Trubetskoy and others in an attempt to discover what types of vowel and consonant systems are possible and their relative frequency and area of appearance.

If genetic comparison establishes classes of languages, i.e., language families in the accepted sense, does not typological classification do this also? The answer, of course, is that it can but that, as opposed to genetic classification, it has no specific historic implications and is arbitrary, i.e., will lead to different results depending on the criterion or combination of criteria selected.

In this respect it is like racial classification based on a number of arbitrarily selected traits. If, for example, we select such a purely phonetic criterion as the presence or absence of lip rounding as a feature distinguishing pairs of vowel phonemes, the languages of the world will fall into two groups, those that avail themselves of this particular principle of contrast and those that do not. English and Italian, which do not, will fall in class A with innumerable other languages; and French and German, along with a smaller number of other languages from different parts of the world, will fall into class B. If some other typological trait is selected, say the position of the dependent genetive relative to the noun, again two classes of languages will emerge, but they will not coincide with those obtained by the criterion of rounded versus unrounded vowel. Taking both factors into consideration, there will be four classes. Certain characteristics will allow of more than two classes. If languages are classified semantically on the basis of their numerical system, we shall obtain a number of classes of languages: binary, quinary, decimal, duodecimal, and no doubt others as well. In short, in contrast to genetic classification, the number of language groups and their membership will differ with the number and particular selection of linguistic traits utilized for the comparison. At one extreme, if some such feature as the presence of a vowel system is employed as the sole criterion, the languages of the world will fall into two groups, those with (and this group will include all the languages of the world) and those without. This latter class will, of course, have no member. At the other extreme, one can specify so many traits that each language becomes the only member of a specific type.

Many such classifications, as should be evident from the examples just cited, are not very useful. We seek to establish typologies which involve characteristics of fundamental importance in language and which are useful for a variety of reasons. Such a classification does exist, the nineteenth-century division of languages which, in its classical version, was threefold: isolating, agglutinative, and inflective types.

This *trop fameuse classification*, to use Meillet's trenchant phrase, betrays fundamental weaknesses which have inevitably led to its present state of disrepute. Yet the problem itself *is* of sufficient important for Sapir, in the only major contribution to the subject since the nineteenth century, to have made it the central topic of his book *Language*. However inadequate the nineteenth-century discussion of this topic now appears, the major virtue of the schemes advanced remains. Something of fundamental importance to the over-all characterization of a language, the morphological structure of the word, was instinctively seized upon as the basis of classification, and Sapir's contribution simply continued this essential feature of the earlier approach, in revised form. Other typologies, particularly phonological, are possible, and these latter have been the chief center of interest in typological discussions in recent years. However, the problem of a morphological typology remains, as evidenced by Rulon Wells's recent statement, "It is shocking that there is no established taxonomy of the languages of the world" (1950, p. 31). The revived interest in this topic is further evidenced by the virtually simultaneous and independent development by Charles Hockett of Cornell and myself of the ideas presented in this paper.[1] In short, the time seems propitious to re-examine the nineteenth-century approach to the problem, discarding what the intervening period of linguistic criticism has demonstrated as invalid and incorporating recent methodological advances in order to reformulate the hypotheses along more rigorous lines. A brief critical review of earlier attempts may serve to place the present treatment in its proper perspective.

The germ of all later classifications is found in the distinction, first set forth by Friedrich von Schlegel in his essay "Ueber die Sprache und Weisheit der Inder" (1808), between languages with affixes and languages with inflections. The valuational attitudes so prominent throughout the later history of the theory are already present in this earliest formulation. The affix-languages express relations through a merely mechanical process. In a striking figure they are likened to a "heap of atoms which every wind of chance scatters or sweeps together" (p. 51). Only Indo-European languages are inflectional, but Semitic is tending in that direction.

This twofold classification was elaborated into a tripartite one by Friedrich's brother, August von Schlegel. In an essay "Sur la littérature provençale" (1818), Schlegel describes three classes of languages: "languages without grammatical structure, affixing and inflectional languages" (p. 159). Of his first class, called by later writers isolating or root languages, he says, "One might say that all their words are roots, but sterile roots which produce neither plants nor trees" (p. 159). To create a literature of science in such a language is a *tour de force*. The affixing languages use added elements ("affixes") to express the relations and nuances of the root ideas, but these affixes still have an independent meaning. Regarding inflectional languages in which such affixes are mean-

---

[1] The same basic approach was presented by Charles Hockett in an unpublished paper read at the annual meeting of the Linguistic Society of America, Philadelphia, 1949, and in a talk I gave before the Linguistic Circle of New York at Columbia University, January 1950.

ingless (i.e., devoid of concrete meaning), we learn that to them
can be attributed a kind of organic life ("organisme") in that "they
contain a vital principle of development and growth" (p. 159). As
with later writers, Chinese is his model of a root-language; only
the Semitic and Indo-European languages belong to the inflectional group; all the others belong to the vast and heterogeneous
intermediate or agglutinative class. The inconvenient fact that
the Indo-European languages have tended to lose their inflection
bothers him as it did other later writers. He therefore introduces
a further subdivision of his inflectional languages, the earlier
synthetic and later analytic. All analytic languages we know result
from the decomposition of synthetic languages. Passing over other
writers who discussed the topic in much the same terms as Schlegel,
we come to Alexander von Humboldt who, in his essay "Ueber die
Verschiedenheit der Menschlichen Sprachen" (1836), placed this
type of analysis at the very heart of his approach to language.
Von Humboldt viewed each language as a distinct self-revelation
of the spirit (*Geist*). Such self-revelations, while each a valid
expression in its own right, exhibit lesser or greater degrees of
perfection. There are four classes of languages in von Humboldt's
scheme. He adds a fourth, incorporating type to the by now traditional threefold classification in order to accommodate certain
American Indian languages whose very complex word-patterns
include instances in which the object of the verb is incorporated
in the same word as the verb root. Von Humboldt is explicit
in rejecting any historical evolutionary interpretation in which
higher types evolve out of lower types. These are ideal types involving different degrees of the unfolding of form. The isolating
languages are "formless," the incorporating languages, through
their overelaboration, betray no true sense of form. As might be
expected, only the inflected languages, by their harmonious fusion
of root and affix in a true unity, are credited with a true sense
of form.

The definitive exposition of the theory is found in the writings
of A. Schleicher, who stood under the twin influences of Darwin
and Hegel. The classes of languages are now interpreted as so

many historical evolutionary phases of the development of languages. The types are limited to three, which are equated to the stages of the Hegelian dialectic. The inflectional class of languages becomes a higher synthesis arising out of a previous opposition. The decay of inflection in historic times introduces a new phase of the *Geist* in which the material side of language no longer counts. In accord with the intellectual currents of the age, and equipped with an impressive set of quasi-algebraic formulas to indicate the various relations of the root to subordinate elements, Schleicher's version of the theory won wide acceptance and provided the basis for the exposition by those two great popularizers of linguistic science, Max Mueller in Europe and Dwight Whitney in the United States. Later versions such as Steinthal-Misteli, which added to the complications of the scheme without any compensating advantages, never became as popular as Schleicher's, which thus established itself as the basic form of the theory.

During this whole period criticism of the ethnocentrism and vagueness of these typologies was by no means lacking. To cite but one instance, Whitney, who was by no means as enthusiastic about the Schleicherian typology as his European contemporary, Max Mueller, declares *"loved* from *love* is as good a preterite as *led* from *lead* or *sang* from *sing"* (1876, p. 362). *Loved* is, of course, an example of agglutinative technique, while *led* and *sing* are inflective. Still, in regard to isolating languages he talks of "this lack of resources possessed by more happily developed languages; . . . thought is but brokenly represented and feebly aided by its instrument." Others, particularly at a later date, were highly critical or even contemptuous as, for example, Mauthner, according to whom ". . . the valuation [of languages] according to whether their inflections are more or less transparent is as foolish as if one judged the merit of European armies according to the greater or lesser visibility of their trouser seams" (1923, p. 309).

Sapir's treatment of the topic in his book *Language* (1921) marks an epoch. He firmly rejects both the valuative and evolutionary aspects of the theory. There is no real reason to suppose that Chinese or Hungarian is not as effective an instrument of thought as

Latin or English. "When it comes to linguistic form, Plato walks with the Macedonian swineherd, Confucius with the head-hunting savage of Assam" (p. 234). Man must have had language for at least 500,000 years; hence, if there is indeed a line of development — isolating, agglutinative, inflective — present-day isolating languages cannot possibly represent the primitive stage. Indeed, the evidence of human paleontology and glacial geology had made this assumption long since untenable. Chinese, the classic instance of an isolating language, was known by Sapir's time to have formerly possessed a more complex morphological system, both from earlier records of the language and comparison with Tibetan and other related languages.

Perhaps more significant than these no longer tenable assumptions were other logical defects which had been pointed out from time to time. The distinctive criteria of the various types had never been either defined with clarity or applied with objectivity. In reading Steinthal-Misteli, one has the feeling that the writer is playing with loaded dice. Whenever, on the basis of his own showing, a non-Aryan, non-Semitic language appears to have a praiseworthy feature, a tacit shift in definition shows that "true form" or "true inflection" is not involved. The definitions were not only vague but partly referred to quite different things, so that a language might well belong to several of the supposedly mutually exclusive classes simultaneously. For example, agglutination was usually taken as referring to a technique of mechanical affixation, so that, in Max Mueller's words, "The difference between an Aryan and Turanian is somewhat the same as between good and bad mosaic. The Aryan words seem made of one piece, the Turanian words clearly show the sutures and fissures where the small stones are cemented together" (1890, p. 292). The contrary term should be *inflection*. But the term *inflection* was also used to indicate the presence of affixes without concrete meaning to denote relations among words of the sentence; e.g., by case endings in the noun or person-number terminations in the verb. On this basis Turkish is both agglutinational (on the basis of technique) and inflectional (because of its case and verb conjugational systems).

A further defect, as was pointed out by some critics, was that a language had to be assigned to a single category, although the features employed might be present to a great or less degree. A term like *agglutinative* applies primarily to a single construction. A language may well and indeed usually does contain some agglutinational as well as some nonagglutinational constructions. In other words, it is a matter of over-all tendency rather than absolute presence or absence of the diagnostic traits. Sapir, by distinguishing among the various criteria which were unconsciously being employed in a confused way in the classical theory, constructs a more complex system in which languages are classified by a number of independent criteria and in which the traditional terms are retained, but in well-defined uses which are often on different axes so that they are no longer mutually exclusive.

One such axis distinguished by Sapir may be said to relate to the gross complexity of the word, i.e., the degree of complexity exhibited on the basis of the number of subordinate meaningful elements it contains. The terms employed here by Sapir are *analytic, synthetic,* and *polysynthetic,* in ascending order of complexity. The theoretic extreme of analysis is represented by languages in which each word consists of only one meaningful unit and thus has no internal structure. Languages which actually approach this extreme are Chinese, Annamite, and Ewe (in West Africa). These are the languages traditionally called isolating, but, as we shall see, Sapir reserved this term for another use. Languages like English with words of little complexity were included by Sapir in the analytic group. However, the degree of synthesis is but one criterion and a relatively superficial one, since it does not tell us in what the complexity of the word consists. A second and quite different consideration refers to technique of construction. The contrast is, roughly, between languages in which the subordinate elements are added to the root elements mechanically, i.e., without either of the elements being modified (the most common meaning of agglutination in the classical scheme), and those involving a process of fusion by which the constituent elements become difficult to recognize and separate. To quote Sapir's examples:

good + *ness* in English is agglutinative, *dep* + *th*, fusional. After treating this topic several times with varying conclusions, Sapir finally sets up a fourfold division: *a*, isolating; *b*, agglutinative; *c*, fusional; *d*, symbolic. Isolation, by which Sapir means significant order of elements, is included here because he thinks of this rubric as concerned with techniques of relating elements. Just as we know that in "John hit Bill" "John" is in construction with "hit" as the subject of the verb by the fact that it precedes the verb, so in *dep-th*, the modification of *deep* to *dep-* indicates that it is in a construction with *-th*. Since the agglutination-fusion contrast refers merely to the mechanics of expression rather than to what is being related, Sapir considers this scale likewise somewhat superficial, though useful as a supplementary criterion.

The division which appears to Sapir the most basic rests on the following considerations. There are two types of concepts which all languages must express, a stock of roots with concrete meanings, e.g., *table, eat,* and pure relational ideas which "serve to relate the concrete elements of the proposition to each other," thus giving it definite syntactic form; e.g., Latin *-um* as a mark of the verb object. As constituting the two extremes of concrete and abstract, Sapir puts these two classes at the ends of his scale as I (concrete), IV (pure relational). Between these, he places two groups of concepts which are dispensable, since some languages have them and others do not. Class II consists of derivational concepts which "differ from type I in expressing ideas irrelevant to the proposition as a whole but that give a radical element a particular increment of significance and that thus are related in a specific way to concepts of type I." Sapir's example is the suffix *-er* in *farmer*, which gives an increment of meaning to *farm-* but is not concerned with the structure of the rest of the sentence. A language which does not have concepts of type II would employ a single unanalyzable element to convey the meaning *farmer*. Concepts of type III (concrete relational concepts) lead over to type IV (pure relational), insofar as they help to relate members of a sentence to each other, but differ in that they have an element of the concrete in their meaning. Examples are the elements indicating gender in a language like German. The *-er* of *d-er* in "der Bauer tötet das Entelein" (the farmer kills the duckling) relates *d-* to *Bauer* by agreement in number, gender, and case. It thus indicates that *d-* modifies *Bauer* and that *Bauer* is singular and subject of the sentence. It does this, however, with the material alloy of the indication of sex gender, in this case, masculine.

Such concepts are called by Sapir concrete-relational. Since we have four types of concepts, of which I and IV are necessary in all languages, but II and III are dispensable, we set up the following four classes of languages: A consists of those with I and IV only. These Sapir calls Simple Pure-Relational Languages, e.g., Chinese. Group B contains those with II as well as the indispensables I and IV. These are Complex (i.e., Deriving) Pure-Relational Languages. Group C is constituted by languages which have I, III, and IV, but not II. These are Simple Mixed-Relational Languages. In group D, finally, we have those languages which have all four types of concepts, i.e., Complex Mixed-Relational Languages. Of the two considerations, the presence or absence of II (derivational) or presence and absence of III (concrete-relational), Sapir considers the latter, which aligns types A and B versus C and D, as the more fundamental. In his final table of classifications, Sapir takes a number of languages and, employing the sets of criteria already discussed, first assigns a particular language to one of the "fundamental types" A, B, C, and D just mentioned. He likewise indicates degree of synthesis.

The third factor, technique, is specified separately for each of the groups of concepts II, III (when they are present), and IV, using the above mentioned scale: *a*, isolating; *b*, agglutinative; *c*, fusional; *d*, symbolic. Sapir often mentions two and sometimes three techniques. If weakly developed, he encloses the symbol in parentheses. He then gives an over-all estimate of the dominant technique of the language, often using compound terms such as agglutinative-fusional to indicate roughly equal use of these two techniques. Note that Sapir does not use the term *inflectional* anywhere in his finished classification. He defines *inflection* as the use of fusional techniques in the sphere of inflectional units. He believes that, so defined, it is not of sufficient importance to figure as a fundamental term in his classification. The presence of inflection is, therefore, indicated by the appearance of *c*, indicating fusion, or *c* and *d*, indicating fusion and symbolism, in association with the concepts of group III (mixed-relational). As an example of Sapir's total scheme, let us take his classification of Semitic. These languages are assigned as a group to D, i.e., complex-mixed relational languages with all four types of concepts present. They are synthetic. In the area of derivational concepts (II) the techniques are listed as *d*, *c*, in that order, i.e., symbolic and fusional. In the area of mixed-relational concepts (III) the techniques are given as *c*, *d*, fusional, symbolic. Under IV the technique is (*a*), isolation, i.e., significant word order, the parentheses indicating its weak development. There is finally an over-all estimate of technique as symbolic-fusional.

The present method utilizes the Sapir classification in revised form. The basic criticisms of Sapir, already voiced by Most (1948, pp. 183–190), boil down to two. The first and most significant is that in his classification into four basic types, Sapir seems to be talking about concepts, but in reality his test is a formal, not a semantic one, a fact which leads to some difficulties in exposition. For example, Sapir discusses the concept of the plural, which he considers highly abstract. However, it can be assigned anywhere along the scale I–IV in a particular language, as he points out. His test, then, as to whether the plural is a root concept (I), a derivational one (II), or relational (III or IV) depends upon which formal class a particular language assigns it to. Sapir recognizes this disparity. "It is because our conceptual scheme is a sliding scale rather than a philosophical analysis of experience that we cannot say in advance just where to put a given concept" (1921, p. 117). In the typology presented here, the approach is formal. It is recognized that there is, in fact, a tendency for meanings of root morphemes (Sapir's I) to be more concrete in meaning than derivational (Sapir's II) or inflectional morphemes (III or IV), but this is too vague to constitute a valid procedure. Here, as elsewhere in modern linguistics, we isolate our distinctive units by a formal, not a semantic, test for purely practical reasons. The second criticism relates to Sapir's scale: *a*, isolating; *b*, agglutinative; *c*, fusional; *d*, symbolic. Isolating is a technique of relating, as are the other devices, but applies almost only between words, relative order being rarely significant within the word. It is therefore out of place here, and this betrays itself in the asymmetry of its occurrence in Sapir's scheme, for it only appears as a technique under IV (pure relational concepts) and does not refer to relations within the word as with the other techniques, but between words.

The method of classification proposed here is fundamentally that of Sapir, with certain modifications in the light of these criticisms. Moreover, in place of intuitive estimates based on over-all impressions, an attempt is made to define each feature involved in this classification in terms of a ratio of two units, each defined with sufficient rigor and by the calculation of a numerical index based on the relative frequency of these two units over stretches of text. Five bases of classification are set up in place of Sapir's three, and a set of one or more indices are established to measure the place of any language in regard to each of them. The first of these parameters is the degree of synthesis or gross complexity of the word. Since Sapir's time the minimum meaningful sequence of phonemes in a language has come to be called the morpheme in American linguistics. For example, the English *sing-ing* contains two morphemes but forms one word. The ratio M/W where M = morpheme and W = word, is a measure of this synthesis and may be called the synthetic index. Its theoretical lower limit is 1.00, since every word must contain at least one meaningful unit. There is no theoretical upper limit, but in practice values over 3.00 are infrequent. Analytic languages will give low results on this index, synthetic higher, and polysynthetic the highest of all.

The second parameter refers to technique. At one extreme are languages in which the meaningful elements are joined with slight or no modification. This is the classic meaning of *agglutination*. The opposite phenomenon is reciprocal modification or merging of the elements. Actually a number of types of constructions can be distinguished, and thus a more subtle typology might be developed. For purposes of the present paper an alternative is selected which seems to correspond most closely to the intent of Sapir and of the usual nineteenth-century analyses. To use contemporary terminology, what is involved is the degree of morphophonemic alternation. The meaningful stretch actually found in an utterance is called a "morph." A number of related morphs are subsumed under a single fundamental unit, the morpheme. The various morphs are then said to be in alternation. For example, in English we relate the morph *lijf* ("leaf") with the morph *lijv-* which only occurs with the plural morph *-z* to form *lijvz* ("leaves"). *Lijf* and *lijv-* are morphs which alternate within the same morphemic unit. The rules for the statement of this alternation belong to the morphophonemic section of the description of English. Where there are no variations among the constituent morphs of a morpheme or where the variations which exist are all automatic, the morpheme itself is said to be automatic. By an automatic alternation is meant one in which all the alternants can be derived from a base form by a set of rules of combination that holds in all similar instances throughout the language. This matter will be discussed in greater detail below. If both morphs in a construction belong to morphemes which are automatic, the construction is called agglutinative.

The index of agglutination is the ratio of agglutinative constructions to morph junctures. There is necessarily always one less morph juncture in a word than the number of morphs. Thus *leaves* has two morphs but one morph juncture. The index of agglutination is A/J, where $A =$ the number of agglutinative constructions and $J =$ the number of morpheme junctures. A language with a high value for this index will be agglutinational, one with a low value fusional. In general, the lower the first, or synthetic, index, the fewer the morph junctures which occur and the less the importance of this second index in characterizing the language. If a language reaches the theoretic lower limit of the synthetic index 1.00, this second index becomes impossible of calculation because no morpheme junctures occur; that is, the agglutinational index becomes 0/0, which is meaningless. In calculating this index, the differences between the degree of agglutination which might be found in constructions involving Sapir's concepts of groups II, III, and IV and which, as we have seen, figures in Sapir's final formulation, have been ignored. Such indices might be calculated on the basis of the distinctions between root, derivational, and inflectional morpheme classes described below, since it is these features which correspond most closely to Sapir's division of concepts. They were not set up, partly in order to avoid too great over-all complications in the typology, partly because of the considerable labor involved in their calculation.

The third parameter corresponds most closely to what for Sapir was the most fundamental basis of classification in languages, the presence or absence of derivational and concrete-relational concepts. Since, as has been seen, an approach in terms of the meaning of concepts is too vague to handle with any degree of rigor, the present treatment is based on the possibility of the exhaustive division of morphemes into three classes, root, derivational, and inflectional. Every word must have at least one root morpheme and many words in many languages have no more. The existence of more than one root morpheme in a word is called compounding. This is a significant feature in which languages differ from each other considerably. There are languages which cannot compound at all, or only very sparingly. Others again compound freely, while most languages are somewhere between. It is remarkable that Sapir nowhere seems to take this into account in his typology. It can easily be measured by a compositional index R/W, where R = number of root morphemes and W = number of words. The second class of morphemes is the derivational. Examples of derivational morphemes in English are *re-* in *re-make*, *-ess* in *lion-ess*, *-er* in *lead-er*. The derivational index is D/W, the ratio of derivational morphemes to words. Languages with a high D/W will belong to Sapir's Complex or Deriving subtypes and will thus fit into classes B or D in his scheme. The inflectional morphemes are the third class. Examples in English are *-s* of *eats* and the *-es* of *houses*.

The inflectional index is I/W, i.e., the proportion of inflectional

morphemes to words. This does not quite cover Sapir's concepts
of type III (concrete relational), as will be shown. However, a language which has these concepts and so belongs to Sapir's mixed-
relational types C and D necessarily has a fairly high value for the
inflectional index; the inverse relation does not necessarily hold.

The fourth parameter refers to a topic discussed by Sapir as
important for the morphological structure of a language but not
included in his final formulation. This is the order of subordinate
elements in relation to the root. The main distinction here is
between the use of prefixes and suffixes. The prefixial index, P/W,
is the ratio of prefixes to the number of words, and the suffixial,
S/W, is the ratio of suffixes to the number of words. An index of
infixing, that is, of the number of subordinate elements which are
incorporated within the root could likewise have been calculated,
but the occurrence of infixes was so rare in the particular languages
investigated that it seemed justifiable to omit it. There are an
indefinite number of further types of relative position of subordinate elements to the root, for example, containment, as in the
Arabic imperfective prefix of the second person feminine which
surrounds the verb morpheme, e.g., *taqtuli·*, "thou (fem.) kill-
est," in which the second person feminine morpheme is *ta---i·*
while "kill" is *-q-t-l* and "imperfect tense" is *-u-*. There is likewise
intercalation, again found in Semitic, in which a portion of the
subordinate element precedes or follows the root and another
portion is incorporated. All these devices are so rare that, at least
for the languages treated, it did not seem worth while to calculate
indices. Sapir's symbolism, which he considers a kind of technique
along with isolation, agglutination, and fusion, really belongs
here. Sapir's symbolism or internal change is, in my opinion, simply
the infixing of an inflective element, e.g., the preterite *-a-* in *sang*.
When the elements are derivational, as in Indonesian languages,
the process is usually called infixing. This brings out the fact that
there are two distinct considerations involved in Sapir's use of
the term *symbolism*, position and regularity. An infixing process
might well be regular, in which case the construction would be
agglutinative. In fact, though, this hardly ever occurs.

The final parameter has to do with the devices employed for relating words to each other. It therefore brings in syntactical as well as morphological considerations. There are three devices that languages may use, inflectional morphemes without concord, significant order, or concord (agreement).

Languages using the first two devices belong to Sapir's pure-relational category, while those using concord are mixed-relational. The inflectional index discussed above would include both non-concordial and concordial inflectional morphemes. This index, which may be called the index of gross inflection, is therefore of limited use for the present problem. It might seem that by distinguishing between concordial and nonconcordial inflectional morphemes and by assigning the words without inflectional morphemes to the isolating class, it would be possible to make a clear threefold division. The extent of isolating, inflectional, and concordial techniques could then be calculated by three indices based on the ratio of each of these types to the total number of words. There are a number of complications that prevent such a simple procedure. Many languages, for example, Latin, merge concordial and nonconcordial features in the same inflectional morpheme. Thus, the -um of the Latin masculine accusative singular of adjectives has two concordial features, gender and number, and a pure inflectional one, case. In such cases, the procedure adopted is to count the same morpheme a number of times, one for each distinct feature. Another difficulty arises in regard to order. Order probably always has some value in relating elements even where inflection exists. We relate the accusative to the nearest verb even where the order is not fixed. Order may even be fixed although other means are present to indicate which words are in construction. This is largely true of German, for example. Significant order should perhaps be restricted to cases where a change of order produces a change of constructional meaning. The criterion employed was closest to this latter one, but easier of application. The absence of an inflectional morpheme in a word was taken as an indication that the method of relating it was order. If we call each instance of the use of a principle to indicate relations between words in the sentence a nexus, then three indices, O/N, Pi/N, and Co/N were calculated, where O = order, Pi = pure inflection, Co = concord, and N = nexus.

The following, in summary, are the typological indices which have been described:

(1) M/W = index of synthesis

(2) A/J = index of agglutination

(3) R/W = compounding index

(4) D/W = derivational index

(5) I/W = gross inflectional index

(6) P/W = prefixial index

(7) S/W = suffixial index

(8) O/N = isolational index

(9) Pi/N = pure inflectional index

(10) Co/N = concordial index

The validity of these indices assumes that we can define the units employed consistently and in such a manner that they may be applied to all languages. In fact, there is hardly one of the units employed in the above formulas which does not admit of a number of alternative definitions. The choices made here are dependent on the particular purposes of the study. We always ask what it is that we want to measure. In certain cases there seems to be no good reason for the choice of one alternative over the other from this point of view, and a purely arbitrary choice was made since some basis of decision had to be reached. It may be of some comfort to note that the theoretically wide range of choice of definitions for certain units only bore on decisions for a relatively small proportion of difficult instances. As evidence of this, the results of the indices calculated for a passage of 100 words of English in 1951, and arrived at by methods no longer fully recoverable by introspection, may be compared with indices for a 100-word passage done recently in accordance with the methods outlined here.

	1951	*1953*
Synthesis	1.62	1.68
Agglutination	.31	.30
Compounding	1.03	1.00
Prefixing	1.00	1.04
Suffixing	.50	.64
Gross inflection	.64	.53

It should be emphasized that other alternatives than those chosen here for the definition of units are equally possible and probably preferable for certain other purposes, for example, writing a grammar of a language.

In the following section the chief problems encountered in defining the units employed in the indices are discussed. These refer to the morph, the morpheme, agglutinative constructions, the distinction of root, derivational and inflexional morphemes, and the word. Nothing approaching an exhaustive treatment of the problems is attempted here. The purpose of the present discussion is merely to point out the chief problems encountered in this study and the reasons for the particular solutions which were adopted.

Basic to the synthetic index as well as most of the others is the possibility of segmenting any utterance in a language into a definite number of meaningful sequences which cannot be subject to further division. Such a unit is called a morph. There are clearly divisions which are completely justified and which every analyst would make. For example, everyone would divide English *eating* into *eat-ing* and say that there were two units. There are other divisions which are just as clearly unjustified. For example, the analysis of *chair* into *ch-*, "wooden object," and *-air*, "something to sit on," would be universally rejected. There is, however, an intermediate area of uncertainty in which opinions differ. Should, for example, English *deceive* be analyzed into *de-* and *-ceive*? It is this intermediate area with which we must be able to deal. We start with a set of forms that will be hereafter called a square. A square exists when there are four meaningful sequences in a language which take the form AC, BC, AD, BD. An example is the English *eating* : *sleeping* : : *eats* : *sleeps*, where A is *eat-*, B is *sleep-*, C is *-ing* and D is *-s*.[2] Where a square exists with corresponding variation of meaning, we are justified in segmenting each of the sequences of which it is composed. Once it has been segmented, each of its segments may then be tested to discover if

[2] One of the four elements may be zero provided the sequences in which it occurs are free forms, i.e., may occur in isolation. For example, hand : hands : : table : tables is a valid square, in which A is *hand*, B is *table*, C is *zero*, and D is *-s*.

it also is a member of a square. If it is, it in turn will be segmented into two morphs. If it is impossible, then we have reached the limit of analysis and cannot divide further. A test of correspondence of meaning is applied to avoid such squares as *hammer* : *ham* : : *badger* : *badge*. A square conforming to these conditions described will always give us valid, generally acceptable analyses. It is too severe, however, in that it excludes some segmentations which everyone would want to accept. The first extension which we make is the following. A sequence which occurs with a member of a square is also recognized elsewhere if with regard to this member (a) the sequence of phonemes is identical except for automatic changes (for which see below) and (b) if the meaning is the same. On this basis we recognize a segmentation of *huckleberry* into *huckle* + *berry*, since *berry* itself is a morph elsewhere. This leaves *huckle-* also as a morph although it never occurs in a square. If now *huckle-* were to occur in some other combination, we would recognize a segmentation there also and so add a new morph. This process is continued until we reach a sequence that does not recur in any other combination. In this instance we have reached it with *huckle-*.

A further extension must be made in the case of what might be called a formally defective square. We should like to analyze men into two morphs, one with the meaning "man" and the other "plural," but there is no square into which it can be put. For example, *man* : *men* : : *boy* : *boys* is formally defective. We set up the following rule. If there can be found a square like the one just cited in which *boy* : *boys* itself is a pair in another valid square, e.g., *boy* : *boys* : : *lad* : *lads*, and if *man* may always substitute for *boy* and *men* for *boys* and produce a grammatical (even though at times semantically improbable) sentence, then *man* : *men* may be subjected to a segmentation analogous to that of *boy* : *boys*, and *men* may be considered two morphs. In the case of *sheep* : *sheep* : : *goat* : *goats* we recognize two morphs for the plural of sheep, one of which is a zero. Such analyses are not to be confused with segmentations into two or more semantic categories, where no valid square exists for substitution. In Latin, for example, we cannot analyze -*us* nominative singular into two morphemes, nominative and singular. The square -*us*:*ō* :: *ī*:*īs* — nominative singular:dative singular :: nominative plural:dative plural — does not have a pair which can be substituted for members of a formally perfect square, and hence the segmentation of these forms is not permitted. Corresponding to formally defective squares we have those which are semantically defective. Here, if there are parallel nonautomatic variations, the analysis is permitted even though definite meanings cannot be assigned to the morphs. Thus, the sets *deceive*:*receive* :: *decep-tion*:*recep-tion* :: *decei-t*:*recei(p)t* justify the segmentations *de* + *ceive* and *re* + *ceive*. This rule permits the usual assumption of morphs for derived forms of the verb in Semitic. In view of the variety of meanings in instances of this kind, it would be difficult to operate without it.

There are certain extensions of the morph concept which are rejected here as inconsistent with the purposes of this study, although entirely legitimate for other purposes. No discontinuous morphs which contain segments in two different words are accepted. This is understandable, since we wish to measure the ratio of morphemes to words and we therefore want each word to contain a definite number of morphemes restricted to the word itself. We likewise do not include meaningful units simultaneous with grammatical stretches longer than the word, e.g., intonation patterns of the sentence. The reason again is clear. We wish morphemes to be parts of words and this they cannot be if they are simultaneous with an entire sequence of words. In this connection it should be noted that neither the index of synthesis nor any of the others utilized in the present study is a general measure of total complexity of a language. Intonational patterns and certain other items which contribute to the over-all complication of a language are not included.

The next step to be taken after the identification of morphs is the establishment of more complex units, morphemes, with morphs as their members. It is this aspect of the problem which has been most frequently discussed in the literature as the chief subject-matter of morphemic analysis by Harris, Hockett, Bloch, Nida,

and others. In general, the principles set forth by Nida are adequate (1948, pp. 414–441). These involve the generally recognized
criteria of sameness of meaning (here applied strictly) and of complementary distribution and the requirement that if morphs of
varying phonemic shape are to be assigned to the same morphemic
unit, there must be at least one nonvarying unit with at least as
wide a distribution.

On this point, however, for reasons to be explained, it is inad-
visable to accept the complementations allowed by Nida in accordance with his rule that "complementary distribution in tactically
different environments constitutes a basis for combining different
forms into one morpheme only on the following condition: that
some other morpheme — belonging to the same distribution class,
and having either a single phonemic shape or phonologically
defined alternant shapes — occurs in all the tactically different
environments where the forms in question are found" (p. 421).
For example, in Arabic there are pronominal suffixes indicating
possession when added to the noun and another set indicating
the verb object when added to the verb. These are tactically different: i.e., the verb in general could not be substituted for the
noun or vice versa. The existence of -ka, "second person singular
masculine," and other phonemically identical forms in both series
would, on the basis of Nida's rule, allow us to unite the morphs
of the first person singular: -ī and -ȳa, noun possessive, and -nī,
verb object, as constituent morphs of the same morpheme. This
alternation is, of course, irregular and in reckoning our agglutinative index, if we accepted this alternative, we should have to call
any construction involving one of the first person singular suffix
forms irregular, or nonagglutinative. We should thus be penalizing
Arabic, as it were, for having some degree of regularity in these
forms. In a language with two totally different sets of pronouns
in these uses, Nida's rule would not allow complementation;
hence there would be no irregular alternations from this source,
although, on a common-sense basis, we should call this the more
irregular situation. Hence only members of the same structural
set, i.e., those substitutable for each other in the same tactical

environment, are considered as possible alternants of the same morpheme.

Given certain morphs as alternants of the same basic morpheme units, we can define an agglutinative construction. It seems consonant with the traditional use of the term to consider its basic reference to be to morphological regularity. However, the term *regular* has been used in a number of different ways. In the discussions of Bloomfield, Wells, and others it is now usual to distinguish types and degrees of regularity and irregularity. The definition of *regularity* adopted here is that which appears to be closest to actual usage in typological discussion. This is the requirement that all the varying phonemic shapes of the morph be derivable from a non-fictive (i.e., actually occurring) base form by rules of combination which hold for all similar combinations throughout the language. This is usually called automatic alternation. The case of a morpheme which does not have alternating morphs, i.e., which involves the same phonemic sequence in all occurrences, is a limiting instance which is, of course, also reckoned as automatic. Sometimes one choice of a base form gives automaticity, i.e., predictability from base forms, while another does not. In cases of doubt those base forms are chosen which give the greatest degree of automaticity for the total description of the language. This is admittedly not a very precise rule, but in practice this does not prove to be a major difficulty.

We define automaticity as the property of the entire morpheme where every morph is in automatic alternation with every other. The morphs may often be grouped in subalternating sets. It is not sufficient for these to be in automatic alternation. The English plural morpheme has the statistically most frequent subset -ən -ən -əz, which are in automatic alternation. However, there are other alternants, e.g., -ən, -zero, etc., which are not in automatic alternation with -sn -zn -əz as a whole. Hence the English plural morpheme is not automatic.

The possibility of calculating compounding, derivational, and inflectional indices depends on our ability to distinguish root, derivational, and inflectional morphemes. Of these the root class is probably the most difficult of formal definition, but the easiest of recognition. By this is meant that in actual practice, there is virtually complete agreement as to which morphemes are to be regarded as root morphemes. The root position in the word is characterized by a large and easily extendible membership and concreteness of meanings. The contrast with inflectional morphemes is greatest in these respects, since these latter tend to be few in number and relational as well as abstract in meaning. Another characteristic would generally be agreed on. Every word must have at least one root morpheme. Hence in a one-morpheme word, that morpheme is necessarily a root. In contrast, derivational and inflectional morphemes need not occur, and there are some languages, so-called root or isolating languages, in which derivational and inflectional morphemes are rare or perhaps do not occur at all. Derivational morphemes may be defined as morphemes which, when in construction with a root morpheme, establish a sequence which may always be substituted for some particular class of single morpheme in all instances without producing a change in the construction. If the class of single morphemes for which the derivational sequence may substitute contains one of the morphemes in the derivational sequence itself, we call the sequence endocentric; if not, then it is exocentric.

For example, *duckling* in English is a derivational sequence, since it may be substituted anywhere for *goose, turkey*, etc. without change of constructional meaning. Since *duck* is included in this class of single morphemes for which *duckling* may substitute, *-ling* is here an endocentric derivational morpheme. *Singer* is an exocentric sequence, since the class of single morpheme sequences for which *singer* may substitute consists of single-morpheme nouns only, and does not include the verb *sing*. Hence *-er* is an exocentric derivational morpheme.

We can now define the inflectional morpheme simple as a nonroot, nonderivational morpheme making the three classes exhaustive and mutually exclusive. Inflectional morphemes, like derivational, need not occur at all in any particular language. When it is part of a word pattern, however, its appearance in the appropriate position is compulsory like that of the root. One member of the class is frequently zero. In these instances, the absence of an overt phonemic sequence shows itself as significant because the word in this form has definite syntactic limitations on its uses; e.g., the nominative singular in Turkish or the noun singular in English.

We finally reach what is in some ways the most difficult problem, the definition of the word unit. It is clearly fundamental to the purpose of the present study inasmuch as all the indices involve the number of words. In most instances this is explicit; sometimes it is tacit, as in the index of agglutination, in which the number of morpheme junctures is always one less than the number of words. There is at present no general agreement on this topic. Some deny the validity of the word as a linguistic unit. Others admit it, but deny that it need be taken into account in the description of a particular language. Some say the word is definable only for each language in a separate *ad hoc* fashion. Some define it in phonological, others in morphological terms. In practice, however, the word continues to be the key unit of most actual language descriptions. Of the two basic types of over-all definitions of the word, the phonological and the morphological, the former is clearly insufficient for the purposes of the present study. In phonological definitions, we define the word in terms of some single phonological characteristic, or through a combination of characteristics which serve as markers. These markers are usually stresses or boundary modifications of phonemes; i.e., junctures. Besides the fact that the use of phonological markers to define the word sometimes leads to the isolation of individual units which we should not wish to call words on other grounds, many languages do not have such phenomena, so that a phonological procedure cannot lead to a universal definition. The other basis has been called morphological, since it is based on the distribution of meaningful elements. Of definitions of this kind, Bloomfield's characterization of the word as the minimum free form is the most satisfactory in that it is universally applicable and points in the right direction to freedom or absence of freedom, that is, bondage as the basic criterion. The actual test of freedom, ability to occur in isolation, is, however, difficult to apply in practice and leads to unusual results. For example, *the* in English would not be a word by Bloomfield's test.

The procedure adopted here can only be briefly outlined. It has led to results satisfactory for this study in the relatively few doubtful cases regarding the existence or nonexistence of a word boundary in the languages under consideration. Instead of asking whether a particular minimal form is bound or free in general, as is usually done, the present treatment is in terms of morphs in particular contexts. This allows us, for example, in Latin to make *ab*, "from," a free form as a preposition but a bound form as a verb prefix in *abduco*, "I lead away." What is specified as bound or free is not a morph as such but a contextually determined class of mutually substitutable morphs. Such a class is here called a morph substitution class (MSC). This notion is expanded to include a sequence of morpheme substitution classes which may in all circumstances be substituted for a particular MSC and none of whose members are identical in membership with it.[3] It is convenient to use the term *nucleus* to cover both individual MSC's and such substitutable sequences. Having broken up an utterance into nuclei in this manner, we now test each nucleus boundary to see if it is a word boundary or not. A nucleus boundary is a word boundary if it is possible to insert an indefinitely long sequence of nuclei. If it is an intraword boundary, either no nucleus can be inserted or a fixed maximum number can be. For example, in the sentence "the farmer killed the ugly duckling" there are nine morphemes: (1) the (2) farm (3) er (4) kill (5) ed (6) the (7) ugly (8) duck (9) ling; seven nuclei: (1) the (2) farmer (3) kill (4) ed (5) the

---

[3] This is necessary in order to exclude endocentric phrases in which a sequence of words can always be substituted for the head or chief number. A sequence of adjectives followed by a single-morph noun would be a nucleus were it not for the proviso of dependence among its members. Adjectives are not bound to nouns in English, for example, because they occur in predicative adjective constructions also. For the basic ideas of the MSC and the derivational sequence, I am largely indebted to the stimulus of the writings of Zellig S. Harris and Rulon S. Wells. The resemblance to the notions of focus class and expansion of the latter writer is particularly close. See especially R. Wells, 1947, pp. 81–117.

(6) ugly (7) duckling; and six words: (1) the (2) farmer (3) killed (4) the (5) ugly (6) duckling. There is an intraword boundary at "kill-ed" because no nucleus may be inserted. On the other hand at the boundary between "farmer" and "killed" there is no fixed maximum number of insertable nuclei. We may talk of the "farmer who killed the man who killed the man who . . . killed the ugly duckling." The contradiction with the phonological word is in certain cases merely apparent. Thus in Latin the enclitic *-que*, "and," which is reckoned as a syllable with any preceding sequence in locating the stress which serves as a phonological word marker, is also part of the word by the present test. *Dō'minus*, "the lord," and *dō'minús* in *dō'minúsque*, "and the lord," are not members of the same MSC because they are not substitutable for each other. *Dō'minús-* belongs to the same nucleus as *legātús-, púer*, and this class is dependent on the class of the following *-que, -ve* since it must be followed by it and hence belongs to the same word. Even with monosyllables, where there is no stress shift, *mū's*, "mouse," and the *mū's* of *mū's-que*, "and the mouse," are members of different nuclei, since the former can be substituted only by *dō'minus, púer*, etc. The latter only by the class of *dō'minús-, púer-*.

A table of the calculated indices follows. The languages selected are chiefly those frequently cited as examples of specific types in

	Sanskrit	Anglo-Saxon	Persian	English	Yakut	Swahili	Annamite	Eskimo
Synthesis	2.59	2.12	1.52	1.68	2.17	2.55	1.06	3.72
Agglutination ..	.09	.11	.34	.30	.51	.67	...	.03
Compounding ..	1.13	1.00	1.03	1.00	1.02	1.00	1.07	1.00
Derivation	.62	.20	.10	.15	.35	.07	.00	1.25
Gross inflection	.84	.90	.39	.53	.82	.80	.00	1.75
Prefixing	.16	.06	.01	.04	.00	1.16	.00	.00
Suffixing	1.18	1.03	.49	.64	1.15	.41	.00	2.72
Isolation	.16	.15	.52	.75	.29	.40	1.00	.02
Pure inflection..	.46	.47	.29	.14	.59	.19	.00	.46
Concord	.38	.38	.19	.11	.12	.41	.00	.38

the existing literature in typology, subject to the limitations of my own knowledge of specific languages. Instead of Turkish, the related Yakut was selected as an example of an agglutinating language, since the extensive Arabic borrowings in Osmanli Turkish have led to irregularities in the vowel harmony and in other respects to such an extent as to render it untypical. Two ancient Indo-European languages, Anglo-Saxon and Sanskrit, were chosen, and two modern languages of the same German and Indo-Iranian branches, modern English and Persian, were also selected to illustrate long-term change in type. Annamite was selected as a representative root isolating language, Eskimo as polysynthetic, and Swahili as an agglutinative, concordial Bantu language.[4] (See accompanying table.)

On the basis of counts such as these, the next step would be to define terms like analytic, synthetic, agglutinative, and prefixing after plotting a frequency distribution curve. There are too few languages here to make this procedure feasible. However, even cursory inspection of the indices set forth here shows that, if we define an analytic language as one with a synthetic index of 1.00–1.99, synthetic as 2.00–2.99, and polysynthetic as 3.00+, the results would conform to the usual nonquantitative judgments. Similarly we might call a language agglutinative if its agglutination index is over 0.50 and similarly for the others.

The present results should also be confirmed by further counts, since they were obtained only for single passages of 100 words each, besides which the probable error should be calculated for each. One might well suspect differences based on the style of the

[4] The passages selected were 100 words long for each language, as follows: Sanskrit, *Hitopadésa*, ed. Max Mueller, p. 5, *varam ekas*, ff.; Anglo-Saxon, *An Anglo-Saxon Reader*, J. W. Bright (New York, 1917), p. 5, *hit gelamp gio*, ff.; Persian, Pizzi, I., *Chrestomathie Persane* (Turin, 1889), p. 107, *ruzi Ibrahimi*, ff.; English, *New Yorker*, December 13, 1952, p. 29, *Anyone who*, ff.; Yakut, *Ueber die Sprache der Yakuten* (St. Petersburg, 1851), p. 29, *min bäɣäsä* ff.; Swahili, C. Sacleux, *Grammaire Swahilie* (Paris, 1909), p. 321, *Kiyana mmoja*, ff.; Annamite, M. B. Emeneau, *Studies in Vietnamese (Annamese) Grammar* (Berkeley and Los Angeles, 1951), p. 226, *mot hom*, etc.; Eskimo W. Thalbitzer in *Handbook of American Indian Languages*, Part I, ed. Franz Boas (Washington, 1911), p. 1066, *kaasasurujuŋuaq*, ff (phonemicized and slightly normalized to conform to Kleinschmidt's grammatical description).

passages selected. The synthetic index was calculated in English and German for a number of passages of varying style, however, with remarkably concordant results.

English

Ladies' Home Journal, January 1950, p. 55 . . . . 1.62
R. Linton, Study of Man, p. 271 . . . . 1.65
O. J. Kaplan, Mental Disorders in Later Life, p. 373 . . . 1.60

German

Baumann, Nama Folk-tale 1.90
Ratsel, Anthropogeographie, p. 447 . . . . 1.92
Cassirer, Philosophie der Symbolischen Formen, p. 1 . . 2.11

This, of course, is no substitute for statistical evaluation. Another topic that can be studied by the present method is the general direction of historical changes in language over an extended period. The coincidences between Sanskrit and Anglo-Saxon on the one hand, and Persian and English on the other hand, are striking. The direction of change for virtually every index is the same from the older to the more recent language. Were more conservative Indo-European languages such as the Slavonic chosen, the results might well be different.

The present study is to be evaluated as purely a preliminary attempt. Some indices may well have to be eliminated and others substituted. The specific definitional choices may likewise be subject to alteration in future studies. However, the general method of the calculation of indices based on text ratios of carefully defined linguistic elements has, I believe, definite value for typological studies.

by OMER C. STEWART

The Forgotten Side of
Ethnogeography

THE relation of primitive man to his physical environment has
been considered important by nearly everyone who has studied
aborigines. An ethnography which did not devote some space to
describing the geographic area in which the people lived would
be an oddity indeed. Even when the adjustment of the natives to
the climate, terrain, and vegetation looms large and when the
physical environment is shown to be an important factor in many
aspects of culture, it has not seemed necessary to identify the study
as ethnogeography. Ethnography, with few exceptions, has been
considered broad enough to include man's relation to nature. Ethnogeography, and its parent anthropogeography, are terms used
almost exclusively by scholars who consider themselves geographers; consequently, they have emphasized the geographical aspects of the relation between man and nature.

The titles under which scholars present their discussions of
man's relation to nature need not, however, indicate whether the
point of departure or the primary training of the author is in
the physical sciences or the social sciences. Ideally, in fact, attention should be given equally to the influence of man on environment and to the influence of geography on man and his culture.
We must recognize, nevertheless, that science has been compart-
mentalized and that in the division of labor anthropologists have
assumed the responsibility for learning about mankind, especially

nonliterate peoples. Geographers have historically begun with the physical world, and have emphasized the influence of the geographic environment when considering the relation of nature to man.

A brief review of the literature of anthropology indicates that "the science of man" has been either passive or negative with regard to the problem of the relation of man to nature. Anthropologists most frequently have simply accepted the views of the natural scientists regarding the physical world. Only when geographers have made extreme claims for the geographical determinism of both racial types and culture have anthropologists been motivated to active analysis of the mutual influence of man and environment. They were able to refute the most extreme assertions of the geographical determinists. Beyond that, anthropologists have accepted from the natural scientists without question both the descriptions of the environment and the reasons for its being as described.

It is my contention that anthropology has failed in its responsibility by not more vigorously seeking out and presenting to other sciences the ways in which primitive man has influenced the world around him. Anthropological literature contains very little information regarding the effect of aborigines upon the terrain, climate, flora, or fauna. Such data are so few that it comes as a distinct surprise to most scholars, including anthropologists, that primitive peoples have had an extremely important influence upon the physical world in which they lived.

Nearly every one, on the other hand, has some ideas about the influence of geography upon humanity, and the written record of such ideas is very long and full. Hippocrates, Plato, Aristotle, Ptolemy, and Lucretius are a few of the ancients who wrote on the subject. Bodin (1580), Montesquieu (1748), Dubos (1770), Taine (1864), and Michelet (1869) are some of the early moderns to do so.

But the great name in anthropogeography is, of course, Friedrich Ratzel (1844–1904), who carried on and refined the interpretations of the famous scientific explorers von Humboldt and von Richthofen. Although a less extreme geographic determinist than his teacher, Ritter, or his principal American student and interpreter, Semple, Ratzel (1898) nevertheless said: "The soil governs the destinies of peoples with a blind brutality. A people should live on the soil which fate has given it; it should die there and submit to the law." Even so, some contemporary geographers, such as Ellsworth Huntington and Griffith Taylor, appear to give greater weight to climate and terrain as factors determining human development than did Ratzel. Because he tempered environmentalism and because he devoted tremendous energy to recording distributions of culture elements and to defining culture areas, Ratzel's writings have enjoyed a sympathetic reception from anthropologists; consequently, he has greatly influenced anthropological research.

Ratzel's temperate environmentalism has dominated American anthropological thinking, first, because it was accepted by Boas, and second, because it has been passed on by Boas's students. Benedict wrote that Boas "embarked on his first trip to the Eskimo specifically to study the reaction of the human mind to the natural environment" (1943, p. 27). This deterministic view was later modified, according to Lowie, who evaluated Boas as follows: "Starting as a geographer, he was disillusioned by his Eskimo experience as to the potency of physical environment, to which he has since then ascribed a preponderantly limiting rather than creative importance" (1937, p. 144). Boas supported geography as the bridge between the physical sciences and social science. In 1887, in an article in *Science* entitled "The Study of Geography," he wrote: ". . . all agree that anthropo-geography — the life of man as far as it depends on the country he lives in — is the true domain of geography" (1940 reprint, p. 640). Among geography's objects is to determine "the mutual influence of the earth and its inhabitants upon each other," he said, and added, "Many are the sciences that must help to reach this end" (p. 647).

Although pronouncing a belief in "the mutual influence of the earth and its inhabitants upon each other" and admitting that many sciences must cooperate to arrive at an understanding of that mutual influence, Boas did not stimulate research which would contribute to that understanding. By 1896 he could approve of the deductions of Ratzel and McGee concerning the influence of geographical environment on culture (p. 272), merely adding the caution that environment "has a certain limited effect upon culture," but cannot be viewed as "the primary moulder of culture" (p. 278). At no time, as far as I can discover, did Boas indicate that he recognized that primitive men influenced their natural environment. Even when he lists the contributions of ethnology to "other sciences, such as psychology, philosophy and history" (p. 638), he relegates its role with regard to anthropogeography to that of correcting the exaggerated claims of geographical determinists (p. 637). It was thus that Boas set a course in American anthropology which has been followed without deviation to the present.

The failure of anthropology to champion the role of primitive man as an active and important agent in "the mutual influence of the earth and its inhabitants upon each other" was not due to a lack of theoretical recognition that such a mutual influence existed. The quotation from Boas shows he recognized it in 1887. Evidence is abundant that the theory of man's influence on nature was widely accepted. Wissler, in his book *The Relation of Nature to Man in Aboriginal America* (1926), phrased it as follows: "The relation between man and nature is fundamental and at no time can he break the bond. This is a generality to which everyone can subscribe . . ." (p. xi). The book reveals, however, that Wissler did not think of a reciprocal relation between man and nature, but rather that "environment is in some way a determiner" of culture (p. 214), insofar as man must adjust to certain ecological conditions. Beyond this, Wissler's idea of the relation of nature to man was to define culture areas and to plot on maps trait distributions.

Another anthropogeographical study by an anthropologist is Kroeber's *Cultural and Natural Areas of Native North America* (1939). Kroeber's objectives were "first, to review the environmental relations of the native cultures of North America," and "second, . . . to examine the historic relations of the culture areas, or geographical units of culture" (p. 1). He made it explicit that his "work in no sense represents a relapse toward the old environmentalism which believed it could find the causes of culture in environment" (p. 1). He reviewed briefly but approvingly the work of Wissler, O. T. Mason, and Ratzel relating cultural to natural areas (pp. 6–7). He then reproduced vegetation maps, climatic maps, physiographic maps, etc., on which to superimpose maps of culture areas, tribes, native populations, etc. I could find no hint in his 242-page monograph that he had recognized the possibility that the natives of North America might have had some influence on their physical environment.

That anthropologists continue to regard man as adjusting to nature without contributing materially to changing his physical environment is evident from the article "Human Ecology" by Marston Bates in the collection of essays in the book *Anthropology Today*, published in 1953. Bates points out that "human ecology" is frequently synonymous with "human geography" (p. 701). In his review of numerous ecological problems relating to man and the methods employed for their solution, he indicates that contemporary research and theory are almost exclusively concerned with man's adaptation to nature. There seems to be no interest in learning how aborigines may have influenced the world about them. Since ecology, possibly more than geography, has emphasized the study of the relations between organisms and their environment, this lack of interest appears to me strange.

The evidence that anthropologists have contributed little toward understanding primitive man's influence on his natural environment could be multiplied. Their theoretical interest has not been enough to counterbalance the points of view of the geographers, botanists, climatologists, soil scientists, etc., who have approached the same problem from their respective disciplines. The ecologists especially, and the plant ecologists above all, have included human factors among those to be considered for an understanding of the life of an area. Unfortunately, however, where natural vegetation was studied or where only aborigines were concerned, the ecologists have too often forgotten their theoretical statements of man's part in the shaping of the total environment.

Notwithstanding their primary interest in plants as such, some plant ecologists, more than anthropologists, have recognized the importance of primitive man's influence upon his physical environment. If anthropologists had, over the years, consciously sought for evidence of changes in the geographic environment resulting from human behavior, they would have helped other sciences. Botanists, foresters, and plant ecologists have long recognized human influence as of utmost importance in limited and special circumstances. Today it is popularly known as a force which can quickly change the vegetation of vast areas. One of humanity's first cultural achievements, fire, was the tool with which primitive man and modern aborigines, as well as civilized man, wrought tremendous changes in the geographic environment over most of the world.

That natives set vegetation on fire has not been unknown to anthropologists. Wissler, for example, in the first edition of his little handbook *North American Indians of the Plains*, published in 1912, reproduced a long description of the fire drive of the Indians of Illinois and Iowa. "The natural inference seems to be," he said, "that the grass firing and impounding methods of taking buffalo were developed before the introduction of the horse and are therefore the most primitive" (p. 23). Again in 1940, in *Indians of the United States*, he wrote: "The discovery of America by these early hunters was a great event, with consequences as momentous as those following 1492. At first the animals had the land to themselves. The largest animals had nothing to to fear, but when man, the disturber and destroyer of nature came, nothing was safe. He set fire to the grass and the forest to drive out the game. . . . Students of climate tell us that many significant changes have occurred since the days [of the early hunters]" (pp. 10–11).

But in spite of this awareness of the Indian practice of setting grass fires and of the tremendous force of such fires, Wissler failed when he wrote *The Relation of Nature to Man in Aboriginal*

America to see what conclusions might be drawn from such data. Although he expressed the opinion "that man's relation to the faunae and florae of the country is very close and that a change even in one of them will have a marked influence upon the mode of life pursued by the tribe" (p. 213), he seems not to have suspected that the Indians in aboriginal times could have brought about such a change. He leaves to the ecologist the evaluation of the relation of life forms to the landscape. "Whatever may be the truth of the matter, it is beyond dispute," he wrote, "that the environment is a determiner of some sort, insofar as living forms are forced to adjust themselves to the conditions it imposes. We have, in fact, a recognized division of science, known as ecology, which considers questions of this kind. The method usually followed in ecological studies is to seek correlations between the characters of life forms and specific characters of the environment and, if it be found that these usually happen together, it is assumed that some causal relation exists between them" (p. 212). Correspondences between an ecological map of North America which charted florae and climatic distinctions and a map of culture areas were for Wissler a satisfactory test. He was particularly impressed by "a tongue of true prairie land [which] reaches across Illinois and expands over northern Indiana, a geographical fact often overlooked; but ethnic phenomena did not overlook it, because we find in this pocket a tribe of Indians having striking prairie characteristics, though, for the most part, surrounded by forest tribes. Our test is, therefore, conclusive, for it proves that there is a close correlation between the geographical area and the type of culture" (p. 214).

It is unfortunate that Wissler was willing to accept this ecological map without raising the question whether the Indians and their particular Plains cultural habits may not in some way have contributed to the presence of that tongue of prairie protruding into the forest environment. An opportunity to contribute materially to the solution of a problem involving the Indians of that area which had been debated for over a century thus was lost. The true origin of this "prairie peninsula," as it was later called, extending through Illinois and into Indiana and Ohio, had been the subject of a scientific argument since 1818. It was in that year, in the first number of the *American Journal of Science*, that an article appeared by Caleb Atwater entitled "On the Prairies and Barrens of the West."

Atwater proposed that the grasslands of Ohio and all the states west of the Allegheny Mountains were a result of soil conditions. He denied the popular opinion that "our prairies and barrens . . . were occasioned entirely by burning woods by Indians to take game" (p. 120). The next year, 1819, first R. W. Wells and then A. Bourne answered Atwater. Wells set out to "prove that they [prairies] were occasioned by the combustion of vegetables." Claiming experience in Ohio, Indiana, and Illinois "and having been employed by the United States as a surveyor in the prairie country of the Missouri and Mississippi," Wells maintained that "prairies and barrens [were] primitively occasioned and continued" by fire (pp. 331–332).

Wells went on to say: "The Indians . . . burn the woods, not *ordinarily* for the purpose of taking or catching game, as suggested by Mr. Atwater, but for many other advantages attending that practice. If the woods be not burned as usual, the hunter finds it impossible to kill the game, which, alarmed at the great noise made in walking through the dry grass and leaves, flee in all directions at his approach. Also the Indians travel much during the winter, from one village to another, and hunting . . . which becomes extremely painful and laborious from the quantity of briers, vines, grass, etc. To remedy these and many other inconveniences, even the woods were originally burned so as to cause prairies. . . . Woodland is not commonly changed to prairie by one burning, but by successive conflagrations. . . . Ordinarily, all the country, of a nature to become prairie, is already in that state; yet the writer . . . has seen, in the country between the Missouri and Mississippi, after unusual dry seasons, more than one hundred acres of woodland together converted into prairie. And again, where the grass has been prevented from burning by accidental causes, or the prairie has been depastured by large herds of domestic cattle, it will assume, in a few years, the appearance of a young forest." (P. 335)

Bourne reinforced Wells's argument with additional reasons why the Indians of the prairie peninsula frequently set vegetation on fire, such as "to insure a good crop of grass for the next summer." Then Bourne reported: "When the white people settle on the barrens . . . fires are seldom seen, a young growth of trees, healthy and vigorous soon springs up. . . . That the barrens are frequently burned; and that when the burnings cease, a . . . vigorous growth of trees soon springs up, are facts which can be attested by the most respectable people of this country" (pp. 32–33).

If Wissler had been curious about the possible effect of fires upon the so-called natural vegetation, he would have discovered a great wealth of literature following the line of the debate in the first volumes of the *American Journal of Science*. From 1819 the Indians were given credit for either causing or extending all tall-grass prairies. In 1911 B. Shimek, Professor of Botany of the State University of Iowa, wrote one of the more definitive papers on the subject, entitled "The Prairies," in which he reviewed most of the published material which had appeared previously. Over a hundred different authors had written regarding the origin of the prairies. The extensive areas of pure stands of tall grass were said to result from geological formation, soil, rainfall, temperature, wind, evaporation, grazing, etc., by different writers. Notwithstanding the attention devoted to the prairies by the various natural sciences, Shimek reported: "Fire has been considered the cause of the treelessness of the prairies more frequently than any other factor. It was so considered in some of the earliest known references, and has received a varying degree of attention to the present time" (p. 217).

Of the dozens of papers containing evidence and argument that Indian burning of the vegetation had been the determining factor in the formation and preservation of that tongue of prairie extending into a region well suited for tree growth, not one is by an anthropologist. Yet the ethnologists studying the tribes of the plains must have known that many botanists, geographers, and ecologists believed that there would have been no tall-grass prairies at the time of discovery by Europeans if the Indians had not regularly set fire to the vegetation of the region. Without the aid of the specialists on Indians the scientific and scholarly attack on the problem was incomplete. Of primary importance would have been the broader and longer perspective such specialists could have supplied. On the question of the length of time that the burning of vegetation had been practiced in the area, an anthropologist would have been led to the conclusion that intentional burning was a universal pattern in the new world, and was consequently probably practiced the world over. From this would follow that it was probably very ancient in Illinois. Extinct bison quarries containing Folsom points, furthermore, suggest that in game drives fire was used as a tool by America's earliest known inhabitants. Since Folsom points have been found in Illinois and Ohio, it is not unreasonable to suppose that fire has been applied to the vegetation of the prairie peninsula for thousands of years. In assessing the potentiality of fire as the determining factor in prairie formation, time perspective is essential, and without the aid of anthropologists the scientists working on the problem did not have it.

Anthropologists would also have brought to the prairie problem what might be called an enlarged base for the exercise of the comparative point of view. Once it is recognized that grass- and tree-burning is a universal pattern, the question of its effect elsewhere arises; and to understand what fire could do in the area of Illinois and Indiana, it is helpful to know what it did in areas even more ideally suited to tree growth. That the whole Shenandoah Valley was kept as a clean, open grassland by Indian fires indicates the power of this cultural tool.[1] Not only the Shenandoah but the barrens of Kentucky[2] and the prairies of Texas[3] were quickly covered with woods when grass-burning was stopped or when its effectiveness was reduced by overgrazing.

[1] Maxwell, 1910, pp. 94–95.
[2] Sauer, 1927, pp. 123–130.
[3] Cook, 1908, pp. 1–16; Stewart, 1951, pp. 317–320.

Anthropologists backed away from the problem of the prairies because they had capitulated so completely to the idea that aborigines adjusted to their physical environment. They accepted Ratzel's environmentalism so entirely that they abandoned their own province and allowed the other sciences to work with inadequate data.

Once it is recognized that the prairie peninsula was probably caused and was certainly maintained by human action, the implications of primitive man's influence on the physical world become very extensive. Since the character of the soils of the tall-grass prairies differs from that of the forest soils adjacent, the soil scientists proposed that the soil was the determiner. Several recent studies, however, have shown that soil changes rapidly in response to the vegetation growing upon it. The deep black earth of Illinois and other prairie regions is now attributed to its grass cover instead of the grass cover being attributed to the soil. Rich prairie earth becomes degraded in a decade or two when oak woods are allowed to grow on it. It has been proposed that the blackness of grassland soil itself is in part due to the ash from burnt grass regularly added to the soil over the millennia. The importance of ancient man's influence on his environment is greatly enhanced when we conceive of him as frequently a determiner of soil types as well as of vegetation.[4]

We should not overlook the effect of primitives upon climate, for it is now established that the plant cover has measurable and significant influence on ground temperature, evaporation, wind, and precipitation. For example, Hursh and Connaughton (1938) studied intensively the local climate of 19,000 acres deforested by smelter fumes and of the surrounding hardwood forest in Copper Basin, Tennessee. The climatic differences between the two adjacent regions are impressive (pp. 864–866). A two-year record showed temperatures averaged three to four degrees higher on the denuded and grassy area than in the adjoining forests. Wind velocity was 7 to 10 times greater in winter and 34 to 40 times greater in summer on the deforested 19,000 acres than in the nearby woods. Pre-

[4] Thorp, 1948, p. 55; Billings, 1941, pp. 448–456; Christy, 1892, pp. 78–100.

cipitation was less by 25 per cent on the open grassland and denuded area. The accumulative effect which might be achieved over millions of acres during thousands of years might be great. These facts are of utmost importance for evaluating the climatic conditions which could prevail if forests were allowed to invade grasslands. That forests could slowly invade tall-grass prairies is well known, and it should be remembered that as they spread upon the grassland, climate would be improved decidedly in favor of the trees.

Although the influence of the American Indian on the vegetation of the prairie peninsula has been the most fully debated, some biologists have long considered fires set by the natives as the crucial determining factor in other grasslands. As early as 1892 Miller Christy published a long article in London presenting the evidence that the treelessness of the Canadian plains and prairies was due to repeated burning over by Indians (pp. 78–100). In 1927 O. Schmieder made a convincing case for the view that the Argentine Pampa was dependent on fire for its pure grass cover (pp. 255–270). Even without the help of anthropological documentation of the full extent of aboriginal grass burning, in 1950 Sauer wrote: "I know of no basis for a climatic grassland climax, but only of a fire grass climax for soils permitting deep rooting" (p. 20). I have assembled hundreds of references, mostly from travelers' accounts, which support Sauer's views. Were it not for fires set by Indians over thousands of years the western high plains would probably have supported drought-resistant trees like juniper, ponderosa pine, and hackberry, as well as sage brush in the north and mesquite in the south. The brush and pines of the plains would have met and intermingled with the eastern hardwood forest in the region where the tall-grass prairie now merges into short-grass plains.[5]

Natural scientists are sometimes reluctant to assign to primitive man the power to change millions of acres of woods into grassland even when the evidence is overwhelming that fire was the determining factor. When it becomes obvious that fire was essential for the formation and preservation of the prairies, the botanists and

[5] Stewart, 1953.

foresters seem to prefer to attribute their existence to fires set by lightning. A careful search of the available records, however, fails to reveal a single instance of lightning-caused grass fires in contrast to hundreds of records of such conflagrations due to Indian incendiarism. Without the full story from the ethnologists of the extent, frequency, and duration of culture patterns of aboriginal vegetation-burning, it was almost inevitable that the biologists should fail to give proper weight to the ancient human influences.

Primitive man's role in affecting the type of vegetation appearing as natural vegetation was undoubtedly as great in other areas as it was in the New World. The grasslands of Africa, for example, appear almost entirely dependent upon repeated burning. Some ecologists, such as Bews (1929, p. 293) and Brawn-Blanquet (1932, pp. 278–283), have said as much. Notwithstanding the conviction of such plant scientists, an outstanding ethnologist like Evans-Pritchard seems to prefer to disregard or minimize any possible effect the natives may have had on the physical environment. In his excellent account of the Nuer (1940), "who live in the swamps and open savannah that stretch on both sides of the Nile south of its junction with the Sobat and Bahr el Ghazal" in southern Anglo-Egyptian Sudan (p. 1), he dismisses man's effect on the environment with a single phrase and devotes the rest of his book to describing the influence of the environment on man and his culture. Knowing that the very grassy nature of Nuer territory was determined by Nuer cultural habits, one is justified in being disappointed that Evans-Pritchard did not emphasize the role of man as a determiner of his culture. In Africa as in America, one has a right to expect the anthropologist to serve as advocate for man in the question of man's relation to nature.

It appears that Ratzel's mild environmentalism dominates British anthropology as it does American, if Evans-Pritchard may be used as an example. "By the end of December," Evans-Pritchard wrote, "a great part of the country has been burnt and is cracked into deep fissures" (p. 54). He was not completely unaware of the effect of such burning on the plant cover, for later, while discussing the absence of harmful tsetse from Nuerland, he said: "This immunity is undoubtedly due to the absence of shady forest which, in its turn, is probably due in the main to flooding and partly to firing" (pp. 67–68). But even this half-admission that man influenced his environment was canceled by numerous statements about the natural conditions which produced the vegetation, such as, "The grasses necessary for the welfare of the herds depend for existence on suitable conditions of soil and water" (p. 51).

Rather than assuming that the area was grassy because of soil and water, it would have been interesting to start with the assumption that trees congenial to the moisture, soil, and temperature of the area would have dominated the region. Consider the different emphasis and the reordering of the material if Evans-Pritchard had pointed out how the Nuer culture had brought into being the precise physical conditions on which that culture depended. Not only would man be seen as responsible for the immunity from harmful tsetse infection through his having kept the area free from trees, but as responsible for the pure stand of grass itself. Without the influence of human beings on the environment the Nuer country would have been covered by thick woods. Under such conditions Nuer culture would have been different in many respects.

Similarly, failure to appreciate the role of fire kept Nadel from a fuller documentation of the cultural influence on the environment by the Nupe in the heart of Nigeria. This inadequacy is evident in spite of Nadel's statement that "communication and culture contact have helped to mould the physical environment of today" (1942, p. 3). Had he known that fires, ancient and modern, had been the deciding factor in the relation between savannahs and forests in that region of over sixty inches of annual rainfall, the force of culture to mold the physical environment would have appeared much larger.

Although not presented as an example of cultural conditioning of the physical environment, Madeline Manoukian's account of the peoples of the Gold Coast (1950) contains evidence on how the relative areas of forest and savannah may change. "*Savanna Zone*: Orchard bush and grassland lying immediately north of the forest zone; it also extends in the east right down to the coast and with deforestation is steadily advancing westwards along the coast in a wedge shape; it has now reached Sekondi. . . . where vegetation exists black soil a few inches in depth is found, formed by vegetable decay and ash from annual fires" (p. 16).

The obligation of anthropologists to discover how the African Negro has changed the natural environment, and to contribute to the scientific world information upon this influence, is all the greater because they are those who concentrate on understanding culture. For West Africa, our record of broadcast burning starts about 500 B.C. with Hanno's observation and, according to Werner, "very good description of a bush-fire on a large scale" (1906, pp. 9–12). Not only the distribution of vegetation but the concomitant differences in soil, temperature, wind, evaporation, rainfall, and animal life need to be considered as cultural problems. African vegetation, like that of the Americas, is with few exceptions a fire vegetation. The exceptions are areas where there is too little plant cover to burn and where it is too moist to burn. Yet even in the latter area, because of the slash and burn techniques of milpa agriculture, the fire factor should not be ignored.

That anthropologists need to investigate fully and carefully the extent to which vegetation is culturally determined is indirectly set forth by B. H. Farmer in a short notice in the January 1953 issue of *Geographical Review*. He said in part:

Tropical Grassland of Ceylon.
"The savanna is one of the most widespread landscapes of Africa. . . . It results from the tropical climate with a moderate amount of rainfall and a long spell of drought." Many of us were brought up at school to believe this statement from M. E. Hardy's *Geography of Plants* (Oxford, 1920). But few would now agree that African savanna, at least in its present aspect, is a true climax vegetation, and the same might be said of other tropical grasslands, such as the *llanos* and *campos* of South America and the *cogonales* of the Philippines. The conviction has grown that such grasslands, as we see them today, are wholly or partly man-made, the product of shifting cultivation and periodic burning. Savanna, in this view, is a fire-climax; and the implications in terms of soil

erosion and soil degradation are of great importance to the human geographer. . . . A careful study . . . is C. H. Holmes's valuable and well illustrated paper "The Grass, Fern, and Savannah Lands of Ceylon, Their Nature and Ecological Significance." . . . Holmes analyzes the climate of Ceylon and concludes that the climax vegetation of all seven present types is a closed forest. . . . All seven types as they stand today are secondary, the result of clearing, burning, cultivation, and, thereafter, periodic burning. [Pp. 115–117]

If the partisan of geographical determinism and the specialists in plants and climate have been forced to recognize the primary importance of cultural behavior as a final determinant of plant distributions, it behooves the students of man to contribute their special abilities to the solution of this fundamental problem.

The ultimate influence of fire upon the vegetation depends upon many natural conditions in addition to the amount of burning. Topography, wind, moisture, temperature, and soil, as well as the original vegetation, combine to determine the effect fires will produce. It is obvious that the vegetation of a relatively flat terrain, subject to periodic dry spells and to frequent strong winds and getting forty inches of rain annually, will be affected differently by annual fires than will the vegetation of a mountainous area getting the same amount of rain annually. Setting an extensive plain on fire regularly once a year might keep the plain completely free from woody growth; whereas an area of similar size, but broken by hills and canyons, might support scattered groves and some brush even if the area were set on fire annually. The rough terrain would protect some trees and inhibit complete burning over. Furthermore, the vegetation of a region with a thirty-inch annual rainfall will react differently to periodic conflagrations from one with a sixty-inch annual rainfall. Burning does not always produce a grassland. Where natural conditions are strongly in favor of tree growth, even regular burning may only serve to keep one forest type dominant at the expense of other trees. There are numerous woods which are dependent upon fire to survive competition with trees which would otherwise take over. A few examples will illustrate this point.

The teak forests of Burma will disappear under complete fire protection. The natives of the region had burned out the teak forests from time immemorial until prohibited by British forest management. Twenty-five years of experience indicated that fire prevention stopped teak reproduction and allowed other, less valuable trees to take over the areas that had been dominated by teak. When the ancient custom of annual burning was resumed, the teak again returned to its former importance.[6]

The long-leafed chir pine of India was also discovered to be a subclimax vegetation in the region where it grew. Because of its commercial value chir pine forest management was carefully studied. The story of the Burmese teak was repeated in the chir of India. Fire prevention was harmful to chir pine. To maintain itself chir needs the help of fire.[7]

More fully documented is the story of the long-leaf pine of the American southern states. Here, as on the plains and prairies, man's role as the determiner of which vegetation shall dominate the landscape has been established without the aid of anthropologists. The absence of ethnological insight applied to the pine forest of the South delayed the solution to the problem and permitted a faulty reconstruction of its history. Both Mooney and Swanton were aware that Indians had frequently set fire to the vegetation in the southeastern United States, but neither seemed to consider it of sufficient importance to give it more than passing reference, in connection with communal hunting. Swanton quotes Smith, Strachey, Spelman, Lawson, Catesby, Byrd, and Calderon regarding the use of fire in game drives. Catesby (1731) wrote: "Their annual custom of fire hunting is usually in October. At this sport some hundreds of Indians, who, spreading themselves in length through a great extent of country, set the woods on fire."[8]

It was an historian, Hu Maxwell, who clearly established in 1910 that the open, park-like, woods, free from undergrowth, which were characteristic of Virginia when discovered resulted from the incendiarism of the Indians. The abundance of straw-

[6] Chapman, 1950a, pp. 131–132.
[7] Gorrie, 1935, pp. 807–811.
[8] Swanton, 1946, p. 318.

berries, blackberries, and raspberries was a result of fire. Not only was the Shenandoah Valley a treeless prairie of over 1,000 square miles in one body, but many other grassy savannahs were described by the early explorers.

Maxwell's historical research led him to write: "The promptness with which forests take possession of cleared ground in Virginia is proof that the meadows and savannahs described by Lederer, Fallows, Beverley, Fontaine, and others, had not been long exempt from periodic fires which kept seedling trees out. At the present day, woods quickly spring up at the first opportunity, and the following extract from Beverley shows that they did the same thing two hundred years ago: 'Wood grows at every man's door so fast that after it has been cut down it will in seven years' time grow up again from seed to substantial firewood, and in eighteen or twenty years it will come to be very good board timber'" (p. 94). Maxwell's conclusion was: "Virginia, between its mountains and the sea, was passing through a crisis, at the time the colonists snatched the fagot from the Indian's hand. The tribes were burning everything that would burn, and it can be said . . . that if the discovery of America had been postponed five hundred years, Virginia would have been pasture land or desert" (p. 103).

Research done since Maxwell wrote has shown that there are other effects of frequent burning besides removing or thinning the trees. It is now clear that the pine forests of the South were present at the time of discovery and have persisted to the present because of the aboriginal and modern culture pattern of firing the woods. The famous plant ecologists Weaver and Clements wrote in their textbook in 1929: "The extent of this great fire belt has naturally led to the assumption that it is climax in nature, but its ecological character, as well as actual successional studies at widely separated points, leaves little or no doubt that it is essentially a fire sub-climax" (p. 512).

An indication of the failure of Weaver and Clements convincingly to establish their view of fire's importance in the southern pines comes from Vestal, who reviewed "Plant Ecology" in the

STEWART

journal *Ecology* in 1931 (pp. 232–239). Vestal frankly stated his
doubt that fire played the dominant role in the formation of
long-leaf pine forest which Weaver and Clements attributed to it.
Support for fire came a few months later in an article entitled
"The Forest That Fire Made," by S. W. Greene, which appeared,
surprisingly enough, in *American Forests,* monthly journal of the
American Forestry Association. The long comment by the Editor
which preceded the article indicates something of the feeling on
the subject at the time. Said the Editor:

> [S. W. Greene] raises questions that will be warmly controverted.
> His conclusions that the long-leaf forests of the South are the
> result of long years of grass fires and that continued fires are essen-
> tial to the perpetuation of the species as a type will come as a
> startling revolutionary theory to readers schooled to the belief
> that fire in any form is the arch enemy of forests and forestry. . . .
> Mr. Greene . . . is not a forester. For the past fifteen years, he
> has represented the Bureau of Animal Industry at the Coastal
> Plains Experiment Station at McNeill, Mississippi, in the study
> of the effect of ground fires upon forage. . . . For a number of
> years, his work has been in cooperation with the United States
> Forest Service in its study of the influence of fire upon forest
> growth. His conclusions . . . have been arrived at through study
> and observation at first hand.
> . . . *American Forests* does not vouch for the accuracy of Mr.
> Greene's conclusions.

A long quotation will best illustrate Mr. Greene's "revolution-
ary theory":

> Fire was the only effective tool that primitive man had for the
> clearing of forest land and it has remained throughout the ages
> as the prime force for land clearing, which must still go on to
> open up the most fertile soils for cultivation and grazing and push
> the forests back to less productive soils.
> All fires in the woods are by no means forest fires that destroy
> useful timber, even though they are uncontrolled, and not all
> foresters are fanatics on the subject of fires. . . . As early as 1855
> a trained ecologist (Hilgarde), working in the long-leaf pine area
> of southern Mississippi, discovered that ground fires in the forest
> were understood by the natives and were applied for a useful pur-
> pose which he mentioned in one short sentence. Secrets of nature

239

were so commonplace to woodsmen that they were considered hardly worth mentioning and so the story of "The Forest That Fire Made" is just coming to general notice although "The Fire Made Forest" itself was the most amazing physical characteristic of the South when traversed by De Soto and his men from 1539–42 and has remained as such for centuries.

Long-leaf pine (*Pinus palustris*) stretched in unbroken, almost pure stands, from Virginia into eastern Texas, a distance of more than 1200 miles, and De Soto and his men traveled the length and breadth of it, for here was a highway free of underbrush, where a deer could be seen through the timber as far as the eye could reach. . . .

No forest of such extent in pure stands and of such commercial value has been found on the face of the earth. Here was a poser, indeed, for the ecologist to ferret out the force of nature responsible for so favoring a single species of tree. . . . In a region of heavy rainfall and mild temperature, one would expect a forest growth of great variety with a jungle undergrowth of vines and shrubs. . . . There was no lack of a variety of seed trees of other species. . . . It was noticeable that other species crowded out long-leaf only in the absence of annual grass fires. . . . Fire then was a good clue and when approached from every angle the scent of fire became constantly stronger. But how could fire stop everything else yet encourage long-leaf?

A peculiar habit of growth of long-leaf possessed by no other pine gave the clue. . . . It forms a bundle of leaves in the grass and for a period of five, ten and no one knows how many years, it builds a root system and stores its reserve food there. If fire causes it to shed its needles it merely calls on the reserve food supply in the roots to form a new set and goes on growing. No one knows what determines the start of its upward growth but when it is ready it sends up a husky shoot and makes a rapid growth, often three feet or more in one year. . . .

The long-leaf pine has two serious enemies — the hog and the brown spot needle disease. Hogs root the seedlings up and can live on the stored food material in the roots. However, hogs had no effect on the virgin stand for there were no hogs until the Spaniards introduced them. The needle disease is caused by a fungus which is often a very serious enemy of the young seedlings underneath a "rough" of dead grass. Burning the dead grass in winter is an effective means of control.

The picture now clears up. Where seed trees are available all that is necessary to get a pure stand of long-leaf without a hard-wood undergrowth is to have frequent grass fires. Indians and lightning could and did set fire to the dead grass and strawfall and the material was ready to burn expanses hundreds of miles in extent any time after frost and in the summer if it had not burned the previous year. Fires offered no threat to the life or property of the Indian for they were not forest fires but merely grass fires that cleared the undergrowth of grass and hardwoods, making travel easy as it does today. No roads or fields were in the way and fire could go across or around the head of small streams until it reached large river courses or was rained out. In the year 1773 the famous botanist William Bartram traveled with the Indians over much the same trail as De Soto from South Carolina to the Mississippi River and gave detailed descriptions of the long-leaf pine country. He speaks repeatedly of the open pine forests, describes Indians chasing deer on horseback through the woods and says of Indians setting fires: ". . . which happens almost every day throughout the year, in some part or other, by the Indians, for the purpose of rousing game, as also by the lightning. The very upper surface of the earth being mixed with the ashes of burnt vegetables, renders it of sufficient strength or fertility to clothe itself perfectly with a very great variety of grasses. The cattle were as large and fat as those of the rich grazing pastures of Moyomensing . . ." Thus two hundred years after De Soto, the Indians were still burning the grass and the white men, no doubt continued the practice directly after them. [Pp. 583–584]

Mr. Greene states his case strongly and convincingly. The sur-prise is that the influence of fires in the southern woods was not recognized and documented earlier. No anthropologist, to my knowledge, has recognized the great importance of fires set by Indians in determining the type of vegetation found in the South-east. Certainly, if Mr. Greene's theory is correct, some recognition should have been given the Indians as an ecological force by the specialists in Indian cultures and history. Does Mr. Greene stand alone?

Without mentioning the article "The Forest That Fire Made" or Mr. Greene, H. H. Chapman of the Yale School of Forestry, presented the same idea in 1932 in an article entitled "Is the Long-Leaf Type a Climax?" in *Ecology*. Chapman said: "The conclusion that the species owed its existence and survival to fires and would disappear were it not for the continuance of fire was definitely stated by Mrs. Ellen Call Long in 1888 and by Dr. Roland M. Harper in 1911–13 (p. 331). Chapman had been experimenting for fifteen years and presented the results of his experiments to substantiate the thesis that fire is essential to the maintenance of the long-leaf pine. His experiments indicated that burning at two- to three-year intervals was better than annual burning.

The statement of Michaux, made in 1802, took on more meaning after the results of modern experiments were obtained. He said of the Carolinas and Georgia: "Seven-tenths of the country are covered with pines of one species, or *Pinus palustris* . . . These . . . are not damaged by the fire that they make here annually in the woods, at the commencement of spring to burn the grass and other plants that the frost has killed" (p. 301). Michaux added that the oaks which came up among the pines were "only fit to burn."

Of course, Weaver and Clements had recognized that fire was important in the southern pines before Greene and Chapman published the studies quoted. Tracy had clearly described the open woodlands of the Gulf Coast as having "very little undergrowth" in 1898 (pp. 1–15), but he did not mention fire. Ashe recognized in 1915 that fire was an essential factor in the production of loblolly pine in North Carolina. It has been, however, in the last twenty years, since the article of Greene, that data have been amassed to give complete and irrefutable evidence that the long-leaf forest was fire-made and is fire-maintained. In addition to the references cited, I reviewed thirty-five articles, all reporting results of controlled experiments which support the general thesis presented by Greene.

Professor H. H. Chapman, who became Dean of Yale's School of Forestry, continued his experimentation and wrote thirteen articles explaining the best methods for producing long-leaf pine. In a second article in 1932, published in the *Journal of Forestry*, he concluded: ". . . if complete fire protection must be enforced . . . the long-leaf pine will disappear as a species" (p. 603).

It is from the region of the southern woods that we get some of our most convincing evidence of aboriginal influence on the soil. Ecologists will admit, as do Weaver and Clements, that "vegetation has played a remarkable role in the formation" of soil (p. 173), yet their research reports so greatly emphasize the part played by soil in determining plant growth that one gets the impression that they forget in their actual work their own statements that vegetation plays a part in soil formation. Wackerman may serve as an example, for, speaking in 1929 of the prairies in Arkansas and Louisiana, he remarked that the "natives long resident in the country, say that the prairies have grown noticeably smaller within memory", yet he attributed the presence of these prairies to poor drainage of the soil (p. 731).

Heyward offers data of vital importance to an understanding of the relation between soil and vegetation. He found, in 1937, that "the greatest percentage of long-leaf pine forest soils is morphologically more similar to grasslands soils than the forest soils." Heyward thought this unusual phenomenon was directly due to the effect of frequent fires. Of equal importance were Heyward's data establishing the fact that in the Southern Woodland "ten years' protection from burning changes the character of the soil" (pp. 23, 27). Billings reviewed the literature on the subject, especially analyses conducted in Switzerland and Estonia as well as in the United States, which agreed with his own research; and, in 1941, he presented quantitative correlations showing that plant cover determines the type of soil.

In spite of these findings and many others regarding the fertility of frequently burned prairie soils, Wilde, writing in 1946 on "Forest Soils and Forest Growth" and referring specifically to the Atlantic Coastal Plains of America, said: "Aside from the fire hazard, burning of forest floor is objectionable because it results in a total loss of the most valuable fertilizer ingredients, nitrogen . . . These ill effects of burning have been emphasized by many writers (p. 153). It should be noted that such ideas have been "emphasized" without sound experimental support. The studies by Heyward and Billings mentioned above, and others, including that of Bruce, made in 1951 (pp. 25–28), provide sound facts with which to refute the facile deduction that burning harms the soil.

The Indians said they burned off the fields and forests to improve the availability of game, and early travelers observed all types of wild animals and birds in greater abundance on the open grasslands than in the thick forests. The proponents of complete forest-fire prevention have taken the opposite side. The wildlife organizations have been convinced that all forest and grass fires damage wild life and reduce game animals. Sportsmen have been sold on the idea that absolute fire prevention is best. Neither the Indians nor the country folk in the southern states have agreed with this, and the later have clung to aboriginal notions that woods-burning improves hunting. Knowing the popular belief that has been built up by extensive, well-financed, long-term publicity against fires, it is surprising to find Mr. Stoddard's report of 1935, thoroughly documented, establishing that periodic controlled burning in the southeastern upland has a "demonstrated value" in game management. Not only grazing game are aided, but mention is made of increased population of wild turkey, quail, and other wild life in burned-over areas, as compared to areas protected from fire (pp. 346–350).

The southeastern portion of the Eastern Woodland vegetation and culture area is unique in providing modern experimental data to verify the correctness of the Indians' theories presented to justify their culture pattern of periodically setting fire to the grasslands and forests. Experimental studies have further demonstrated that the southern pine forest as a type must have been established by Indians, by means of fire, and that its continuation depends on continued frequent burning. The peculiarities of the major southern pine tree, the long-leaf, which have allowed it to become dominant because of the periodic burning over extended periods of time, raises an important question which the foresters have only partially answered. Vestal, in 1931, raised the question in an offhand way, when he expressed doubt that fire determined the composition of southern pine forests and he wrote: "Furthermore, if fire is a constantly recurring condition in a certain climate, then it is a feature of that climate, and as expectable as rainfall, though far more irregular" (p. 236). Unfortunately neither anthropologists, foresters, botanists, nor ecologists have placed fire on an equal footing with moisture, wind, elevation, or soil as an important causative factor to be carefully evaluated, past and present, in order to understand the vegetation of a region, large or small.

Professor Chapman restated this general thesis in 1947, but greatly diminished the force of his otherwise excellent pronouncement by minimizing the extent of vegetation-burning by Indians. He said:

Natural areas (in southeastern states) . . . consist first of such old growth as might be capable of preservation, and which should be burned over every two to five years to perpetuate the conditions which Ponce de Leon found in his first trip, and to secure naturally grouped reproduction. . . . If fire is kept out, the whole character of the long-leaf forest undergoes a complete change.

The forester in his praiseworthy desire to improve upon nature for the production of desired species, quality and volume, may frequently fail dismally in the outcome by actually going against the most deep-seated natural laws — laws which gave rise to different species and attuned them each to a niche in the environment. Those niches are the result of the recurrence of fire, wind, insects, and disease; as well as the fertility and moisture content of soils, climate, and the inflammability of ground cover and brush. [P. 193]

It was undoubtedly because Chapman did not know that forest- and grass-burning was a general American Indian habit that he weakened his statement by adding, "Actually, we started out in this country with the entire continent as a great natural area, modified only slightly by man by the Indian habit of burning the woods" (pp. 193–194).

Here Chapman falls into the almost universal error of ecologists, which is to limit one's deductions as to the influence of aboriginal burning to a small area. If Chapman had known that the northern part of the Eastern Woodland had been subjected to fires as had the southern part, that plains and prairies had been constantly fired by Indians, and that the mountains and valleys of the West had been regularly subjected to fire, I doubt that he would have said the continent had been "modified only slightly . . . by the Indian habit of burning." Chapman himself proved that Indian fires in the southern pine forest made the forest what it was. Indian fires made Virginian and Kentucky landscapes what they were. There is ample evidence that Indian fires made prairies and plains what they were when first viewed by Europeans. The facts from each area must be used for a full understanding of the forces which determined the vegetation in all other areas.

Chapman's error in properly evaluating the full influence of Indian burning of fields and forests appears to stem also from another failure very common among ecologists — the failure to appreciate the length of time man has occupied this hemisphere. That this is true of Chapman is clear from his article entitled "Lightning in the Long-Leaf," published in 1950 (pp. 10–12). He so clearly realized that the growth habits of the long-leaf pine were unusually well adapted to surviving frequent fires that he made the wise suggestion that we have here a plant that has made a fundamental genetic, probably evolutionary, adjustment to fire. This appears to be a valid conclusion, for there is no doubt of the long-leaf pine's excellent adaptation to survive being burned to the ground several times and then to produce quickly a remarkably large and healthy tree. The weakness in Chapman's argument lies in attributing the burning to which the long-leaf had to adjust exclusively to lightning fires.

Admitting our almost complete lack of knowledge of the time required for plants to accommodate themselves to particular environmental conditions, Chapman's conclusion that the long-leaf adjusted to "lightning fires, starting millions of years ago" and continuing to the present, appears weak because it does not take into consideration the comparative influence of lightning fires in other areas. If lightning fires were to have a special, unusual influence in the southern pine forest as compared with other forests, one would expect to find an exceptionally large number of fires started by lightning in the area. Chapman tells us that between

1940 and 1947 there were 612 fires attributed to lightning in the forests of Alabama, Florida, Louisiana, Mississippi, and Texas. That is a very small number if compared with 4,410 lightning fires for California for only one year, 1947, or California's yearly average of lightning-caused fires, 1943–1947, of 4,829. There are more fires in the southern states than in the rest of the nation. For 1930 the South had 90 per cent of the 190,000 forest fires that occurred in the United States. Wackerman reported that only 1 per cent of the fires in the South were caused by lightning (1939, p. 63). Of California's recorded forest fires from 1911 to 1920, 41.5 per cent were started by lightning. Compare the 1 per cent of the fires by lightning in the southern states with these figures from the 1949 Department of Agriculture Yearbook (p. 25): Rocky Mountains, 70 per cent of fires started by lightning; Northwest, 50 per cent of fires started by lightning; California, 23 per cent of fires started by lightning. With these data before us, it is difficult to justify the unusual development of fire resistance in the long-leaf pine as a response to lightning fires.

But is it necessary to postulate that "millions of years" were necessary for the evolution to take place? Would not "thousands of years" be enough? No one knows. By guessing that ten to twenty-five thousand years would have been sufficient for the remarkable adaptation of the long-leaf pine, we can assume that the adjustment was to man-made fires. The Vero and Melbourne (Florida) sites, at which human skeletons were in association with mastodon bones, suggests that the southeastern section of the Eastern Woodland area has been inhabited as long as any of the New World. If it were thought that a hundred thousand years were required for evolutionary development of long-leaf pine peculiarities, it could be taken as support for the authenticity of the Abilene flints, placed in the third interglacial.

In any event, by recognizing that man has occupied the New World for at least ten thousand years, that he has been here probably twenty-five thousand years, and possibly one hundred thousand years, and by admitting the probability that during his entire history here he has set fire to vegetation, we can account for such adaptations as that of the long-leaf pine. This time-perspective permits an understanding of many ecological adjustments otherwise impossible to comprehend.

The materials I have presented establish that aboriginal man has had a tremendous and decisive influence on several aspects of his physical environment. Our knowledge of such effect is far from complete because anthropologists, to a large degree, have assumed that though natives adjusted to their environment, they did not change the physical world sufficiently to warrant careful investigation. It is time that anthropologists revised their thinking on this matter. The evidence others have collected now makes it mandatory that we start with the assumption that nearly every area in the world has been modified by ancient man. Wherever and whenever man has occupied a region, the chances are that the flora, fauna, climate, and soil have responded to culture in some measurable and important manner. A half million years of the use of fire must be evaluated. Since it is now clear that setting fire to plant cover is a universal culture pattern, it is imperative that the fire factor be fully weighed along with geographic influence in order to arrive at a proper appreciation of the relation of man to nature. It is time for ethnologists to contribute their proper share to the understanding of the interrelations between primitive man and his physical environment.

A RELATED BEHAVIORAL FIELD, SOCIOLOGY

by RAYMOND V. BOWERS

Research Methodology in Sociology:
The First Half-Century

A RECAPITULATION of the methodological progress and problems of a science is perhaps of periodic use, particularly in a young science and at a time when the demand for scientific contributions to the national welfare and security is at its highest peak in history. The objective here is not, however, an exhaustive critique of individual methods. Such could not be accomplished in a single paper and cannot, in any case, be accomplished properly because of the inadequacy of most methodological reporting. It is, instead, an attempt to focus on major trends and some of the general problems still to be resolved — a view of the forest rather than the trees. The discussion is centered in four topics: (1) the occasions for research; (2) the design of research; (3) the resort to observation; (4) readiness for the job ahead.

It has been only slightly more than half a century since the first issue of the first wholly sociological journal was published, and

NOTE. This is a condensation and revision of a paper presented before the American Sociological Society, 28 December 1947. It was prepared at the request of President Louis Wirth as a status report on the field of research methods, but was withheld from publication by the author at that time in order to augment certain sections. In preparing it for publication now, the author wishes to acknowledge his debt to Professor Wallis for orientation into many of the basic methodological issues of the behavioral sciences.

A number of sociologists were circularized for comments of relevance to this paper, and their contributions are gratefully acknowledged. The word "research" is used throughout in its broadest sense, as including "basic research," "applied research," "development," "operational research," etc.

that date is perhaps as relevant a reference point as any for this methodological survey. In the editorial foreword to this first issue of the *American Journal of Sociology*, in July 1895, Albion W. Small gave some advice to his readers which turned out to be prophetic of the main trend of sociology in the intervening years. He said: ". . . precisely because permanent enlargement of human welfare is not a matter of shreds and patches . . . the program most directly adapted to the furtherance of that end is suppression of the riot of imagination and substitution of the order of investigation." This trend toward "the order of investigation" has been accompanied by an increasing interest in methodological matters, including not only the techniques by which empirical research is accomplished but also the logic underlying the process itself.

That this methodological interest has, at times, seemed to become an end in itself and to have too completely suppressed "the riot of imagination" should be noted, as should the rather heated methodological issues that have dotted the years. But such manifestations were to be expected, owing to the speed with which the substitution was taking place and to the tremendous backlog of research problems and data waiting to be exploited, a context which tended to yield rewards for unstructured description and *ad hoc* interpretation more readily than for efforts towards greater methodological elegance.

THE OCCASIONS FOR SOCIOLOGICAL RESEARCH

The major occasions for research in any science are to refine knowledge and to resolve practical problems through the application of such knowledge. In actuality, however, the practical problems have often — perhaps usually — been the prime impetus to research, the necessity for their solution being the major stimulus to the development of more useful knowledge and the techniques for producing it. As the same first issue of the *American Journal of Sociology* put it in 1895:

It is a very callow sociologist who imagines that he and his collaborers are inventing the subject matter of a new science. They are trying to perfect means of answering obtrusive questions about society which the ordinary man is proposing every hour. They are not creating but merely representing popular curiosity. Life is so much more real to the people than to the schools that the people are no sooner possessed of some of the tools of thought and some means of observation, than they proceed to grapple with more vital questions than the scholars have raised. Hence, social philosophies popular in source, partial in content, but potent in political effect, get vogue before scholars know the terms of the conditions which these rule-of-thumb philosophies claim to explain. The doctrines of professional sociologists are attempting to substitute revised second thought for the hasty first thoughts composing the popular sociologies in which busy men outside the schools utter their impressions.

In the half century since this statement was made, sociologists have functioned in a world of incredible change and crises and of increasing public concern over them, including the most serious depression in our history and the two most destructive wars. This, in turn, has led to a greatly increased need for a more useful understanding of society and to techniques for acquiring it. However, it is probably correct to say that the sociological bases for action have been more extended than refined during this period. The vogue has been to explore new sources of data and thus add to the horizontal surface of the science rather than to increase its vertical dimension by digging increasingly deeper into fields whose sod had been turned. Some of the reasons for this — and they are not confined to sociology during this period nor are they characteristic of all sociological research — are not hard to discover. The chief reason is that sociologists and others whose training was primarily in the humanities were not well trained for scientific research. This training, coupled with the growing reaction against the "riot of imagination" it represented, made them fertile soil for the lure of a radical empiricism which encouraged the unstructured collection of "facts" almost as an end in itself. Heavy teaching responsibilities and the nearly total lack of research funds or facilities provided additional incentives to accept the "horizontal" solution. Under such conditions the consolidation of isolated generalizations into the beginnings of a systematic theory, the integration of such theory with research, and the coordination of research activities concerned with common problems were generally underemphasized. There has, however, been a notable increase in attention to these basic matters in the past few years. To exploit more fully in the future the occasions for research in sociology, two main challenges are evident:

1. We shall have to place greater emphasis on the consolidation of our empirical findings. This will involve, at its simplest, what Lazarsfeld has called "codification," the development of hypotheses which contain a relationship common to empirical generalizations in apparently different spheres of behavior. It will involve, at its most difficult, the construction of systematic theory with its ancillary semantic and syntactical considerations. The need for such consolidations has been increasingly pointed out in recent years. It is time that we rewarded those contributing to this vertical dimension of sociology equivalently to those interested in expanding the empirical base. Through their efforts we shall begin to put our conceptual house in order, and thus provide the basis for research directed at the testing of hypotheses systematically related to the body of existing sociological knowledge, an occasion for research which has lain relatively fallow so far. In this way we shall dig continually deeper into the complexity of social life.[1]

2. We must also become more sensitive to the opportunities for applying our results to problem situations, and must learn how to do this engineering type of job. There has, of course, been notable recent progress in this *rapprochement* between the research sociologist and the administrator, in both government and business. Moreover, support for such participation is coming from many directions. An early post-war statement by the eminent scientific and educational administrator, James B. Conant, may be cited: "In my belief the methods of certain of the social sciences have already been developed to a point where studies of society

---

[1] The subject of this paragraph has been discussed so frequently in recent years as to preclude extensive citation. However, the various aspects of the problem are admirably covered in the writings of Dodd, Lazarsfeld, Merton, Parsons, and Shils. See also R. M. Williams, 1947; Bowers, 1936.

by competent scholars can provide basic information to assist the leaders of industry and of education. Both fundamental investigations as to the nature of man and society, and immediate studies of specific problems, are required. . . . In particular, certain types of work in sociology, anthropology and social psychology seem full of promise. The point of view of the younger men in these fields, if coupled with practical experience with industry on the one hand, or public education on the other, and infused with a zeal to move American society along its historic road, we believe might be peculiarly effective at this moment in our history."[2]

That these behavioral sciences are entering an era of great research possibilities is beyond question. But to make the most of it, we shall have to pay closer attention to the systematization of our research findings, and to the gearing of "engineering" efforts to administrative need.

THE DESIGN OF RESEARCH

The successful exploitation of these occasions for research will depend in good measure on our attention to research design, i.e., the methodological plan by which the research worker attacks his problem. During the past fifty years there has been considerable groping in sociology for useful designs.[3] The absence of acceptable research traditions in our own past and the presence around us of formal experimental models in other fields have provided both motivation for this quest and some confusion in its pursuit. The result so far has been a wide range of tactics and considerable disagreement as to their merits, the range extending from the approach of the single worker who claims only to describe what he sees, to a research team's testing a battery of hypotheses under conditions approximating experimental control.

[2] Conant, 1947. Statements by sociologists concerning these "applied" activities include: Leighton, 1945; Mann and Likert, 1952; R. M. Williams, Jr., 1953; Russell Sage Foundation, Annual Report 1951–1952; *Philosophy of Science*, Vol. 16, No. 3, 1949 (articles by Hauser, Merton, and Shils); and Russell Sage Foundation, *Effective Use of Social Science Research in the Federal Services*, 1950.
[3] Chapin, 1947; Stouffer, 1948; Stouffer, 1950 (Vols. 3 & 4); Blumer, 1939; Merton and Lazarsfeld, 1950.

This range is, of course, due in part to the variety of research goals sociologists have followed: taxonomy has proceeded along with the testing of hypotheses, and both have been contemporary with considerable sheer curiosity. It is also in part due to the variety of subjects sociologists have chosen for study; the carefully reported vignette of an unusual case of social isolation obviously requires a different research design from work on the prediction of marital success. However, a factor of considerable importance has been a basic difference of opinion regarding research strategy, some maintaining that greater precision in research design is needed before we can effectively add to our understanding of society, others that greater understanding is needed before precision is appropriate. This issue has tended to become so involved in philosophies of science, status systems, and slogans that we have at times lost sight of the common objectives and have been unable to see the similarities for the claimed differences. It is obvious that research design must include both precision and understanding, but this does not mean that all problems at any one time can or should be approached with the same emphasis. Emphasis on precision may as justifiably be the main approach to a particular demographic problem at the present time as it would be premature in an exploratory study of the social factors in neurosis.

The scientists' research tactics are a complex and creative matter. Their defense lies in their efficiency to produce results. There are, however, certain criteria which constitute necessary, although not necessarily sufficient, guides to good designs, and which are becoming increasingly used in sociological research. These are:

1. *The criterion of research feasibility.* Every research venture is a risk of time and effort. Hence, it should be as calculated a risk as possible, as there are few who wish to waste their time exploring — or building — blind alleys. As Donald Young (1941) has said: "Research feasibility should be tested by examination of the adequacy of (a) the available data, (b) the existing or potential personnel, (c) the applicable research techniques, and (d) the foundation of prerequisite knowledge on which to build. But existing inadequacy," he continues, "should not be considered a

final barrier to work until it has been determined that the deficiency cannot be remedied." Such a determination requires, admittedly, a number of difficult judgments. It should, however, operate among qualified researchers to provide rough estimates of the probability of successfully accomplishing a given research objective, although it is recognized that this is probably more true of applied than of basic research. Hence, if for reasons such as a national emergency it becomes necessary or advisable to apply our knowledge to relatively new problems, the criterion of feasibility would provide an appraisal of expected success and thus minimize the dangers of either over-selling or under-selling our capabilities.

2· *The criterion of explicit formulation of research objectives.* A major consideration in any research design is the explicit formulation of the objective in the detail necessary for developing the design and executing the research. It is becoming increasingly recognized that the measure of the productivity of a research project is determined in large part at this stage, for it is here that previous knowledge can most effectively be brought to bear on the new problem. The probability is high that those who have only a vague understanding of what they are after at the beginning of a project will have an equally vague understanding of what they get at the end. Sociologists have not, however, generally shown sufficient patience with this criterion. We have been too much impressed by the occasional appearance of useful unexpected results in other fields, and have too often overlooked the planning that has almost always preceded such discoveries.

A careful formulation of what one is looking for will determine, in great measure, the specific nature of one's observational devices and the nature of the analysis. Each interview question, for example, and each analytical table will have roots in the research objective, designed to throw light on a research hypothesis. When the objective is not carefully elaborated at the beginning of the study, the selection of observational devices and analytical tools tends to become an independent occasion of planning, i.e., of rethinking and at times unwittingly revising the objectives. The planning judgments in such cases are scattered through the course of the study, are not assembled on the bases of consistency, relevance, etc. It is obvious that if the researcher feels unable to settle such basic matters at the beginning of a study, he is no more likely to be able to settle them in the middle of it or at its end.

Such searching analysis of one's objective, and the careful formulation of its implications in the light of existing knowledge, are hard work. But they constitute a major difference between scientific and prescientific investigation. Fortunately there is an increasing recognition of this in sociology.

3. *The criterion of methodological explicitness.* There is also increasing recognition that it is necessary to record as explicitly as possible all operations involved in executing the research that have a bearing on the outcome. This is important for two reasons: (a) These methodological operations, together with the research objective, constitute the matrix in which the results have been forged and with reference to which they have determinate meaning. To understand the results, and hence to permit their further test and verification, require a knowledge of the process by which they were produced. (b) By recording relevant operations, research experience can more adequately be reviewed, appraised, and shared with others. As a science matures and research procedures are standardized, this job is, of course, simplified. In sociology it should be given increasing attention.

4. *The criterion of specifying the research outcome.* Presumably results are the aim of research — a new item of knowledge, a new methodological tool, or a technique for resolving practical problems. The objective has raised questions, and the methodological design has selected and funneled empirical data appropriate to these questions. The researcher's job is not over until he has made the most of this activity. In some research this may be relatively easy, since the situation is so structured that a "yes" or "no" answer is possible. In sociology this is not often the case. We have to deal with small differences, low correlations, exceptions, and unanticipated odds and ends. The inclination has too often been to tell others to make the most of them. It is obvious, however,

that no one is in a more strategic spot to appraise the results than the researcher himself. His responsibility cannot end at hurried cataloguing of his results. He must come to his most considered judgment as to their significance in the light of his research operations and his professional background. He must tell what the study failed to accomplish as well as what he thinks it accomplished, and both must be stated in as precise, formal terms as the context permits. Furthermore, he has the responsibility of reporting hunches as to why the results were inconclusive and of suggesting more appropriate methods for future research.

In summary, it may be stated that sociologists during the past half century have shown notable progress in the field of research design.[4] We inherited a tradition of grand concern over large topics in which the end far overshadowed the means for attaining it. We have corrected this scientific imbalance, but in doing so we have sometimes lost sight of the end in our experimentation with means. It is now time that we place as much emphasis on our research objectives and on the outcome of our research as on the methods by which the objectives are implemented and the outcome reached.

THE RESULT OF OBSERVATION

The resort to highly disciplined forms of observation is the distinctive mark of the scientist. During the past fifty years sociologists and other behavioral scientists have made notable progress in pursuing this methodological goal, their attention being increasingly turned to problems of sampling, the selection of items to be observed, the consistency of response, observer bias, and the other factors involved in reliable and valid observation.[5]

[4] With reference to this point it is suggested that the student of sociological history would find it profitable to compare the research articles in the 1952 issues of the *American Sociological Review* with their predecessors of twenty-five and fifty years ago in the *American Journal of Sociology.*

[5] The range and depth of the contributions to these topics over the years are partially indicated by the following: Stouffer *et al.*, 1948–1950; Festinger and Katz, 1953; Dollard, 1935; Thomas, Loomis, and Arrington, 1933; Chapple and Arensberg, 1940; Kluckhohn, 1940; Moreno, 1953; Chapin, 1947; Lynd and Lynd, 1929; Thomas and Znaniecki, 1918; Rice, 1931.

In principle the problems of observation in social science are not basically different from those in other sciences. In practice, however, there are a number of considerations which continue to make the social scientist's research job one of great difficulty. In formulating his research questions, the social scientist has his professional knowledge to draw on, but he must cope, somewhat more than the natural scientist, with the intervening variables of his life history, deeply entrenched thought-ways and personality syndromes, because these concern his relations to people much more than to the nonsocial components of the environment. Secondly, in observing the actions of human beings, the social scientist is confronted not only with the nonverbal type of behavior available to other scientists but the additional dimensions of verbal behavior and documentary records. That is, he has to deal with what men say and write as well as what they do, and with the unique problem of the relations between them. Thirdly, in his relation to his observational field, the social scientist has somewhat greater difficulty playing the role of the objective manipulator because he is likely to be a participant in an interpersonal situation with research subjects that have independent powers to react significantly for or against the purposes of the study. Finally, in recording the events of his observational field, the social scientist has to cope, again somewhat more than other scientists, with the scientifically irrelevant intercessions of his personal patterns of thought and attitude, for these are more selectively attentive and inattentive to social events than to others and affect the recording of what is observed.

These important facts of life for the social researcher may be challenges rather than unmanageable barriers, and, in some cases, such as the availability of verbal and recorded behavior, have advantages unavailable to other scientists, but they are factors to be considered and solved. The library researcher or the analyst of a social agency's records or the manipulator of statistical series has not avoided these issues. He has merely avoided first-hand implication in them. Buried in these documents are the interpersonal responses and the cultural and psychological interventions of others. Since increasing attention in modern social research has been directed at these problems, let us now turn to the general nature of the solutions that are being developed.

Scientific observation, i.e., observation which is relevant and repeatable, requires that (1) the observational field be delimited, (2) the desired objects of observation be made available, and (3) the observer be prepared to observe them as accurately as possible. Each of these phases is a complex matter.

1. The delimitation of the observational field is obviously a derivative of the study's objective. A study of population growth involves a different field from one of morale. However, it is the more specific, delimitating decisions that constitute the first two important problems for sociological observation: selection of the items of behavior to be observed, and selection of the individuals or groups on whom the observations are to be made. In other words, the problem "What observations on what people?" is the basic one, and the decisions made at this point not only have some effect on the reliability of the study's results but determine their validity for the stated objective.

It is the selection of the specific items to be observed — the referents, for example, of the questions in a test or question-naire — that determines the validity of the observations, their relevance to the objective of the study. All other observational matters — the selection of the individuals or groups to be observed and the controls over them and over the observers — concern obser-vational reliability. This is said, at the risk of stressing the methodologically obvious, because sociological research has made much greater strides in handling reliability than validity and has at times displayed a tendency to find excessive solace in measures of reliability alone.

In general, the selection process represents the researcher's judgment that the items are representative of the types or uni-verses of data specified in the terms and relations of his formulated problem or hypotheses. In the early stages of any field such judg-ments are necessarily informal and intuitive, as the universes are themselves unclear. As experience accumulates, the universes become better defined and the problem of typical instances becomes a matter of more general agreement. Today high-school students can make such selections unerringly in many scientific experiments that were beyond the capability of the experts not so long ago.

In the behavioral sciences, there is growing clarification of many observational universes, but the selection of representative items is still subject to considerable variation, as can be seen by comparing interview schedules, questionnaires, tests, or scales presumably designed to obtain data for the same or comparable objectives (social status, morale, marital adjustment, etc.). Individual researchers vary considerably in their judgments as to the most useful data to collect. Recognition of this has led to much concern over corrective "validating" devices of a *post hoc* character.

Such checks have generally been of two kinds: those confined to an internal analysis of the data (tests of internal consistency, etc.) and those relating the data to external criteria presumably having some more known or accepted connection with the problem in hand. The former assist in determining whether an item yields data from the same universe as other items in the observational design, and whether it yields such data efficiently enough to remain in the design. The latter attempts to test whether the items are, in fact, a part of the universe presumably under study. The usefulness of such devices at the present stage of the behavioral sciences is unquestioned. However, the emphasis given them has tended to draw attention from the more fundamental problem of the original selection of the items for which they constitute the *post hoc*, "validating" check. That is to say, such checks have been interpreted by some as the primary means of selecting items, overlooking the fact that their function is not to initiate judgments concerning the selection of data but to comment on them, to make uncertainty more credible in undeveloped areas of social research. Thus, as our knowledge of our subject matter increases and provides a sounder basis for predesigning our observational instruments, the usefulness of such *post hoc* checks must diminish. Moreover, their current use should not deflect our attention from the basic task of improving the original selection of items in even the most undeveloped areas.[6]

The selection of the individuals or groups on which observations are to be made has been for most research workers during this period a problem of relatively less concern than the one just discussed. This has been due in part to the "practical" necessity of taking what is available within given limitations of time and money. Nevertheless, an increasing interest in formal research designs and statistical analysis has brought sampling procedures into greater vogue, and this has stimulated concern over the problem of representativeness in other types of research. This is, however, a new frontier and will require much patient and skilled attention, even though, as Deming (1944) and others have pointed out, sampling errors are only one of a number of sources of error in social studies and are perhaps small in comparison.

One of the chief problems in the development of appropriate sampling designs is a lack of knowledge of the social universes to be sampled. This lack has led at times to an unreasoning dependence on every nth case or on known demographic factors as principles of stratification. These expedients have already been questioned by some, who claim that such samples have little relation to the way society (i.e., the social universe) is structured and hence are inappropriate for much social research. Others go so far as to question the extent to which the assumptions of mathematical sampling are ever met within social universes. Such questioning is healthy if out of it comes increased interest in finding more adequate bases for sampling social situations.[7]

2. Structuring the observational situation also involves controls over what is to be observed. In studies dealing with people at first hand, the first such control is the important matter of "rapport," or obtaining the respondent's cooperation while being watched, tested, interviewed, circularized by mail, etc. The importance of such factors as the auspices of the observer, differences in such characteristics as age, sex, race, and social status between

[6] Mosier, 1947; Bowers, 1936.
[7] McCormick, 1945; Lee, 1947.

interviewer and respondent, the type of covering letter in mailed schedules, etc., is discussed in the literature. Kluckhohn's statement concerning rapport in anthropological field work is particularly fruitful to the student observing his own kind of people, who may be inclined to overlook the complexity and importance of this problem.[8] Increasingly thoughtful analyses of field experience are being shared with the profession.[9] Interview manuals prepared by research organizations provide practical suggestions based on extensive experience. The literature of social work is likewise rich in experience with this problem. But much systematic experimentation needs still to be undertaken.

A second type of control over the observational field is the various means of manipulating the situation to produce the desired observations and to reduce unwanted response variability. There are two methods: by the use of environmental controls, either artificial, as exemplified by experimental group situations, or natural, such as "before and after" studies;[10] and/or by manipulating the stimulus situation by asking predesigned questions, using predesigned tests, etc. Much productive attention has been directed at such controls of the stimulus situation. Level of language, order of questions, stimulus uniformity, degree of directness, etc. have been increasingly discussed. A whole literature is developing around such topics, for example, as nondirective interviewing or sociometric tests. But it is well to realize that such methodological developments are still in their infancy.

Such growing restrictions on the observational situation have their opponents, who complain that the richness of reality is being strait-jacketed. This is, of course, true, but it is irrelevant. Asking specific questions of nature and structuring the observational field to get as specific answers as possible are the method of science, and sociologists are developing means of so structuring the observational situation that they can ask increasingly specific and pertinent questions and get increasingly useful answers.

[8] Gottschalk, Kluckhohn, and Angell, 1945.
[9] Leighton, 1945; Gardner and Whyte, 1947; Merton, 1947.
[10] Greenwood, 1945; Chapin, 1947.

3. Structuring the observational situation also involves controls over the observer, i.e., techniques which will increase observer reliability and reduce observer distortion, for human observation is an interpretative process, the translation of stimuli in a setting filled with the well-worn paths and well-structured road blocks of the life history. Interviewer bias, for example, is well recognized, and increasing precautions are being taken by opinion-survey groups and others to curtail it,[11] but much more needs to be known about the personality and social coordinates of observers before bias can be understood and systematically corrected or adjusted for in the analysis. It is, of course, unrealistic to expect completely unbiased observers; the problem is rather one of reducing biases as much as possible, and developing means of taking them into consideration as do samplers in their use of biased samples.

Attempts to determine observer error have taken many forms. Two or more observers have been assigned to the same observational situation, or one observer has repeated his observations, or the results of each of a group of observers of comparable situations have been compared, or a written interview record has been compared with a mechanical recording of the interview, and so on. Every study should include some analysis of observer error and the results should be made available to the reader.

Attempts to reduce observer error have also taken many forms. All of them may be said to be aimed at making the observer's job more definite and explicit and at reducing the number and importance of the decisions he is required to make in the process of observation. This is accomplished by greater emphasis on research design and planning, particularly the more careful specification of objectives, the delimitation of the observational field, and better observer training. These increase the observer's research motivation, provide him with a more definite mission, and make him more conscious of good practice in performing the mission.

[11] The Social Science Research Council has, for some time, been sponsoring a major project on the isolation, measurement, and control of interviewer effect. The work has been carried out by the National Opinion Research Center, and much of it has appeared in periodical form. A final report is scheduled for early publication.

In summary, in this discussion of factors involved in structuring the observational situation so that more valid and reliable observations may be made, we have purposely centered the discussion on the functional components of the process rather than the various types of observational devices. Questionnaires, interview schedules, field manuals, biogram outlines, tests and scales of all sorts are simply combinations of questions to reach a research objective. They help structure the observational field. In all these devices the important problems are their validity for the objective and their efficiency in extracting the desired responses reliably. However, these matters are still only part of the observational problem. Of equal importance are other types of stage-managing leading to the cooperation of those under observation and to the reduction of bias in the observer. Despite our recognition of these problems, they still remain a relatively new frontier of methodological skill.

READINESS FOR THE JOB AHEAD

So far we have been concerned with the trend of sociology toward an empirical orientation and some quality factors in social-research techniques. But these considerations would not be complete without reference to such quantity factors as the personnel, facilities, and organization required to put the techniques to their most effective use. How ready are we to handle the magnitude of the job ahead?[12]

It is now evident that the rapid changes and recurrent crises of the twentieth century have not only stimulated the growth of the social sciences but have provided increasing occasions for their application outside the universities. That this process has undoubtedly been accelerated by the high prestige of the other sciences in contemporary affairs, providing coattails on which we have possibly ridden faster than our performance alone would warrant, should not be overlooked. However, the situation remains that government and industry are becoming increasingly good customers of social-science skills.

The growing dependence on science in recent years is mirrored

[12] Hauser, 1946; Taylor, 1946.

in the growth of research budgets from $166,000,000 in 1930 to approximately $3,000,000,000 in 1952, and in the increasing sponsorship of research by the public at large through the Federal Government. For even though the three major sources of research moneys (industry, government, and the university-foundation institutions) have all greatly expanded their support since 1930, the proportion borne by the government has increased from 15% to 56%, while the proportion supported by industry has decreased from 70% to 40%, and that by universities and foundations from 15% to 4%. Despite this shift, however, it is interesting to note that the same percentage of the totals (10%) has continued to be spent in the universities, indicating that university research facilities have continued to expand with the research tide, although to an increasing extent under the new auspices of government and industry. In 1952 the government alone obligated $90,000,000 to university research contracts and grants.[13]

Separate data for the social sciences are not available, but they are known to follow the upward trend. Since 1947 the military research program, which has been the most generous new sponsor of social-science research, has increased its social-science funds from practically nothing to several million dollars in 1952. Other new government programs such as those of the National Institutes of Health and the Department of State have also entered the field, as have new programs sponsored by the business community and such new agencies as the Ford Foundation. In the case of the social sciences, however, a much higher percentage of these funds has undoubtedly gone to the universities, probably more than 50% as compared to the 10% for all research funds.

This rapid increase in social-science research funds has, however, been accompanied by growing concern over the capability of the social sciences to absorb them, and this fact, coupled with increasing competition for the taxpayer's research dollar, has already (1953) led to recessions in government support. This should be only a temporary loss, but it raises important questions

[13] Scott, ed., 1952; Research and Development Board and Bureau of Labor Statistics, 1953, *Industrial Research and Development*.

as to our current readiness for the responsibility others are thrusting upon us. On the surface, at least, the problem appears primarily a quantitative one — a shortage of qualified personnel to fill jobs at all levels: at the working level to accomplish the required research, at the management level to plan and monitor the program, and at the action level to assist in translating research results into operationally useful products. But even granting that appropriate research workers are not plentiful, the problem is also one of inadequate communication of the new opportunities to the profession. There is an obvious lag between our opportunities to participate in the great research programs of the day and our organization to effect this participation. The research funds which could be used to expand social-research facilities and increase the skill of social-research personnel have already begun to go by default. The result may be a widening of the gap between the social and natural sciences, a trend that social scientists themselves have been the most eloquent in deploring.

The organizational problem in sociology has been slowly recognized in recent years, resulting in the establishment of a small central secretariat to conduct the American Sociological Society's necessary business more efficiently. But the profession is still subject to the charge made after World War II by the four great research councils that "many professional societies have given little serious attention to their responsibilities for analyzing the present and future demands of society on their professions, or to the planning and action necessary to fulfill their obligations to society." [14] Problems of the efficient utilization of the profession's resources — job placement, professional standards, liaison with new opportunities of support and service — are only vaguely defined as corporate concerns. The traditional arguments against such corporate responsibility must be reappraised, for sociology is changing, as have other sciences, from a profession mainly devoted to teaching to one primarily engaged in research and "engineering" activities.

[14] Quoted from *Practices in Collection and Maintenance of Information on Highly Trained and Specialized Personnel in the U.S.; Report to the Conference Board of the Associated Research Council*, National Research Council, Washington, D.C., 1947.

National reorganization of the profession is, however, not alone enough. Research facilities and team research at the local level must be increasingly developed if the research opportunities of the future are to be fully exploited. Recent developments in this direction are encouraging.[15] We have added research centers or become cooperating parts of research centers in many universities, and plans are under way for others. Such facilities have obvious advantages for training as well as for research. They provide greater assurance of research continuity, and permit more cooperation and integration of research skills within departments and between departments. Moreover, cooperation between social-research institutes will provide a quicker means of testing conclusions on different populations, of conducting comparable studies in various parts of the country, etc. The good research of the future will increasingly involve such cooperation, as many have pointed out. However, such facilities are still too few in number. For their increase we must obviously look for funds beyond the universities and foundations to government and industry, which means that we must consider the new responsibilities and perhaps even the new demands that such sources of support may entail.

It is somewhat ironic that our opportunities for research are outrunning our resources, since opportunity has, in the past, been the elusive factor. However, it is somewhat reassuring that the problem is less the qualitative state of our research art than it is our unreadiness to practice this art in the quantity required.

SUMMARY AND CONCLUSIONS

In these comments on the first half century of sociological research, certain trends appear evident:

1. Sociology has itself been passing through a period of rapid change from a "social study" to a "social science" — from a grand concern over the origin and meaning of society to a preoccupation with its empirical variety and, finally, towards a balance between the two.

[15] Social Science Research Council, *Directory of Univ. Soc. Sci. Research Organizations.*

2. During this period the major methodological emphasis has been on problems of observation — how best to recognize the significant and observe it with a minimum of distortion or variation. This has resulted in a multiplicity of techniques and devices for "controlling" the observational situation and recording its results, and, despite the uncertainties over appropriateness and the disagreements over utility, the gains have been substantial.

3. Also during this period, matters of research design and analysis have become increasing targets of development, although the great advances in these methodological fields are still to come.

4. Finally, the record of these years, together with the deepening crisis in world affairs and the growing dependence on science to resolve it, is providing occasions for sociological research of considerable magnitude and challenge. To exploit these occasions, certain matters would appear to require attention:

a. Greater emphasis on the consolidation of empirical knowledge into theory, to provide a more adequate conceptual basis for fundamental research.

b. Continued creativity in observational and analytical techniques, particularly with reference to their relevance or "validity" for the problem at hand.

c. Increased concern over the application of existing knowledge to the problems of the day, and, consequently, the development of the necessary "engineering" techniques.

d. Improved organizational means of facilitating research participation, sharing research experience, and combining research skills to increase the utilization of the profession's resources.

We have centered our attention, verbally at least, on sociological research. But professional pigeonholes are becoming increasingly difficult to maintain. The common considerations are the development of a science of human relations and the solution of problems in human relations. In both cases methodological and theoretical considerations cut across professional lines. The future should not be jettied by the artificial barriers of the past. The job ahead requires not only the combined skills of the social sciences but also of the mathematician, the humanist, and the administrator.

CONCLUSION

by A. L. KROEBER

Critical Summary and Commentary

I HAVE been asked to comment on the preceding papers and to bind them together, so far as they allow, each author having first freely chosen his own topic. Fortunately, each paper has theoretical import. The order in which I take them up is not quite the order in which they occur in the book. I have chosen to begin with Acker-knecht's essay "On the Comparative Method" and to follow it with an appraisal of Spencer's on "The Humanities in Cultural Anthropology," since these essays bring up the broad subject of the history and constitution of anthropology. A consideration of the comparative method, moreover, takes us beyond autonomous anthropology into related fields of science: the comparative method is biological as well as sociocultural. I next discuss Linton's essay "The Problem of Universal Values," and from that pass on to the papers that are more specifically concerned with method and technique or are oriented toward a particular branch of anthro-pological studies.

ACKERKNECHT

I subscribe whole-heartedly to Ackerknecht's position. My one criticism would be that he does not go far enough. He sees the comparative method as something that must and will be revived. I would say that it has never gone out; it has only changed its tactic.

All science or disinterested intellectual inquiry ultimately seeks knowledge of process. This must be preceded, however, by descrip-tion of the properties of the form and substance of the phenomena, their ordering or classification upon analysis of their structure, and the tracing of their changes or events.

It so happens that on the inorganic level, or at least certain of its aspects, this phenomenological-classificatory-historical approach can be transcended with relative ease. Though the qualitative properties of inanimate substances and objects intergrade endlessly and are difficult to separate out, others of their properties, such as extension, direction, duration, weight, rigidity, motion, are rather readily measured or quantitatively approximated by simple devices of mensuration originally developed for the practical purposes of daily life and having rude counterparts even among backward peoples. And therewith regularities or laws could be formulated. So it was that some important elements of the science of physics were developed early, along with the basic branches of mathematics; whereas the more qualitative properties that we call chemical, resisted resolution into precise processes several thousand years longer.

Somewhat analogously, the beginnings of a science of the earth we live on were developed much later — paradoxical as this may seem — than the systematic foundations of knowledge about the bodies remote in the heavens; perhaps because these latter phenomena, on account of their very distance, had their appearance freed from most qualitative complexities and distractions. Also, in their long perspective the regularities of their movements were the more easily apparent. At any rate, physics, astronomy, mathematics began to grow organizedly more than two thousand years ago, and hand in hand; but chemistry and geology have been sciences for less than two centuries.

The science of living things is old. A case could be made for Aristotle's having been a better biologist than physicist. But biology was a science of static classification rather than of dynamic process; and it remained almost wholly such until very nearly the same period when geology and chemistry were gestating. We have a name for its incipient form then: natural history. We retain the name because we still practice natural history.

Medieval bestiaries and herbals were mixtures of descriptions from common and from recondite knowledge, of hearsay and folk-lore magic, of accounts of uses and imputed virtues. They were catalogues of miscellanies with minimal organization. But exploration and curiosity increased the mass of fact, and diminished the proportion of fable, until Linnaeus was able to present the whole of the ranks and order of organic nature as then known: descriptive indeed, but definite, indeed strictly defined as to fact, and thoroughly organized in classification. This whole great effort of course was based on comparison — exact comparison, and a marshalling according to principles. Cuvier carried the work forward by more conscious concern with "type" or pattern: the larger configurations inherent in the multitudinous data: configurations or classes that carried hidden in themselves their derivations, their historical relations.

Why these genetic-historical implications remained so long un-recognized is a most interesting problem in the history of ideas or cultural psychology. One thinks at once of the influence of Christianity, committed, as an accidental of its insistent monotheism, also to a monogenesis of the world, and therewith to a frozen nature. Yet established religion is insufficient as an explanation, for eighteenth-century Enlightenment developed some overt disbelievers and more scoffers and underminers of Christianity. It is evident that strong positive habits of thinking in terms of fixity rather than flow had grown up within science itself, and were confirmed by the alliance of physics, astronomy, and immutable geometry. Mechanics after all is aimed at fixity. A machine "runs"; but, however complicated, it remains the same machine in structure. A by-product of this positive thinking was the nearly total suppression of sensitivity for intellectual perspective — a lack that seems almost incredible to contemporary minds. Not even to experience uneasiness in viewing six hundred million years of events compressed into six thousand argues a lack of feeling for all time beyond the most immediately recent: a basic lack of sense of the past. That pressures against this must have been building up is shown by the sweepingness of the revolution that Darwin, half-unwitting of its scope, touched off in 1859. Yet it remains difficult today to imagine the intellectual world that geologists, biologists, and other scientists lived in until then.

Ackerknecht is right when he says that "the evolutionary idea," at least that of progress, was more nearly expressed around 1800 by the socially-minded — he cites Voltaire and Condorcet — than in the contemporary biology. It was we men, or at least it was the men of the enlightened seventeenth and eighteenth centuries of reason, that were proclaimed to have made progress. The planet, with its population of unreasoning animals and plants, was still viewed as constant and timeless.

In one sense this condition of arrearage from Voltaire to Darwin might be considered fortunate. Their very innocence of any notion that life might have had a history on this earth kept biologists from premature and probably wild speculation upon what the course of such a history might have been. So they went on collecting, comparing, classifying, revising their classifications, pushing deeper into anatomical and then physiological structure. They steadily enlarged their knowledge and deepened their understanding of its organization. Not only was there the influence of Cuvier's concept of types, but the "natural" classification of plants was being worked out in this period. Lamarck did set up an imaginary mechanism accounting for adaptive changes; but his idea exercised relatively little influence on the general thought of his day, as one looks back. By 1859 geology had attained a notable development, and paleontology was well under way. But how all the events which these sciences were uncovering could have been crowded into a scant few millennia — this question was scarcely raised overtly and certainly not widely.

By the time Darwin finally promulgated his mechanism of selection as the cause of adaptations (a mechanism that was very difficult to reject altogether) and change was thus admitted as an ever present and continuing phenomenon (and therewith the principle of a *history* of life on earth was established), the water behind the dam of ideas had risen to its top and "evolution" carried all before it in one of the dramatic great revolutions of thought. But one reason for the overwhelming character of the success of the doctrine of evolution was the century and more of humble but solid cumulative work of assemblage, analysis, comparison, and classificatory organization of knowledge about the forms of life. It was the capital of marshalled empirical data which systematic natural history had accumulated that swept the evolutionary point of view to its swift decisive victory.

A generation later, with evolution established as a *de facto* history, it was possible for genetics to effect its momentous revolution by demonstrating a main mechanism of this history. And it accomplished this by experiment — that is, artificial isolation of phenomena — and achieved exact quantitative results in the manner of the inorganic sciences. But what underlay and made possible both successful overturns, that of evolution and that of genetics, was the natural history which had preceded them. And this natural history is still being prosecuted, and interpretatively so, whether one call the work taxonomics, systematics, comparative morphology, or by some other term. Thus, only recently the tree shrews have been transferred from the primitively generalized order of insectivores to the more specialized order of primates, the route of the development of man being straightened thereby.

Within two years of 1859 the evolutionist school of anthropology had started up in full cry and motion to reconstruct a history of human cultural development by means of its "comparative method." Within a decade it had produced its most thoughtful and balanced member, Tylor. Others recruited themselves from jurists: Bachofen, Morgan, Maine, and McLennan; and, somewhat later, from classical scholars: Lang and Frazer.

Apart from Frazer, whose greatness and influence lay outside of anthropology much more than within, the strong impact of the movement came in its early years. By 1896, as Ackerknecht points out, Boas, the first anthropologist trained in physics, had openly challenged the validity of the comparative method of the evolutionists; and by 1915 their activity was about over. Even in England, first Rivers and then Malinowski disavowed the point of view in favor respectively of diffusionism and functionalism.

It is plain what brought about the short-livedness. There was available to the evolutionist anthropologists no body of systematically classified knowledge on human customs and institutions corresponding to that which the natural historians had assembled on animals and plants for a century or two, and had worked and reworked with increasing refinement of organization. What the evolutionary anthropologists operated with was, first, a good presumption, after 1859, that there had been evolution in culture as well as in living forms. Second, they operated with more or less happy speculations or naive guesses on what the over-all course of the evolution had been, and particularly what its starting points were. And third, they had available a mass of accounts of the peoples of the world by explorers, travelers, missionaries, compilers, and "collectors of customs" — a mass similar in its haphazardness and lack of organization to the medieval bestiaries, even if less inclined to acceptance of magical inclusions. Into this caldron they dipped with something of the zest of a medieval recounter of oddities and wonders, selecting what items fitted their thesis. Except for the general thesis maintained by each author, the items had no context: they were extracted, wrenched, from the matrix of their natural context of occurrence. It was, so to speak, like bringing into free association the eight feet of the spider with the eight of the octopus, instead of relating the eight-footed spider to the decapod crabs and the hexapod insects, but the octopus to squids and snails. There was no real classification extant of peoples and their cultures, and for most of them no history; but the anthropological evolutionists blithely thought they could do without. Except for Tylor, they scarcely even tried to use the scraps of data which prehistory had begun to provide.

In brief, it was the comparative method run wild and uncontrolled, and a schema of evolution attained by a short cut instead of the evidence of laboriously acquired and organized knowledge.

I am wholly in agreement with Ackerknecht that the development of culture must be traced by the persistent application of the comparative method. It was only the overhasty misuse of the method that broke down in the later nineteenth century. Step by step the archaeologies and ethnographies of regions are being consolidated into histories of the culture of larger areas, and then into histories of the interrelations of these. From this larger body of organized knowledge of what the structure and context and development of particular cultures and groups of cultures actually were, we can then proceed to infer abstracted generalizations with increasing reliability.

It is really remarkable how resistive our human minds are, on the whole, to nonspeculative, genuinely historic comprehension of phenomena, — to their historic interrelations. The exceptions to the resistance are such brief and personal histories as we all experience in our own lives and those of our kin and friends, and those collocations of similarly personal biographies which still largely constitute conventional "history." Even a simple but organized historic record is almost lacking for some major civilizations, such as the Indian. In fact, an organized and reasonably authentic history seems to be a near-impossibility without the aid of written records.

When it comes to all subhuman fields, — we might almost say subpersonality fields, — to an ordered intellectual apprehension of these *as developments*, to a scientific approach which deserves the name of a history of nature, — any of this begins far later in time than we are generally aware of. It is evidently much easier to discover certain repetitive mechanical regularities, whose recognition constitutes the basis of physics, but which are, so to speak, static events. Their dynamism is that of an isolated and brief moment, as of a falling body, the lift of a lever, a liquid finding its level — not of long and interacting sequences. Throughout the early stages of the sciences, wherever we encounter formulations that seem to be developmental explanations or histories, they are pseudohistories, such as Thales deriving the cosmos from the first principle of water, some of the early anthropological evolutionists deriving culture from female primacy, but Freud from an Oedipus event resulting in totem and taboo. There are essentially only Gordian hackings at a knot too vast for would-be conquerors.

Today astronomy is classed as an historical science. It was not historical — in the sense of developmental — to the Babylonians, the Greeks, not even to Copernicus. They dealt with motions, of course, but not with larger change: the motions were recurrent and fixed. It was not until LaPlace and Kant with their nebular hypotheses, until the reinforcements of larger telescopes, the spectroscope, photography contributed by physics in the eighteenth and nineteenth centuries, that astronomy began to deal with long-range change and became aware of history and development in planetary and stellar bodies and systems.

The historical sister science of geology began roughly about the same time; that is, as an activity operating on an organized, verifiable body of sought evidence, in place of the speculative lunges of Neptunists and Vulcanists that had preceded. The biological sciences were roughly contemporaneous with astronomy and geology in developing their historical bent, at least their implied historical bent, although overtly they did not declare themselves evolutionistic until 1859. The name "natural history" has acquired an old-fashioned ring, somewhat like "natural philosophy"; but as a mode of intellectual activity the endeavor to learn the history of nature is *late* in science — only one to two centuries old.

Two reasons may be suggested for this lateness, though there may be others also. The first is that repetitive regularities, timeless universals, are conceptually simple and rigid as compared with the plasticity of any historical flux. Being simple, they were sought; and being sought, some of the more simple ones were found early, and were prized. The second reason is that what the simpler basic "laws" or constants need for their discovery is concentration, extraction, definition and limitation of focus; but even a first fragmentary and approximative history requires the accumulation and organization of large bodies of knowledge.

It seems reasonable to infer that the historical sciences, far from being of a more immature order at which they have been arrested, really represent a late, complex stage possible only in an unusually highly advanced civilization. Of course, this does not lend the historical sciences any intrinsic superiority over the experimental ones. Nor is there reason for assuming that because they develop later they will displace the others. Both approaches will presumably go on flourishing, side by side and reciprocally stimulative; and additional approaches may be added to them.

On the other hand, it is now evident that the historic approach is applicable everywhere in the phenomenal cosmos. The movement is thus one of magnitude, which will no doubt require considerable time to realize; and as it is still youthful, we may anticipate that the full flourishing of historical science is still ahead of us.

Another fact also points to this inference. Since the Renaissance, in Occidental civilization, human culture has been studied chiefly by humanists in what are called the humanities — and studied with fervor and devotion. The humanities have dealt with things humane, but hardly with things broadly human; with high culture rather than with culture as such, culture as the most characteristic human property. They have preferred to stay outside the natural sciences, free to be ethnocentric, patriotic, propagandist, or normative. But with all this, the humanities have, since the later eighteenth century, been increasingly comparative and historical in their interest, and less and less prescriptive, dogmatic, and willful. Since this change coincides in period and spread with the development of the historical approach in natural science, the two trends are evidently parts of one larger current. We may therefore expect a continuance of *rapprochement*: humanistic studies becoming increasingly pan-human in their range, and increasingly historical at the expense of their normative constituent; and natural science taking cognizance and making greater use of the humanistic data and the results of humanistic studies. In fact, anthropology may with a degree of justice be conceived, at least in part, as an *avant-garde* of natural science moving toward the area of conjunction — as linguistics is extending toward natural science from the side of the humanities.

And in this surge of historical attitude, comparison — the contextual comparative method, I should like to call it — is necessarily involved as a foundation. Sound comparison inevitably carries historic implication, as soon as there are intellects ready to apperceive historic significances.

CONCLUSION

Spencer's position as to the humanities and anthropology is one that I have of course great sympathy with; but, in line with what I have just said as to comparison, I do not see a permanent opposition to natural science, or danger from it to us in anthropology. In fact, it is my basic premise that anthropology is a natural science and must continue to want to be one, if it is to realize itself; but that its own field can be developed only under partial autonomy and by procedures of its own. These procedures are about as different as is possible, within science, from the approved and productive procedures of physics. They are almost certainly more similar to biological procedures. And many of the data in the human field are those which tradition relegates to the humanists. We cannot however accept this relegation as validly excluding us from any human area. Since we cannot hope to perform nearly as well as the humanists the kind of achievements they have attained with their intensivity of focus and depth of knowledge, anthropological concern with specifically humanistic data — as part of the data of total human culture — is warranted insofar as we can learn adequately to treat these data as part of nature; which means: in the general manner of natural science as a whole, with ourselves nonresidually included in nature.

The following are some of Spencer's more notable points, with my personal reactions to them.

Science can ameliorate human living; the humanities, with their retrospective gaze, cannot. I would add that genuinely fundamental science probably tends to result in eventual amelioration, but does not as such seek it; whereas most social science seeks amelioration almost as overtly as do such recognizedly applied natural sciences as medicine and engineering.

Spencer describes the humanities as wanting to be outside natural science; as being evaluative — that is, normative; and third, as lacking system. Their results are meaningful, but not meaningfully coherent. — This seems a wholly fair factual description.

He sees anthropology using the initial steps of the scientific method, namely the propounding of hypotheses; but in testing these, it uses largely nonmeasurable data. I would subjoin that they are not necessarily nonmeasurable even in the field of the humanities, although many humanists profess to abhor the quantitative. Moreover, facts are facts, even if unmeasurable; and red was positively distinguishable from blue even before we knew their wave length. Ornithologists separate orioles and cardinal birds from bluejays by color and by some hundreds of other descriptive traits, which are far more significant for classification than the measurements they may also make. It just happens that the particular materials and problems of classical physics made a mathematical approach easy and productive, and a degree of experimentation also. It is gratuitous to assume that measurement and experiment are the equally necessary criteria of successful prosecution of other sciences. How much did Darwin measure or experiment?

How far may anthropology invade the field of the humanities? Certainly so far as it is more broadly comparative, says Spencer. And less selective, I would add; and not normative; though the evaluative function of the humanities may be accorded to anthropology also, so far as evaluation is comparably descriptive instead of normative. Biologists evaluate (though they do not call it that): the seal is a good swimmer, but a poor walker.

Anthropology deals, among other things, with culture wholes, whereas the humanities tend to assume them. In the investigation of national or supernational culture wholes (civilizations), anthropology must necessarily take most of its data from historians and other humanists; but its task is the association of the parts.— I agree, and would add that at least some of us are more willing to try than many humanists.

LINTON

Linton takes up the important and timely subject of universal values. Any modern thought on this basic topic is most welcome.

Personally, I should have felt happier had Linton foregone his pragmatic justifications for broaching the theme, namely: The peoples of the world must find common areas of understanding or die; and: Unless they come to some sort of agreement on what is important and desirable, we are headed for catastrophe. The imminence of the wreck and ruin of civilization seems far from proved, as I see it. So is the view that another world war will occur unless something specific be immediately done to prevent it. The future really remains quite difficult to know; what is certain is the present fact that statements such as these contain an ingredient of emotion. And a problem like that of universal values is intellectually fundamental enough to warrant attention in its own right, rather than because we are alarmed about our future.

Still, however motivated, the attempt is desirable; and Linton begins with a psychologically slanted definition of values as: anything capable of producing similar responses to choices in a society or segment thereof. Formally, "anything" of course needs limiting by the addition of "cultural" or some such word, in order to shut out physiological values shared with subhuman animals. We should probably all accept Linton's further points that values may be negative as well as positive; that "a value-attitude system" can usually be profitably substituted for indefinite "value"; and his distinction between instrumental and conceptual values — means and ends values — and recognition of the generally higher affective charge of the instrumental ones because of their greater concreteness.

Then for the values themselves. Here is the enumeration:[1]

(1) Belief in supernatural beings or in a pervading, impersonal supernatural force. (2) Immortality, persistence of personality. (*3) The nonethical character of the supernatural, except in ancestor worship and monotheistic religion. (*4) Trend toward expansion of societies. (5) Reciprocity and fair dealing. (*6) Leadership, management, power drive. (*7) Therefore few wholly egalitarian societies. (8) The family as chief instrument of education and cultural perpetuation. (*8a) Chief forms of the family: the

[1] Asterisks mark those formulations that seem descriptive of near-universal actual *conditions* in cultures rather than outright value-attitude systems of ideals in them.

conjugal and the consanguine. (*8b) Alternative value set on premarital chastity and on spouses' adjustment. (9) Prescription of roles in the family. (10) Property concepts (arising genetically in part from subhuman identifications with particular territories). (11) Knowledge, both useful and for its own sake. (12) Escapes from reality: games, literature, arts. (13) Unformulated common denominators underlying the varieties of esthetic expressions.

The "hierarchical" or preferential groupings among these value systems are recognized as varying; and the insistence on conformity to values, or tolerance of individual deviation from them, is also variable in diverse societies.

Herewith we have at least an outline or sample of universal values, which has the virtue of a motion made in a deliberative body: if imperfect it can be improved by amendment. Nor would anyone be likely to quarrel with any part of the list as improper or too narrow in scope. Nevertheless there is a certain vagueness, a haziness of contour, in the formulations. Could such a list not have been drawn up reasonably well by any interested person with an adequate background of general reading and intelligence? It scarcely seems the quintessence of a prolonged and refined experience in anthropological dealing with cultures. Possibly so in an impressionistic-residual way; but it is not professional through the use of specific methods and techniques, such as for instance Murdock's *Social Structure* employs on a world-wide basis — though it applies them to the one small segment of kinship.

I would incline to take issue with Linton's hope that the current preoccupation with cultural differences is only a passing phase in anthropology. I do not believe that there is such a preoccupation. Our concern is with likenesses *and* differences. There are some who prefer a small field and to cut analysis fine, which results in minor distinctions being made explicit while resemblances tend to be taken for granted. But who will cast a stone at analytic precision in science? And if common features are left implicit by the analyst himself, those who gather his work into the greater syntheses will make them explicit then: if sufficiently pregnant, they will not be permanently overlooked. If it be said that science is the determination of order in phenomena, and therefore of regularities and recurrences, that is true. But each actual differentiation is presumptive evidence also of some competing regularity; and where these regularities are numerous and *nuancés* as in the field of man and his culture, there is real risk that, our patience giving out, we force our way through to an illusory order, a mainly verbal one, by ignoring complicating diversities in the phenomena. It is plain that real understanding can be achieved only by meeting and mastering differences as well as likenesses.

When Linton says that recognition of the relativity of culture leads to tolerance but remains essentially a negative principle, he is of course right. Realization of relativity is a needed first step, not the end of a journey. It is an indispensable step because it means the breach with dogmatism — with the attitude which refuses to see any problem because the answer is evident without investigation. Successful discovery of regularities in human history and culture can begin after a high degree of relativity (= complexity) of culture is assumed as a premise. Insistent recognition only of phenomenal variety, however true and however satisfying esthetically, is necessarily sterile as an intellectual aim or achievement; just as belittling of the variety is an intellectual evasion. The variety must be overcome, not deplored, denied, or shrugged off.

HERSKOVITS

Herskovits's review of problems of method in ethnography is marked by balance and his accustomed good sense. Sometimes indeed he points out the need of common sense so ardently as to give a first impression of advocacy of an extremist position; or to leave one in doubt whether it is a real or hypothetical devil that is being put into his place. What disciplines, for instance, are among those that attempt to by-pass psychocultural dynamics and thereby give a pseudoscientific stamp to an unreality? Is it perhaps "culturology" that is meant? I thought first of modern linguistics, which has rejected or is in process of casting out psychology *and* meaning *and* explanation. But linguistics is scarcely setting up an unreality, nor pretending to more scientificness than it has; and I do not think Herskovits means it.

I find myself, and believe most anthropologists will find themselves, in agreement with what Herskovits says on the interrelation of the atomistic and the functional-integrative approaches, the specifically social and the specifically cultural, the static and the dynamic interest. Only — who actually is an advocate of primacy of the static? We all like to think of ourselves as dynamically attacking problems of dynamics. Perhaps a useful commonplace is the realization that beginnings of inquiry must normally be made with the simpler static situations. One trouble with the pioneers of the great decade of ninety years ago of first evolutionistic thinking about culture is that they were all operating dynamically on anthropology's very birthday.

Herskovits grants these pioneers, in spite of their inadequate method, a comparative approach and "historical depth"— which I take to be a euphemism for their a priori conviction of evolution, since "disregard for a cultural context" is mentioned. As a student, like Herskovits, under Boas, I am however a little startled by the statement that "a new tool came to hand" with the development of acculturation studies. Yes, it did; but it came after a thirty- or forty-year gap, which was dominated by the figure of our joint *guru*. Acculturation studies seem to me to represent rather an innovation away from Boas, an innovation in which Herskovits participated, whereas for instance Lowie and Spier and I did not. As the very etymology of the term expresses movement and change, it is true that acculturation studies were bound to be historical in a sense; but usually to a very short-term degree only. They dealt with "history in the making," which tends to boil down to process — and mostly very slightly diachronic process: almost achronic. Herskovits himself possesses a sense of historic depth; possibly he has failed to realize how shallow that sense is in many acculturation studies by others. Keesing's *Menomini* is an honorable exception.

Nor could I quite agree that "one of the contributions of acculturation research to the methods of anthropology has been to put the historical component in anthropological science on a sure footing." That component is much older and much broader and solider than what acculturationism has contributed. Herskovits has apparently expressed himself enthusiastically here; I have always assumed from his work that our positions on historical approach and results were quite close.

The distinction of micro-ethnography from macro-ethnography is useful. One deals with small variations of culture, down to idiosyncracies and personal uniques; the other with the total range of variation in human behavior. However, there is more than one kind of macro-ethnography. Herskovits evidently means the approach which determines, say, what kinds of descent reckoning there are the world over in all historic time, how they associate with moieties, totemism, residence, and so on; or, again, the motivations that can enter into visual art, such as functional decoration, ornateness, religious symbolism, naturalism, conceptual representation, social prestige, and their combinations. Much of Boas's ethnography was of this type; and so was Wundt's when he was analyzing and not speculating. The results, however, are essentially static, even if historical context is observed. They define a frame of reference. A more directly historical macro-ethnography deals with the development and interrelations of larger culture wholes sequentially, and is the outright history of culture, not excluding such problems as that of progress.

As to ethnographic "truth," Herskovits sagely points out that no one can make up a culture, any more than a language. Bits of the truth can be denied or warped here and there, from shame, or for propaganda; but they are bound to be found out if the culture is still living, and are likely to be if it is dead. The worry about verity of data comes nine-tenths from people whose first-hand experience of culture is limited to their own.

SISTER INEZ

Sister Inez Hilger's field method is essentially field technique, but it is slanted ethnographically as indubitably as is Herskovits's paper. It is all sound; and it carries a strong personal appeal to me because I did ethnography with one of her tribes fifty-three and fifty-four years ago. The fundamental approach is still comfortingly the same; and so is the equipment: pencil and a stoutish notebook. Even the results attainable are astonishingly corroborative, in fields like social relations — rituals already by 1900 no longer practiced have of course been much more largely forgotten.

At a few points, the technique of field inquiry is now more systematic and smoother than then. In some cases at least, Sister Inez was able to profit by contacts previously established by missionaries. She worked to some degree from a previously compiled Field Guide on child development. An assistant wrote down the notes. This last should be a great help. It leaves the questioner-listener far freer to watch expressions, gestures, movements of bystanders.

It is also evident that while there has always been some memory loss of the old culture, and often a great deal, the Indians of today sense the ethnologists' motivation far better, appreciate it, and respond accordingly. The days are over when an informant furnishing even a vocabulary felt marked, ashamed, and afraid. The change is one I experienced for myself when rturning to the Mohave early in 1953 after a forty-five years' absence.

COLSON

Miss Colson's interesting problem is related to that of Sister Inez, but differs in three essentials. Her cultures are still functioning, not mainly a matter of memory; her societies are not tiny, half-submerged enclaves, but populations numbering tens and hundreds of thousands; and her study is made to aid the better administration and development of these populations. Consequently, regional variabilities are larger, the question of validity of sampling obviously becomes important (whereas it is largely pedantic for tribes like the Arapaho), and the detailed, slow-moving, face-to-face approach, with its emphasis on individuals and personal rapport, must give way to something more summary and businesslike. Ground just has got to be covered, and efficiency replaces the feeling-charged relationships of the old-line ethnographer as a goal.

The result is a sort of census, with trained native assistants, a corps of cooperating workers, coverage of area, and a general atmosphere reminiscent of sociology rather than of ideal ethnography as Malinowski portrayed it. The census, on a minute scale, is not new even in ethnology, as Colson points out; in fact, Rivers' once-famous "genealogical method" yielded a cross-sectional census of up to a hundred persons as a by-product. The real points about a census attack however are, When does it become basic, and How broad should its informational spread be? And there Colson's procedure seems both sound and genuinely effective.

Of course, different procedures are not mutually exclusive. They can be applied to the same peoples for different purposes. Most of my own field ethnography has been done in the single-handed, stroll-in, pencil-and-notebook way. But I once instituted a survey in which a half-million items of ethnographic fact were secured from two hundred and fifty groups of Indians in western North America, and did not feel that thereby my world had crashed. It was just that the older method with its emphasis on unsystematic intensivity left an infinity of gaps and noncomparables in the data, which a census survey that was aimed at continuity and equivalence would largely remedy. Of course we were then making a census of items of culture content: Colson and her colleagues, a census of persons and their relations.

It is also of interest to consider how far the fact that studies like Colson's seem to us in America to have a sociological cast, may be due to American anthropologists' taking for granted that they will normally be surrounded by larger numbers of sociologists, whereas Britain hardly recognizes the subject of sociology by name. Much of what some of us have recently been pointing out, namely that British social anthropology does not correspond too well in emphasis with American ethnology and cultural anthropology, is evidently due to this fact that their social anthropology has *de facto* to do duty for sociology as well as anthropology.

BOWERS

While we are at sociology, I should like to say something about Bowers' "Research Methodology," but I fear once I begin I may say too much. I consider the development of fundamental science, whether of human relations or of anything else, a different matter from the solution of pragmatic problems. The practical problems can no doubt be solved more wisely if there exists genuine science to draw on. But the science as science will not develop better or faster for having its pursuit mixed with problems of application. Physics helps engineering solve its problems, but engineering as such can help physics only by providing it with sharper tools. It obviously cannot contribute to the solution of the problems of physics as such, or to the basic methods.

The contrary assumption underlies the paper of Bowers. It says that by combining the two approaches, by mixing their motivations, sociology will improve and get farther — has already got farther. I flatly disbelieve this premise; and there seems no use arguing differences of opinion directly derived from this premise and my opposite one.

MANDELBAUM

Mandelbaum's descriptive contribution I find it hard to say anything about, except that I admire the perfection of its workmanship. It is description, analysis, and interpretation all in one. It presents the cultural form of a ritual, its social and cultural meaning, and its individual meanings and variability. It is vivid, fluent, and interesting; it makes the culture and the people live and have significance; and it is a model job, ranking with the Tikopia, the Nuer, and some of Malinowski's best.

HOLMBERG

Holmberg is one of the few anthropologists that have been able to experiment with culture; and he feels half-guilty over it! His "Adventures in Culture Change" were really that; and they are most interesting. Both his situation and that of the Siriono were too unusual to serve as much of a point of departure for talk of a "method"; but they resulted in a most stimulating episode which the reader is likely to remember when most methodological discussions have receded into gray dimness of mind.

CONCLUSION

Wilford also writes about method — in eastern United States archaeology. He deals with two issues: Walter Taylor's criticism, and problems of classification involving diffusion and chronology.

Taylor's charge is that American archaeologists tend to stop when they have achieved a chronology. They do not go on to historiographic contextual integration of their materials, he says; and still less to the comparative study of the nature of culture — that is, abstract generalizations. Archaeology as such is only a technique for the securing of certain kinds of cultural information, he maintains; its contextual and its abstracted generalizations are respectively parts of general history and general anthropology.

I see nothing of principle to quarrel with in this position. But I agree with Wilford that Taylor is captious — or perhaps perfectionist — in his specific criticism that his colleagues devote too much attention to the external relations of their finds at ancient sites, and too little to the internal or "conjunctive" relations. A small, poor group with a meager culture, living long ago in a destructive climate — how much *can* they leave? To be sure, presumably no internal comparison is ever absolutely exhausted: future ingenuities can always hope to make additional findings. But the law of diminishing returns sets in early, as Wilford points out, especially on the rather pitifully poor discoveries characteristic of Eastern Woodland prehistory. The bulk of presently possible meaning does and must lie in the external relations of particular excavations, in this eastern area.

Perhaps Gordon Childe is the student most gifted today in squeezing rich and sound meaning out of archaeological data; but he aims consistently at external as well as internal relations, and is perhaps most notable for his skill in tying down similarities of wide geographical range. And in addition he is operating on the whole Near East and Europe over five thousand years, with all their cultural wealth and variety!

Not only are the data for the United States and Canada immeasurably thin and monotonous by comparison, but it is under forty years since we Americans first began to think at all in terms of temporal succession for our home materials in the Southwest; and less long ago than that in the East. With our archaeologists of 1914 having not even climbed to Taylor's step three, namely chronologizing, small wonder that they are not yet abstracting many laws on level five in 1954.

And the parts of Wilford's paper that so usefully summarize both the achievements and the limitations of diffusion studies and chronology in the East, accentuate again how tremendously difficult it is to attain broad and significant results in that area. The Woodland culture pops in and out, before, during, and after Hopewell, into the very historic period, but is so starkly gaunt that those who have given it a lifetime of study sometimes have difficulty assigning given sites to periods nearly three thousand years apart!

It is a truism that what archaeology can give us more directly and fully than any other approach to culture is true depth: the actual record of continuity with a minimum of lacunae. And this is of course a vital dimension. When it comes to finding out how the complex machine of culture runs, what its "workings" or "laws" are, it is directly reported history and living ethnology that are evidently going to be immeasurably more productive — although weaker on time, as soon as the brief dating of recorded history runs out. I for one am thankful that our eastern archaeologists have got out of their extraordinarily refractory material as much areal classification, spatial relation, evidence of diffusion, and relative chronology as they have. For decades I faced an equally difficult body of material — the remains in California, and mostly potteryless at that. I did not even dent the data as to their interpretation, through having begun by bestowing primary attention on ethnology and linguistics. It was not until Heizer gave Californian archaeology its full right of way that it began to yield constructive results. And constructive results are what archaeologists of the eastern area have been getting — not as rapidly as one might wish if wishing did the job, but at a cumulative rate.

CONCLUSION

GREENBERG

Greenberg revives an idea of Sapir's which has lain practically fallow for thirty years, and carries it a step farther by devising a series of quantitative indices expressing types of language.

He reviews the history of typological versus genetic-historical classification of languages, beginning with Friedrich and August von Schlegel, going on through Wilhelm von Humboldt, and crystallizing in Schleicher, with carry-on by Max Mueller, Whitney, and Steinthal. This linguistic eddy of the German current of transcendental idealism was both valuative and ethnocentric, and seems anachronistic as well as crass in the contemporary state of linguistic science.

However, its very naiveté may have intrigued Sapir. At any rate, he rolled it out and played with it to see what he might make of it, in the sixth chapter of his 1921 *Language*, sixty years after the Germans had had their say. It was an intellectually sensitive inquiry of the imagination, free of value-preference judgments, of course, and operating with ratings along several scales instead of a single one. Some anthropologists were impressed; but they were not actively classifying languages, and they did nothing further with the scheme. Of late, Sapir's chapter on "Drift" has attracted more attention than the one on classification, perhaps because of its implications of immanences.

Linguists have left the Sapir typological classification rather severely alone; it lay pretty well outside the climate in which they were operating; as the years passed, it was remembered perhaps chiefly as an oddity of a great mind. In not only dusting the Sapir typology off but attempting to revalidate it by devising objective indices of some of its criteria, Greenberg has accordingly departed from the orthodox custom of contemporary linguistics, as he had also previously done in advocating preliminary probability judgments on genetic relationship without total reconstruction of earlier stages.

Linguists, being perfectionists by virtue of their profession, have not taken too kindly to Greenberg's findings on relationship; whereas the attitude of anthropologists has been more sympathetic.

This is because, in connection with cultural situations, they are more apt to be interested in even provisional linguistic results than they are likely to be concerned over upholding the purity of linguistic method. The same reactions are likely to be provoked by Greenberg's present typological computations, except that anthropologists and historians will probably find less grist for their mill in type similarities than in historic relationships, and linguists may entertain an added objection against the indices. I have the impression that Greenberg will need more space than his present article allows to do himself full justice. The Sapir chapter has not been easy reading for the undedicated; and Greenberg has the additional task of justifying the measurement bases of his indices.

His approach however is basically simple and practical, and one of common sense; which, if he were a nonlinguist, might be construed as presumption of incompetence in linguistic matters. But since his competence is beyond cavil, his essay probably reflects chiefly a deviation from the modal temperament of his profession. He wants to push on, and would rather have provisional results soon than to wait indefinitely for the attainment of ruthlessly perfect ones. Toward that inclination outsiders can only be sympathetic. If his measures contain an element of subjective judgment and inexactness, that can presumably be corrected. In principle, there is nothing unsound about the indices. The difficulties they may bring would be technical.

The nonlinguist can draw certain inferences from Greenberg's table without knowing too precisely what each index represents. For instance, two pairs of Indo-European languages are tested, each pair containing one member historically derivative or near-derivative from the other. In each of ten structural traits, English differs from Anglo-Saxon in the same *direction* (as expressed by index figure) as modern Persian has changed from Sanskrit as representative of Indo-Iranian. In both pairs, the values for "index of synthesis" have gone down with time — from 2.12 to 1.68, and from 2.59 to 1.52 — and those for "index of agglutination" have gone up — from .11 to .30, and from .09 to .34. And similarly for the eight other indices. This consistency of trend of change certainly suggests that the method must be mainly reliable, even if it should be judged to be somewhat imperfectly accurate. And it would involve chiefly labor to increase the number of Indo-European pairs, and to add non-Indo-European ones from Semitic or Hamitic.

Other inferences can be drawn from the tabulation. Of the eight languages tested, four are Indo-European, four non-Indo-European. If however we consider highest and lowest value attained in each index among the eight idioms, only two of twenty [2] such extreme values attach to the four Indo-European languages. Are they therefore to be construed as standing consistently somewhere near the middle of the total range of human languages, in feature after feature? If the method were applied to eighty languages and this run of middling values then still persisted for Indo-European, we should of course be surer of the fact. We might even find the figures and the indices themselves suggesting some explanation of the situation.

Again, it is interesting that Annamese, the one language included that is usually labeled isolating, six times out of nine registers the absolute minimum of .00, once the low of 1.06 (absolute potential minimum 1.00, other languages running from 1.52 to 3.79), and once the absolute maximum of 1.00 — for the property of isolation. One could well infer from these figures alone what has usually been ascribed to the East Asiatic languages: they stand, morphologically, at one extreme of the total range of possibilities of linguistic type.

Eskimo, on the contrary, four times attains maximum index values among the eight idioms examined, and four times minimum. It is therefore suggested as strongly characterized in different directions in several features; whereas Annamese is also strongly characterized, but consistently in one direction and trend. Swahili also scores three maxima — in agglutination, prefixing, and concord — as against only one maximum for four Indo-European languages

[2] Actually one and a half out of nineteen because of shared minima, and because the theoretical maximum for agglutination is meaningless.

(by Sanskrit for compounding). The general impression one has, from non-indicial description, of these three languages — Annamese, Eskimo, Bantu — is indeed one of salient characterization of structure. On the other hand, we are not in the habit of thinking of our own speech as only moderately characterized but balanced and average in quality. Greenberg's index method has certainly brought us a long way from the idealistic ratings of the Germans with our own speech regularly placed at the summit.

There is one other relevant question. What do we do with a morphological classification of world languages when we have it? This question has probably not been asked much in present-day linguistics, and certainly not answered. A typology might, but would probably not, furnish clues to buried genetic relationships. The typologic findings would presumably be too over-all or gross to serve as indicators of historical connection, for which the evidence that linguists insist on is refined. The typologic classification might or might not suggest language mixture cutting across genetic relationship. It would also ultimately help to define the total range, the extremes and frequency norms, of the structure of human speech, both as potentiality and actuality, and in this way delimit empirically a part of "human nature," of that potential equipment which underlies our varied individual and social behavior. This would amount to a sort of psychology — though a sort very different from that currently practiced by psychologists. It would at any rate be likely to help raise new questions as to what men are; how they are really constituted, precisely.

But I also sense that for a long time to come typological classifications are likely to be sporadic affairs, compared with the constant reconstruction of genetic history. For one thing, I am not clear as to what their counterpart is in biological science, as genetic linguistics and culture history are the counterparts of biological evolution.

STEWART

Omer Stewart makes an important point in showing how the burning over of natural vegetation by natives in much of North

CONCLUSION

America was far more extensive and influential than usually supposed by anthropologists or admitted by foresters and botanists. He goes on to read his colleagues a little lecture on being one-sided instead of two-way environmentalists: primitive man, he says, partly made his environment as well as passively accepted and adapted to it.

There seems no question that fire was the earliest and long the most powerful tool with which man could affect nature. There exist strange spottinesses in this general domain. Beavers perhaps come second to ourselves in their influence: their dams seem to have materially altered at least smaller drainages. In deserts, perhaps in some steppes, in the wet tropics, the over-all effects of fire were probably limited. Yet in regions like much of the United States the effects were considerable, though they have been generally underestimated.

In part this underestimation appears to be due to forestry having in the United States, during the last generation or two, got itself entangled in a liaison with the reformist conservation movement. The result, since there existed among us some shocking wastes through forest fires, was that a tradition grew up that good foresters are against any fire in any timber at any time; and this tradition gradually acquired the sanctity of an unquestioned a priori, and the partially contrary evidence was dismissed, often simply brushed aside. It is to my mind an instance illustrating how deleterious the result to fundamental science can be when its autonomy is infringed by the injection of practical considerations, even laudable ones, which sooner or later are bound to have emotional or conative involvements.

What Stewart can present in the space available to him is only a fraction of his evidence on the extent to which our Indians burned over the land, sometimes making grassland but often also maintaining and improving forests; and — this a theoretical point — contributing to their environment. If in the ardor of this proof Stewart sometimes overstates his case, the error more often touches what is said about anthropologists than what is said about the landscape. I would say that it is wholly because of his emphasis on distributions and areal classifications that Ratzel has influenced American anthropologists, not because of his tempered environmentalism. Even at that the influence was indirect and not too strong. Ratzel influenced Boas little and that chiefly negatively, at least in his middle and late years when Boas's prestige was greatest. I believe any of Boas's students will confirm me in this. It is true that American anthropology did not seriously or explicitly consider the reciprocal influence of man and environment; but that was an oversight while we were busy discovering culture, relativism, diffusion, patterning, acculturation and other intracultural things, and too busy on the whole to pay much attention to extracultural relations. But it was not from malice prepense, nor a sin against the Holy Ghost. Stewart has well made his point about the Indian custom of burning and its effects upon the landscape, and this in turn leads to an interesting consideration of general principle. For which we shall all be grateful and leave it there.

REFERENCES AND INDEX

REFERENCES

An Ethnographic Field Method, by Sister M. Inez Hilger

Augusta, Félix José de
   1916. *Diccionario araucano-español y español-araucano.* 2 vols.
   1934. *Lecturas araucanas.* Santiago.
Cooper, John M.
   1946. "The Araucanians," in *Handbook of the Indians of South America,* Vol. 2, Bureau of American Ethnology, Bulletin 143. Washington, D.C.
Densmore, Frances
   1929. *Chippewa Customs,* Bureau of American Ethnology, Bulletin 86. Washington, D.C.
Hilger, Sister M. Inez
   1951. *Chippewa Child Life and Its Cultural Background,* Bureau of American Ethnology, Bulletin 146. Washington, D.C.
   1952. *Arapaho Child Life and Its Cultural Background,* Bureau of American Ethnology, Bulletin 148. Washington, D.C.
   n.d. "*Araucanian Child Life and Its Cultural Background,*" unpublished ms.
Klopfer, Bruno, and Douglas Kelly
   1942. *The Rorschach Technique.* New York.
Kroeber, A. L.
   1902. *The Arapaho,* American Museum of Natural History, Bulletin 18, Parts 1 and 2.
Valenzuela, Pedro Armengol
   1914. "Glosario etimológico de nombres de personas, animales, plantas, ríos, y lugares aborigenes de Chile y de algunas otras partes de America," *Revista Chilena de Historia y Geografía,* Vol. 10, pp. 154–155.

The Intensive Study of Small Sample Communities, by Elizabeth Colson

Barnes, J. A.
   1951. "Marriage in a Changing Society," *Rhodes-Livingstone Papers.*
   1952. "Measures of Divorce Frequency in Simple Societies," *Journal of the Royal Anthropological Institute,* Vol. 79, pp. 37–62.
Colson, Elizabeth
   1951. "Residence and Village Stability among the Plateau Tonga," *Rhodes-Livingstone Journal,* No. 12.
Driver, H. E.
   1953. "Statistics in Anthropology," *American Anthropologist,* Vol. 55, pp. 42–59.

REFERENCES

Gifford, E. W.
1926. "Clear Lake Pomo Society," *University of California Publications in American Archaeology and Ethnology*, Vol. 18, pp. 287–390.

Gluckman, M. G.
1950. "Kinship and Marriage among the Lozi of Northern Rhodesia and the Zulu of Natal," in A. R. Radcliffe-Brown and D. C. Forde, eds., *African Systems of Kinship and Marriage*. Oxford University Press.

Kluckhohn, C.
1939. "Theoretical Basis for an Empirical Method of Studying the Acquisition of Culture by Individuals," *Man*, Vol. 89, pp. 1–6.

Mead, Margaret, ed.
1937. *Cooperation and Competition among Primitive Peoples*. New York.

Mitchell, J. C., and J. Barnes
1950. *The Lamba Village*. University of Cape Town.

Murdock, G. P.
1949. *Social Structure*. New York.

Nadel, S. F.
1947. *The Nuba*. Oxford University Press.

Richards, A. I.
1935. "The Village Census in the Study of Culture Contact," *Africa*, Vol. 8, pp. 20–33.

Streib, G. F.
1952. "The Use of Survey Methods among the Navaho," *American Anthropologist*, Vol. 54, pp. 30–40.

Wilson, Monica
1951. *Good Company*. Oxford University Press.

On the Comparative Method in Anthropology, by Erwin H. Ackerknecht

Ackerknecht, E. H.
1948. "Hygiene in France, 1815–1848," *Bulletin of the History of Medicine*, Vol. 22.

Balzac, H.
1859. *Oeuvres Complètes*. Paris.

Bidney, D.
1953. "The Concept of Value in Modern Anthropology," in A. L. Kroeber, ed., *Anthropology Today*, pp. 682–699. Chicago.

Boas, F., ed.
1938. *General Anthropology*. New York.

Gomme, Sir G. Lawrence
1908. *Folklore as an Historical Science*. London.

Harnack, A.
1917. *Aus Wissenschaft und Leben*, Vol. 1.

Lawrence, W.
1822. *Lectures on Physiology, Zoology and the Natural History of Man*. London.

Lowie, Robert H.
1937. *The History of Ethnological Theory*. New York.

Merz, J. T.
n.d. *A History of European Thought in the 19th Century*.

REFERENCES

Muehlmann, W. E.
n.d. *Geschichte der Anthropologie*. Bonn.
Nadel, S. F.
1951. *Foundations of Social Anthropology*. Glencoe, Ill.
Nordenskjöld, E.
1935. *History of Biology*. New York.
Rothacker, Ed.
1947. *Logik und Systematik der Geisteswissenschaften*. Bonn.

The Humanities and Cultural Anthropology, by Robert F. Spencer

Benedict, Ruth
1946. *The Chrysanthemum and the Sword*. New York.
1948. "Anthropology and the Humanities," *American Anthropologist*, Vol. 50, pp. 585–593.
Bryson, Frederick R.
1938. *The XVI-Century Italian Duel*. Chicago.
Cohen, Albert K.
1946. "An Evaluation of 'Themes' and Kindred Concepts," *American Journal of Sociology*, Vol. 52, No. 1, Part 1.
Commager, Henry Steele
1950. *The American Mind*. New Haven.
Evans-Pritchard, E. E.
1951. *Social Anthropology*. London.
Goldschmidt, Walter
1951. "Ethics and the Structure of Society: An Ethnological Contribution to the Sociology of Knowledge," *American Anthropologist*, Vol. 53, pp. 506–524.
Kany, Charles E.
1932. *Life and Manners in Madrid, 1750–1800*. Berkeley.
Kirk, Russell
1953. *The Conservative Mind*. New York.
Kluckhohn, Clyde
1941. "Patterning as Exemplified in Navaho Culture," in L. Spier, ed., *Language, Culture and Personality*, pp. 109–130. Menasha.
Kroeber, A. L.
1944. *Configurations of Culture Growth*. Berkeley.
1951. "The Novel in Asia and Europe," *University of California Publications in Semitic Philology*, Vol. 11, pp. 233–241.
Lowie, Robert H.
1945. *The German People: A Social Portrait to 1914*. New York.
Mandelbaum, David G.
1953. "On the Study of National Character," *American Anthropologist*, Vol. 55, pp. 174–187.
Northrup, F. S. C.
1947. *The Meeting of East and West: An Inquiry concerning World Understanding*. New York.
Opler, Morris E.
1945. "Themes as Dynamic Forces in Culture," *American Journal of Sociology*, Vol. 51, pp. 198–206.

REFERENCES

1946. "An Application of the Theory of Themes in Culture," *Journal of the Washington Academy of Sciences*, Vol. 36, pp. 137–166.

Pearce, Roy H.
1953. *The Savages of America: A Study of the Indian and the Idea of Civilization.* Baltimore.

Redfield, Robert
1953. "Relations of Anthropology to the Social Sciences and to the Humanities," in A. L. Kroeber, ed., *Anthropology Today*, pp. 728–738. Chicago.

Sapir, Edward
1924. "Culture, Genuine and Spurious," *American Journal of Sociology*, Vol. 29, pp. 401–429.

Tax, Sol, *et al.*
1953. *An Appraisal of Anthropology Today.* Chicago.

Trevelyan, G. M.
1942. *English Social History.* London.

White, Leslie A.
1949. *The Science of Culture.* New York.

Whorf, B. L.
1941. "The Relation of Habitual Thought and Behavior to Language," in L. Spier, ed., *Language, Culture and Personality*, pp. 75–93. Menasha.

Archaeological Method in the Eastern United States, by Lloyd A. Wilford

Fewkes, Valdimir J.
1937. "Aboriginal Potsherds from Red River, Manitoba," *American Antiquity*, Vol. 3, No. 2. Menasha.

Griffin, James B.
1951a. "Some Adena and Hopewell Radiocarbon Dates," in *Radiocarbon Dating: A Report on the Program to Aid in the Development of the Method of Dating* (Frederick Johnson, assembler), Society for American Archaeology, Memoir No. 8. Salt Lake City.

———, ed.
1951b. *Essays on Archaeological Methods* (Proceedings of a Conference Held under Auspices of the Viking Fund), Anthropological Papers of the Museum of Anthropology, University of Michigan, No. 8. Ann Arbor.

Hoffman, Bernard G.
1952. "Implications of Radiocarbon Datings for the Origins of the Dorset Culture," *American Antiquity*, Vol. 18, No. 1. Salt Lake City.

Holmes, William H.
1903. "Aboriginal Pottery of the Eastern United States," *Twentieth Annual Report*, Bureau of American Ethnology, 1898–1899. Washington, D.C.
1919. *Handbook of Aboriginal American Antiquities*, Part I, "Introductory: The Lithic Industries," Bureau of American Ethnology, Bulletin 60. Washington, D.C.

Johnson, Frederick
1951. "Collaboration among Scientific Fields with Special Reference to Archaeology," in James B. Griffin, ed., *Essays on Archaeological Methods* (Proceedings of a Conference Held under Auspices of the Viking Fund), Anthropological Papers of the Museum of Anthropology, University of Michigan, No. 8. Ann Arbor.

REFERENCES

Krieger, Alex D.
1951. "A Radiocarbon Date on the Davis Site in East Texas," *American Antiquity*, Vol. 17, No. 2. Salt Lake City.

Kroeber, A. L.
1948. *Anthropology*. New York.

Linton, Ralph
1936. *The Study of Man*. New York.

McKern, W. C.
1937. "An Hypothesis for the Asiatic Origin of the Woodland Culture," *American Antiquity*, Vol. 3, No. 2. Menasha.

Martin, Paul S., George I. Quimby, Jr., and Donald Collier
1947. *Indians Before Columbus*. Chicago.

Newell, H. Perry, and Alex D. Krieger
1949. *The George C. Davis Site, Cherokee County, Texas*, Society for American Archaeology, Memoir No. 5. Menasha.

Priest, Josiah
1835. *American Antiquities and Discoveries in the West*, 5th ed. Albany.

Ritchie, William A.
1951. "A Current Synthesis of New York Prehistory," *American Antiquity*, Vol. 17, No. 2. Salt Lake City.

Shepard, Anna O.
1953. Review of *Essays on Archaeological Methods* (Proceedings of a Conference Held under the Auspices of the Viking Fund), ed. James B. Griffin, *American Antiquity*, Vol. 18, No. 3. Salt Lake City.

Shetrone, Henry C.
1920. "The Culture Problem in Ohio Archaeology," *American Anthropologist*, N.S., Vol. 22, pp. 144–172. Lancaster.

Strong, William Duncan
1935. *An Introduction to Nebraska Archaeology*, Smithsonian Miscellaneous Collections, Vol. 93, No. 10. Washington, D.C.

Taylor, Walter W.
1948. *A Study of Archaeology*, American Anthropological Association, Memoir 69. Menasha.

Wissler, Clark
1922. *The American Indian*, 2nd ed. New York.

A Quantitative Approach to the Morphological Typology of Language, by Joseph H. Greenberg

Mauthner, F.
1923. *Beiträge zu einer Kritik der Sprache*, 3rd ed., Vol. 2. Leipzig.

Most, M.
1948. In *Actes du sixième Congrès International des Linguistes*. Paris.

Mueller, M.
1890. *Lectures on the Science of Language*. New York (from 2nd London ed., rev.).

Nida, E.
1948. "The Identification of Morphemes," *Language*, Vol. 24.

Sapir, E.
1921. *Language*. New York.

REFERENCES

Schlegel, A. von
1818. *Sur la littérature provençale.* (Printed as pp. 149–209 in Vol. 2 of his collected French works, edited by Edouard Börking, Leipzig, 1846. The quoted passage occurs on p. 159 of this edition.)
Schlegel, F. von
1808. *Ueber die Sprache und Weisheit der Inder.* Leipzig.
Wells, R.
1947. "Immediate Constituents," *Language,* Vol. 23.
1950. *The State and Prospects of Semantics.* Lithographed.
Whitney, D.
1876. *Language and the Study of Language,* 5th ed. New York.

The Forgotten Side of Ethnogeography,
by Omer C. Stewart

Ashe, W. W.
1915. *Loblolly or North Carolina Pine,* North Carolina Geological and Economic Survey, Bulletin 24.
Atwater, Caleb.
1818. "On the Prairies and Barrens of the West," *American Journal of Science,* Vol. 1.
Bates, Marston
1953. "Human Ecology," in A. L. Kroeber, ed., *Anthropology Today.* Chicago.
Benedict, Ruth
1943. "Franz Boas as an Ethnologist," in *Franz Boas, 1858–1942,* American Anthropological Association Memoir, No. 61.
Bews, J. W.
1929. *The World's Grasses.* New York.
Billings, W. D.
1941. "Quantitative Correlations between Vegetational Changes and Soil Development," *Ecology,* Vol. 22.
Boas, Franz
1940. *Race, Language and Culture.* New York. (Reprinted articles: "The Study of Geography," *Science,* Vol. 9, 1887; "The Limitations of the Comparative Method of Anthropology," *Science,* N.S., Vol. 4, 1896; "The Aims of Ethnology," 1888.)
Bourne, A.
1819. "On the Prairies and Barrens of the West," *American Journal of Science,* Vol. 2.
Brawn-Blanquet, J.
1932. *Plant Sociology.* New York.
Bruce, David
1951. "Fire, Site, and Longleaf Height Growth," *Journal of Forestry,* Vol. 56.
Chapman, H. H.
1932a. "Some Further Relations of Fire to Longleaf Pine," *Journal of Forestry,* Vol. 48.
1932b. "Is the Longleaf Type a Climax?" *Ecology,* Vol. 13.
1947. "Natural Areas,"*Ecology,* Vol. 28.
1950a. "An Unknown Pioneer in Prescribed Burning in Burma," *Journal of Forestry,* Vol. 48.
1950b. "Lightning in the Longleaf," *American Forests,* Vol. 56.

REFERENCES

Christy, Miller
   1892. "Why are the Prairies Treeless?" *Proceedings of the Royal Geographical Society and Monthly Record of Geography.* London.
Cook, O. F.
   1908. *Change of Vegetation on the South Texas Prairies,* U.S. Department of Agriculture, Bureau of Plant Ind. Contribution, Vol. 14.
Evans-Pritchard, E. E.
   1940. *The Nuer.* Oxford.
Farmer, B. H.
   1953. "Tropical Grasslands of Ceylon," *Geographical Review,* Vol. 43.
Gorrie, R. Maclagen
   1935. "Protective Burning in Himalayan Pine," *Journal of Forestry,* Vol. 33.
Greene, S. W.
   1931. "The Forest That Fire Made," *American Forests,* Vol. 37.
Heyward, Frank
   1937. "The Effect of Frequent Fires on Profile Development of Longleaf Pine Forest Soil," *Journal of Forestry,* Vol. 37.
Hursh, C. R., and C. A. Connaughton
   1938. "Effects of Forest upon Local Climate," *Journal of Forestry,* Vol. 38.
Kroeber, A. L.
   1939. *Cultural and Natural Areas of Native North America,* University of California Publications in American Archaeology and Ethnology, Vol. 38. Berkeley.
Lowie, Robert H.
   1937. *The History of Ethnological Theory.* New York.
Manoukian, Madeline
   1950. *Akan and Ga-Adangme Peoples of the Gold Coast,* International African Institute. Oxford.
Maxwell, H.
   1910. "The Use and Abuse of Forests by the Virginia Indians," *William and Mary College Historical Magazine,* Vol. 19.
Michaux, F. A.
   1802. "Travels in America," in *Early Western Travels.* Cleveland: A. H. Clark Co., 1904.
Nadel, S. F.
   1942. *A Black Byzantium.* Oxford.
Ratzel, Friedrich
   1898. "Le Sol, La Société et L'Etat," *Année Sociologique,* Vol. 3.
Sauer, Carl O.
   1927. *Geography of the Pennyroyal,* Kentucky Geological Survey, Series VI, Vol. 25.
   1950. "Grassland Climax, Fire, and Man," *Journal of Range Management,* Vol. 3.
Schmieder, O.
   1927. *The Pampa,* University of California Publications in Geography, Vol. 2.
Shimek, B.
   1911. *The Prairies,* State University of Iowa, Bulletin 35, and Contributions from the Laboratories of Natural History, Vol. 6 (2).
Stewart, Omer C.
   1951. "Burning and Natural Vegetation in the United States," *Geographical Review,* Vol. 41.
   1953. "Why the Great Plains are Treeless," *Colorado Quarterly,* Vol. 2.

REFERENCES

Stoddard, Herbert L.
1935. "Use of Controlled Fire in Southeastern Upland Game Management,"
Journal of Forestry, Vol. 33.
Swanton, John R.
1946. *The Indians of the Southeastern United States*, Bureau of American
Ethnology, Bulletin 137. Washington, D.C.
Thorp, James
1948. "How Soils Develop under Grass," *U.S. Department of Agriculture
Yearbook*. Washington, D.C.
Tracy, S. M.
1898. *Forage Plants and Forage Resources of the Gulf States*, U.S. Depart-
ment of Agriculture, Division of Agrostology, Bulletin 15. Washington,
D.C.
Vestal, A. G.
1931. Review of *Plant Ecology*, by Weaver and Clements, *Ecology*, Vol. 72.
Wackerman, A. E.
1929. "Why Prairies in Arkansas and Louisiana?" *Journal of Forestry*, Vol.
37.
1939. "Fire: The Greatest Threat to Southern Forests," *Journal of Forestry*,
Vol. 37.
Weaver, J. E., and F. E. Clements
1929. *Plant Ecology*. New York.
Wells, R. W.
1819. "On the Origin of Prairies," *American Journal of Science*, Vol. 1.
Werner, Alice
1906. *The Natives of British Central Africa*. London.
Wilde, S. A.
1946. *Forest Soils and Forest Growth*. Waltham, Mass.: Chronica Botanica
Co.
Wissler, Clark
1912. *North American Indians of the Plains*, Handbook Series No. 1., American Museum of Natural History. New York.
1926. *The Relation of Nature to Man in Aboriginal America*. New York.
1940. *Indians of the United States*. New York.

Research Methodology in Sociology: The First Half-Century,
by Raymond V. Bowers

Blumer, H.
1939. *An Appraisal of Thomas and Znanieki's Polish Peasant in Europe and
America*, Social Science Research Council, Bulletin 44.
Bowers, R.
1936. "An Analysis of the Problem of Validity," *American Sociological Review*, Vol. 1., No. 1.
Chapin, F. S.
1947. *Experimental Designs in Sociological Research*.
Chapple, E. D., and C. Arensberg
1940. *Measuring Human Relations*, Genetic Psychology Monographs, No. 22.
Conant, James B.
1947. *American Fitness to Survive* (An Address Delivered before the Boston
Conference on Distribution, 21 October 1947).
Deming, W. E.
1944. "On Errors in Surveys," *American Sociological Review*, Vol. 9, No. 4.

REFERENCES

Dollard, J.
1935. *Criteria for the Life History*. New Haven.
Festinger, Leon, and Daniel Katz, eds.
1953. *Research Methods in the Behavioral Sciences*. New York.
Gardner, B., and W. F. Whyte
1947. "Methods for the Study of Human Relations in Industry," *American Sociological Review*, Vol. 11, No. 5.
Gottschalk, L., C. Kluckhohn, and R. Angell
1945. *The Use of Personal Documents in History, Anthropology and Sociology*, Social Science Research Council, Bulletin 53.
Greenwood, E.
1945. *Experimental Sociology*. New York.
Hauser, P. M.
1946. "Are the Social Sciences Ready," *American Sociological Review*, Vol. 11, No. 4.
Kluckhohn, F.
1940. "The Participant Observer Techniques in Small Communities," *American Journal of Sociology*, Vol. 46.
Lee, A. M.
1947. "Sociological Theory and Opinion Research," *American Sociological Review*, Vol. 11, No. 4.
Leighton, A.
1945. *The Governing of Men*. New York.
Lynd, R. S. and H. M.
1929. *Middletown*. New York.
McCormick, T. C.
1945. "Simple Percentage Analysis of Attitude Questionnaires," *American Journal of Sociology*, Vol. 50, No. 5.
Mann, Floyd, and Rensis Likert
1952. "The Need for Research on the Communication of Research Results," *Human Organization*, Vol. 11, No. 4.
Merton, R. K.
1947. "Selected Problems of Field Work in the Planned Community," *American Sociological Review*, Vol. 12, No. 3.
———, and P. F. Lazarsfeld, eds.
1950. *Continuities in Social Research*. Glencoe, Ill.
Moreno, J. L.
1953. *Who Shall Survive?* Rev. ed. New York.
Mosier, C. I.
1953. "A Critical Examination of the Concepts of Face Validity," *Educational and Psychological Measurement*, Vol. 7, No. 2.
Research and Development Board and Bureau of Labor Statistics
1953. *Industrial Research and Development*. Washington, D.C.
Rice, S. A., ed.
1952. *Methods in Social Science*. 1931.
Scott, E., ed.
1952. *Applied Research in the United States*, National Research Council, Publication 210. Washington, D.C.
Stouffer, S. A., *et al.*
1948. *The American Soldier*, 4 vols.
1948–1950. *Studies in Social Psychology in World War II*, 4 vols. Princeton.

REFERENCES

Taylor, C. C.

    1946. "The Social Responsibilities of the Social Sciences — The Federal Level," *American Sociological Review*, Vol. 11, No. 4.

Thomas, D. S., A. M. Loomis, and R. Arrington

    1933. *Observational Studies of Social Behaviour*. New Haven.

Thomas, W. I., and F. Znaniecki

    1918. *The Polish Peasant in Europe and America*, Vol. 1. Boston.

Williams, R. M., Jr.

    1947. *Reduction of Inter-Group Tensions*, Social Science Research Council, Bulletin 57.

    1953. "Application of Research to Practice," *American Sociological Review*, Vol. 18, No. 1.

Young, Donald

    1941. "Memorandum on Suggestions for Research in the Field of Social Adjustments," *American Journal of Sociology*, Vol. 46, No. 6.

INDEX

Abbey Theater, 137
Abilene flints, 247
Academia Argentina de Letras, 40
Acculturation, 19–21, 287–288; *see also* Siriono tribe, Tonga tribe
Ackerknecht, Erwin H., on comparative method, 117–125; commentary on, 273–281
Adena culture, 183, 189
Adler, M., 131
Agglutinating languages, *see* Language
Agriculture, diffusion of, 177–178
Alternative behavior in ceremony, 76
American archaeology, 171–191
American Forests, 239
American Indian and natural environment, 226ff
American Museum of Natural History, 40
American Philosophical Society, 25*n*
American Sociological Society, 251, 268
Ancestor worship, 156
Angell, R., 264*n*
Anglo-Irish literature, 137
Anglo-Saxon language, 218–219
Annamite language, 218–219, 296
Anthropogeography, 221–248; *see also* Ethnogeography
Anthropology, *see* Archaeology, Comparative method, Culture, Ethnography, Field techniques, Humanities, Linguistics, Society
Anthropology: and comparative method, 117–125; and the humanities, 126–144, 281–283; and natural science, 273–281; evolutionist school, 277; relations to history, 135, 141, 172
Anthropology Today, 124, 225
Arapaho Indians, 26, 29, 41–42
Arapesh tribe (New Guinea), 44
Araucanian Indians (South America), 26, 29–42: astronomy, 30; foods, 42;

marital predictions by inkblots, 36–38; naming system, 39; personality predictions by drunkenness, 37–38; sib organization, 38–40; weaving, 30–31
Archaeological method, 171–191, 292–293; criticisms of, 171–175
Archaeology: Adena culture, 183, 189; and historical documentation, 188; archaic level, 179, 180–181; categories in, 173–175; chronology, 183–191, 292–293; culture classifications, 183ff; Davis site (Texas), 180; definitions of, 171ff; dendrochronology, 188ff; diffusion, 175–183, 293; distributional studies, 184ff; Dorset culture, 180; Eskimo cultures, 180–181; evaluation of cultures, 187; Fort Ancient site, 185; Hopewellian cultures, 178ff; methods of, 171–191, 292–293; Minnesota cultures, 182; Mississippi cultures, 178ff; of eastern United States, 171–191; of Meso-America, 176–177; of Southwest, 176–177; Ohio cultures, 182; radiocarbon dating, 188ff; regional conferences, 186; relations between Asia and North America, 176–177; relations with other sciences, 188ff; stratigraphy, 184–186; taxonomy of, 172–175, 178, 186–187; Tchefuncte culture, 189, 190; Woodland cultures, 178ff
Area studies, in archaeology, 176
Arensberg, C., 259*n*
Aristotle, 222, 274
Arnold, M., 129, 143
Art, universal quality of, 165–166
Atheism, 157
Attitudes: and values, 148–149; changes in culture, 20
Atwater, C., 228–229
Augusta, Fr. F. J. de, 32

INDEX

INDEX

Emeneau, M. B., 219*n*

Emotional effects of values, 146ff

Empirical approaches: in archaeology, 173–174; in cultural anthropology, 130–131; in sociology, 254–255, 266

English language, 218–220

Environment, natural, influenced by man, 221–248

Environmentalism, 223

Eschatology, 153–154, 156

Eskimo cultures, 180–181; language, 218–219, 296

Esthetic expression, 144, 165–166

Ethnocentrism, 7

Ethnogeography, 221–248: anthropological approaches to, 221–228; influences of man on the natural environment, 225ff; uses of fire by man in control of environment, 228–248, 298

Ethnography, 3–113: analysis, 100–101; census data in, 13, 43–59, 290; descriptive, 3–4; field work and methods, 3–42; field work, examples of, 25–113; functionalist approaches, 4, 287; methodology of, 286–288; process in, 287; quantitative approaches in, 12–13, 43–59; recording of textual materials in, 9; techniques of field inquiry in, 3–113, 289; traditional, 25; trait lists, 3, 6, 290; validity of data in, 5, 14, 21, 25–42, 288; *see also* Field techniques

Ethnology, *see* Ethnography

Ethos, 135

Euroamerican culture, 20

Evans-Pritchard, E. E., 130, 131, 233–234

Evolution, doctrine of, 121–124, 276–277

Evolutionary school, 5, 117, 123, 277–278

Experimental methodology, in science, 123, 127, 283

Experiments, in culture change, 103–113

Family: as human institution and value, 160–161; functions, 161

Farmer, B. H., 235–236

Festinger, L., 259*n*

Fewkes, V. J., 180

Field methods, *see* Field techniques

Field techniques (in ethnography), 3–113; accuracy, 22–23; analysis of cross-cousin marriage, 56–59; census data, 13, 43–59, 290; census forms, kinship and personal data, 53–54; checking by use of native words, 41–42; commentary on, 288–290; communication, 6, 9–11, 25–42; comparative methods, 18–21; contact-making, 29; corroboration of data, 5–42, 52, 58; cross-checking, 33–34; culture area concept, 23–24; definition of problems, 3–6, 42–58; description, 59; determination of group size, 49–50; determination of group representativeness, 50; determination of sample units, 51–52; duration, 6–8; elicitation of native traits, 35–36; field assistants, 26, 28–29; field guide, 25ff; field plan, 42; genealogies, 52; historical depth, 18–21; independent checking by investigators, 21–22; informants, 26ff; interpreters, 10, 28, 51; interviewing, 27, 29–31, 35; kinship data, 53; language, 9; motivating the informant, 32–33; museum collections, 40–41; note-taking, 29–32; observations, 27–33; participant observation, 34; payment of informants, 26–27; personal documentation, 53–54; photography, 26; problem of unit size, 48; problems of variation, 15, 75ff; procedures, 5–42; quantitative approaches, 12–13, 43–59; questionnaires, 12–13, 14, 53–54; rapport, 11–18, 28, 52; reactions of observers, 12; sampling, 13–16, 43–59; selection of informants, 28; statistical appraisals, 13, 43–59; team research, 16–18; validity, 5, 14, 21, 25–42, 51–59, 288; variations in behavior, 100

Fire, and human ecology, 226–248, 298–299

Fire prevention in forestry, 244

Fischer, E., 121*n*

Folk culture, 137–138

Folklore, 141

Folsom culture, 230

Ford Foundation, 267

Forests, 226–248

INDEX

INDEX

INDEX

Residence, in marriage, 45
Revista Chilena de Historia y Geografía, 40
Rhodesia, 46–59
Rhodes-Livingstone Institute, 47, 51
Richards, A., 48
Richthofen, F. von, 222
Ritualism, elements of, 90
Rivers, W. H. R., 121*n*, 277, 290
Rivet, P., 121*n*
Roman Catholic Church, 55
Romanticism, 138, 139
Rorschach tests, 36–37
Russell Sage Foundation, 255*n*

Sacleux, C., 219*n*
Sacrifice, 62, 72, 102, 155
Sanskrit language, 218–219, 295
Sapir, E., 131–132, 138, 144, 195, 198–199, 200–204, 205, 294, 295: linguistic typology of, 200–204; treatment of "genuine and spurious" cultures, 131–132
Sauer, C., 230*n*, 232
Schlegel, A. von, 196, 197, 294
Schlegel, Fr. von, 119, 196, 294
Scholarship, as social value, 165
Schurtz, H., 123
Science: development of classifications, 274–276; historical development of, 274–279
Scientific method, 5, 59, 117–125, 126, 130, 131, 133, 147, 273–283; in sociology, 253–271
Scott, E., 267*n*
Semper, C., 119
Semple, E., 223
Seventh Day Adventists, 55
Shakespeare, 142
Shaw, G. B., 137
Shepard, A. O., 190
Shikamatsu, 135
Shils, E. A., 147*n*, 254*n*, 255*n*
Shimek, B., 229
Siriono tribe (Bolivia), 103–113, 291: agriculture, 103, 108–110; changes in agricultural patterns, 108–110; economy, 104ff; in-group hostility, 108; introduction of domesticated animals, 110–111; introduction of domesticated fowl, 111–112; of firearms, 112–113; native beer, 108; patterns of

livelihood, 103–113; use of digging stick, 104, 107; of palm cabbage, wild honey, 107; of watermelons, 109–110
Small, A., 252
Smith, G. E., 121*n*
Social anthropology, in Britain, 290
Social behavior, 4, 60–102, 135, 149–168; *see also* Culture, Culture patterns
Social controls, 167: imperatives, 149–150, 160–161; mobility, 47–59; relationships, 53–54, 56–58, 64–66
Social science: problems in, 260–270; scientific methodology in, 127, 133–134
Social Science Research Council, 265*n*, 269*n*
Social sciences: research financing in, 266–269; sponsorship of research, 267
Social stratification, 49–59: structure, 4–5, 74–102, 149–164; systems, 149–168
Socialization, trends toward, 167–168
Sociedad Argentina de Americanistas, 40
Society: and culture, 4, 127, 149; and family stability, 160–163; coordination of activity, 159–160; esthetic expression in, 165–166; exchange of labor, 158; inequalities in, 159; role of property in, 163; sexual division of labor in, 158
Sociology: and anthropology, 290; application of results of research, 254; criteria of research feasibility, 256–257; delimitation of observational field, 261; design of research, 255–259; determination of observer error, 265; explicitness in methodology, 258; formulation of research objectives, 257–258; future research, 266–269; occasions for research, 252–255; reliability of data, 261; research methodology in, 251–270; research possibilities, 255ff; results of observation, 259–266; scientific methodology in, 253–254; scientific observation, 261; situational controls, 263–266; specification of research outcome, 258–259; structuring observational situations, 263–266; tests of validity, 262

INDEX

Soils and vegetation, 243
Southwestern archaeology, 176
Spencer, H., 119, 123
Spencer, Robert F., on humanities in cultural anthropology, 126–144; commentary on, 282–283
Spengler, O., 132, 141
Spier, L., 287
Standards of living, 13
Statistical approaches: in community studies, 43–59; in linguistics, 192–220; to cross-cousin marriage, 57; to population mobility, 48; methods, 127, 144
Steele, R., 137
Steinen, K. von den, 121n
Steinthal-Misteli, 198–199, 294
Steward, J., 124
Stewart, Omer C., on the forgotten side of ethnogeography, 221–248; commentary on, 297–299
Stoddard, H. L., 244
Stouffer, S., 255n, 259n
Streib, G. F., 48
Strong, W. D., 188
Study of Archaeology, A., 171–175, 292
Sturm und Drang, 142
Suicide, 46–47
Supernatural, 153–154
"Survivals" in culture, 122
Swahili language, 218–219, 296
Swanton, J. R., 237
Swift, J., 137

Taine, 222
Tamil language (So. India), 60
Taylor, G., 223
Taylor, W. W., 171–175, 191, 292
Tchefuncte culture, 189, 190
Teak forests, Burma, 237
Team research, in ethnography, 16–18
Technological change, 105ff
Tehuelche Indians (South America), 37–38
Thalbitzer, W., 219n
Thales, 279
"Themes" in culture, 132, 134
Theory, relations to method, 6
Thomas, W. I., 259n
Thomas, D. S., 259n
Thomistic theology, 139
Tibaera (Bolivia), 104–112

Toda tribe (So. India), 60, 72, 94
Tokugawa age, 135
Tone, W., 138
Tonga tribe (Africa), 46–59: age of women at marriage, 58; censuses of, 53–57; changes in economy, 56–58; colonial administration, 58; cross-cousin marriage, 56–59; kinship data, 53–57; personal data, 53–57; suicide, 46–47
Toynbee, A., 141
Trevelyan, G. M., 143
Trubetskoy, N. S., 194
Tylor, E. B., 122, 123, 124, 154, 277, 278
Typological approaches to linguistics, 218–220; 294–297

Unconscious behavior patterning, 151
United States: eastern, archaeology of, 171–191; national character, 139; National Museum, 40; Office of Indian Affairs, 28
Universal values, 145–168, 284–285: of esthetic expression, 166; of family, 160–163, 284; of knowledge, 164–166; of leadership, 160, 284; of property, 163–164; of religion, 151–155, 284
University of California, culture element surveys, 3–4, 290
University of Pennsylvania Museum, 40

Value-attitude systems, 148–149, 284
Value judgments, 128, 144, 145; studies, 133, 145–168
Values, 133, 145–168, 284–286: and emotional associations, 146, 150; and individual needs, 163, 168; and religion, 152–153; cultural, 145–168; definition of, 147–148; in-group perpetuation, 158; in marital ties, 161–163; of children in society, 162–163; of family ties, 160–163; of in-group, 158; instrumental and conceptual, 150ff; of knowledge, 164–165; of parenthood, 163; of property, 163–164; of reciprocity, 158–159; of social continuum, 157; problems of social perpetuation, 158; relativism in, 166–167; susceptibility to change, 152; universal, 152–164, 284–285